NOT NATURAL

ELIZABETH BREEN

Ordering Information:

Prime Seven Media
518 Landmann St.
Tomah City, WI 54660

Printed in the United States of America

TABLE OF CONTENTS

I dedicate this book to all of my children, for whom I have nothing but unconditional love. It is my sincere hope that one day you will all come together as the family I tried and failed to create and which was torn apart by secrets and lies.

I wish to offer my deepest gratitude and appreciation to my son, Zach, for the critiquing, advice, and invaluable insight, from a child's perspective, whilst completing this book. You were my rock! I love you. Isabelle and Ben deserve a special thank you for having supported me from the day I finally gathered strength to leave my marriage. I have made your lives, as well as my own, truly miserable for a great portion of the time since that day. I can never change that, I can only say how much I appreciate all that you have done for me and, continue to do, in an effort to prevent my PTSD and depression taking complete hold of me again. I love you. To my eldest daughter, Brianna, I took you into an abusive and untenable situation and I have to live with that every day of that which remains of my life. There are no words adequate enough to express my regret and sorrow tor having made the decisions I did and I can only say to you that 'I you 49 my darling!' I love you. To my beautiful grandchildren Steve and Ebony, without you both I could not go on. Thank you for the love you give me and the strength you pass on to me, it is so magical. I love you. Mitchell, it is with so much love that we were reunited after you being caught in no man's land, trying to maintain a relationship with both of your parents. I am so grateful and appreciative for the fact that you are always there for me no matter your situation. I love you.

From the very moment of your birth, I was in love, so deeply and completely that to be separated from you for seconds caused me agonising pain emotionally and physically. I could not settle without being able to see and touch the most precious little redhead I had ever seen in my life.

The pain of my 12-hour labour evaporated into the joy that was my adorable little baby girl.

I knew from that very second that I would move heaven and earth to protect and provide for you.

All the agonising doubts that had preceded your birth disappeared in a nanosecond. The verbal and psychological abuse I had received at the hands of my mother, brother and sister for bringing a screaming child into their house to disturb their lifestyles was still at the forefront of my mind as we, you and I, had been given only two weeks to find a place to live by ourselves because they were not prepared to tolerate the incursion into their serenity. Mum had dragged me around the streets of Toowoomba to various shops the week before your birth so that I could purchase the final items that I would require to make us a home. I was, at the time, meant to be on strict bed rest as I had already been hospitalised once at St Vincent's Hospital with pre-eclampsia!

That momentous occasion is now, almost 38 years ago, my beautiful baby girl. We have endured both the best times of our lives and the worst times of our lives inside those almost four decades.

It was you and I alone at your birth and it was perfect, just as you were and are—true perfection.

This is the story of the journey through our lives, Brianna, both before and after you were born.

I dedicate this book to all of my children for whom I have nothing but unconditional love.

The hole in my heart caused by the loss of four of my babies from my life can never be filled by anyone or anything else. I am trying to let you go of you so that I may live what remains of my life in peace, love and harmony but that has proven to be very difficult to achieve in the years since I last held each of you in my embrace.

It has been even more difficult for me to reconcile the loss of my grandchildren. They have no blame in the separation of their grandparents, yet one is still allowed to have them in their lives whilst the other is not. My heart aches for them so greatly.

The purpose of this book is to try, by writing everything down, to give you all the truth of my life. I now see how you were all brainwashed by your father as I have certainly had it explained to me enough by the experts and have come to understand that I had also been brainwashed by him. But I still find the practicalities of seemingly and oft self-proclaimed very intelligent people falling for it. And as I hold truth so dear to my heart, my biggest question is 'why has not one of you or your partners ever asked me why I felt that I had to take the action that I did? Why did no one ever ask if I was okay?' The condemnation of your mother on the simple say-so of a true narcissist is, quite frankly, beyond the realms of possibility to not only me but also to all the professionals that I have encountered since 2012.

This helps me when I come to a point of total confusion trying to work it out:

Everything we hear is an opinion, not a fact...
Everything we see is a perspective, not the truth...

-MARCUS AURELIUS

What any child most needs from its parents is understanding, love and care.

-TARA BRACH.

CHAPTER 1

NOT NATURAL

It was a cool and slightly breezy winter's afternoon as I walked home from school at St Joseph's Catholic Primary School in Chinchilla in western Queensland with a friend who lived quite close to me.

My friend talked all the way home, saying, 'I know something about you.'

Of course, my natural response was, 'Tell me what it is.'

'I can't, Mum and Dad said I couldn't,' she replied.

The banter continued back and forth between us and I discovered that her parents had chosen me to be the subject of their previous night's dinner table conversation, in front of their children.

I was desperate to establish what they could possibly know about me that I was, in fact, not allowed to know about myself. My mind was doing somersaults trying to figure it out. I was all of ten years old so I asked her to give me the letters for the word and that way, she would not have actually told me. She did and we parted ways at the bottom of the road, she to continue straight and me to go up one block to my home. I had tried all the variations of the letters she had provided but seemed to be getting nowhere. I was almost home when I gave up and was in the process of storming in the front door to tell

Mum all about this conversation that had so upset me. As I placed my foot over the threshold into the lounge room, it hit me—adoption!

'I am not adopted, am I, Mum?' was all I could say.

'Yes, Ellie, you are and so is Jonathon.'

'Why have you never told me this before, Mum?'

'Don't you remember all the times that I have told you and Jonathon that you were specially chosen?'

To be totally honest, I did not and I still do not remember ever having been given this information but I trusted Mum and said that I did as, at that point in my life, I did not believe that she would lie to me.

'But that is not the same as adopted though, Mum.'

'Well, actually, it is love. You were born of my heart, not under it, love.'

That I did remember and still do.

'Dad and I could not love you any more than we do already, we are your parents. The ones who care for you, feed you, clothe you and care for you when you are hurt or sick. That is what real parents are.'

I was completely satisfied with the explanation that my mother had given me and I never discussed it with another soul from that day on. Not my brother, my father or my sister who was a natural child.

It became blatantly obvious through the years though, what a lot of my aunts, uncles and even my maternal grandmother thought about Jonathon and I. And, in fact, I was even told that I was "not natural"! That really hurt me the first time I heard it and it hurts not a single bit less today, almost 60 years later. I believed it was possibly more difficult for me being a girl and having a "natural sister". Girl cousins would receive gifts from our maternal grandmother and I would try to be polite by commenting on how lovely they were and ask where they had gotten them. I was thinking of the shop they were purchased from but I very quickly learned to recognise the looks on the faces of my aunt and cousins and the fact that it had been received from Nanna, known in many circles as the Super Dragon. I did not believe that Jonathon had quite the same issues as I did, especially as he was 18 before he even realised that he had been adopted! More on that later.

On my paternal grandparents' side, things appeared to be far more civil but I learned as an adult that they were very similar in many ways, especially with the aunts and uncles. I never ever believed that Grandma and Granddad did not love me as though I was flesh and blood but I would never ever know for certain now. To me, they were the kindest, most loving and compassionate people I had ever met. My grandma taught me to cook. I loved and admired them both so much. My grandparents lived in Chinchilla and my Nanna lived in Miles.

I think I "grew up" in Chinchilla even though I was not yet 12 when I left there. The realisation of my heritage not being the same as my beloved father was a blow to me but one that I kept very firmly to myself as I did most things. This proved to be my undoing as I got older. I became an expert at compartmentalisation. A box for everything and they all had their places and time. I was admired by many, decades later, for the way I was able to cope with so many stresses, a view I did not share, by the way. My GP of 30 years of my life would always say that I was a rock and no one would ever be able to break me! I told him many times that he would eat his words one day as there would be a point past which I would start to crumble. When that point arrived, I had long since ceased seeing that GP due to what I perceived as misconduct.

Many things had occurred whilst I lived in Chinchilla, which certainly forced me to take a more mature view of life. I was only 10 when I started to menstruate. That was like a knife to the gut.

'You are a woman now; here, use these, it happens every month and you cannot let boys touch you or you will get pregnant.' That was all I got from my mother. I had agonising lower abdominal pains and was taken around to my grandmother's house so all could be informed. Grandma proceeded to tell me that it went on until you went through "The Change" and that had happened to her when she had been 50! I was absolutely horrified. 40 years kept repeating in my head, over and over like a huge neon sign. I was only 10.

As it turned out, I was 48 when menopause started and 53 years and 1 month when I had my last period. The pain and aggravation of the monthly torture I had endured for all of those decades, I would not have wished on my worst enemy.

It was the assassination of Robert Kennedy in 1968 when I was just 11 that shaped the adult that I would become. I went to a Catholic primary school. The nuns at St Joseph's were less than impressed with me after Bobby's death. I started constantly asking why? Religion lessons were never to be the same again. A statement would be made about God, His work or some other work and I would ask 'why'. The school called my parents in to get me to stop but my curiosity for the truth had been ignited and was off and running faster than the flame heading towards the dynamite. Being told that I just had to believe or that I had to have faith was no longer going to cut it. A man whom I had perceived to be a truly honourable man, a truthful man, had been assassinated just as his brother had been five years earlier. The die had been cast! I would never again blindly follow anyone without questioning the truth of that practice and/or having it proven to me that what I was being told was the absolute truth.

My absolute requirement for the truth in all things also cursed me throughout my life. More on that later.

Many things conspired to shorten my childhood. The fact that I had very little in the way of happy memories from my childhood bothered me greatly. Given what I know today, I was left to wonder what I may have blocked from my memory. My only true memories were of somewhat painful times in my younger life.

I had a memory of my brother Jonathon sitting in the rocking horse our father had made. I was rocking him and next thing he had fallen out and cut his eyebrow. The rocking horse had been too close to the concrete garden edge. I had copped a load of grief for that!

I remember even further back to when Jonathon had been in a pram, very little indeed. I had been younger than three at this point. Mum had been leaning over the bathtub cleaning it, the pram pulled very close to her. I had been eating a small box of sultanas and being a really good girl sharing them with my baby brother. Mum became hysterical when she realised Jonathon was choking!

I attended swimming lessons on a Saturday at the pool at Queens Park in Ipswich, where we lived until I was almost 10. One Saturday, when I had finished my lesson, I went to the bus stop to wait for my bus home as I always did. But the bus never came. I was beside myself with fear and stress. My parents did not have a telephone and there was no back-up plan. All I could think to do was to walk home across Queens Park. The tears were streaming down my face the whole walk back to Whitehill Road. It seemed to be taking an eternity and I was certain that Mum would flog me as it was my brother's birthday party that afternoon. It does seem extremely odd to me now, that I have absolutely no recollection of arriving home that day…I also have no memory of the party or indeed of the birthday party that I had when I was young. My first Holy Communion is blank. I was a member of the Junior Red Cross and have no idea of where we met or what we did. I do recall singing as a group at an aged care facility as part of the Red Cross.

A cousin of my dad, Billy, was killed in Vietnam. I remember vividly walking up and down the side of the Ipswich house, trying to correlate all this information. War, death, grieving, sadness. I was seven or eight.

I remember when my sister Emma was born. I was five years old. Grandma and Granddad had come to look after Jonathon and I. It had been an awesome time. Granddad had taken us for walks down to the shop to get lollies. That awe had ended abruptly when the new baby had been brought home. She was incredulous. She never stopped screaming. Jonathon and I went to Mum and Dad one morning before they were out of bed and very genuinely requested that they take her back to the hospital and get a different one as this one was no good! As I sit here now, I have some very hazy and vague recollection of Jonathon or I saying that they had chosen us and they should be able to choose another baby that didn't scream so much. I remember Mum and Dad explaining that it didn't work that way. I find that a shock that I have that memory now. What else was hidden in the fog of my mind?

I have no memories of good times. What I do have are feelings. That itself makes me awfully suspicious as to what it is that I have pushed to the nether regions of my mind. I have a superb memory for dates, times, events and the like, so why do have I so little memories from childhood? So much so that even the "Fog Brain" of fibromyalgia and the thyroid disease cannot dim the most important dates, times and events of my adult life.

My father, Edward, since he married my mother, Florella, in 1949 had always worked for Queensland Rail. He was a guard. He found that with three small children, the shift work was rather taxing, especially with Emma who was, to say the very least, difficult. Or more truthfully, a total nightmare! At one point, Mum and Dad had all three of us sleeping in the one bedroom, the cot in the middle.

It does now seem to be particularly cruel and unusual punishment for Jonathon and I, looking back on that period with the eyes of a midwife and mother of nine children, especially given that there were three bedrooms in the house!

We had not long had our lunch and Mum and Dad were in the kitchen doing the cleaning and washing up whilst we were all meant to be going to sleep. Emma, of course as always, had very different ideas and was screaming! Jonathon and I could not take it any more so we took up our positions on the floor beside the cot and each patted Emma's back in an effort to get her to go to sleep. At first, I could hear Mum and Dad talking, then I heard Dad say, 'She is finally quiet.' Little did he know why. By the time they came to check before Dad was to leave for his shift at work, Jonathon and I were both fast asleep leaning on the cot and Dad lifted us up onto our beds.

As Emma grew older, she did not get any easier to cope with. So, Mum and Dad decided that it would be much better for the whole family if he were to have a day job. He started to work for MLC selling insurance. The trouble was that they sent him to Chinchilla, the town he had grown up in, and had to try to sell insurance to the farmers that had it tough. Dad not only empathised with them, he had been them as he had grown up on a farm in Chinchilla. He had been the third eldest of seven children and to help the family, Dad had gone to work in the quarry and had given every single bit of his pay to his parents.

It did not help him much that every day when he arrived home, we would ask him how much he had sold that day. Mum and Dad had sold the house they had built in 1958 in Ipswich for this move and as all they had to survive on were their savings, things were looking grim. The decision to try to return to Queensland Rail was made but unfortunately, Dad was sent to Cloncurry as certain senior Queensland Rail members were not best pleased that Dad had left the railway and felt that he needed to be taught a lesson. Mum would always say, 'It was the Masons that caused this.' Mum was to remain in Chinchilla with us children. Dad would come to visit on a Greyhound bus when he could and we had all travelled to Cloncurry once whilst he was there. It was a very long and arduous journey in 1967 but when I saw that dad was the guard on our train from Townsville out west, I was filled with joy.

It seemed that Dad was to be left in this wilderness apart from our family for an indeterminate amount of time but Mum was told by the doctor that she was pregnant again. This swayed the railway and we were all moved to Toowoomba during the Christmas holidays of 1968/1969.

Mum and Dad had bought a house on the range and we settled into family life once again. It turned out that the Mum had suffered a phantom pregnancy so there was not to be another sibling but we were all reunited and extremely happy.

Before I had even managed to start at my new school, Mater Dei in Toowoomba, I managed to dislocate my left knee. Jonathon, Emma and I had all been out on a bike ride with our neighbours, Terry and Gerry (twins) and Tom, their younger brother. We had all headed up to Picnic Point, which had the most magnificent views of the Lockyer Valley below the Toowoomba Range, some 691 metres. It was on our descent from the top heading back home that I was certain the brakes had failed as I had attempted to take a corner. My knee met with a cement pole as I came off the bike and my knee came off much worse than that pole. I had never experienced pain quite like that in my life, despite having had a tonsillectomy at seven and a plantar wart surgically removed in Chinchilla and almost having died due to my allergic reaction to the ether.

One of the boys kept riding home to get Mum and Dad. As they were trying to get me into the back of our station wagon, my patella clicked itself back into place. I was taken to the Toowoomba General Hospital Casualty. I was, henceforth, in an ankle-to-hip bandage of cotton wool/bandages/cotton wool/bandages splint in the hottest part of the summer and had to do physiotherapy raising my leg with weights on it in order to strengthen my knee. I had refused to use crutches and was a sorry sight for some time. I also, in the end, refused to do the physio. That patella has been the bane of my existence—well, one of many actually. I went back to playing tennis and doing ball games but refused to run. I loved swimming and tennis and my knee seemed to cope very well with those. My knee dislocated again when I was 15, a silly turn and out she went but I put it back in. I very successfully completed my three years of nursing training and one year of midwifery training without my knee causing any further issues.

The next time I was to suffer from this issue was in 1989. I was physically in very poor shape at the time, after the birth of my second son. It was a particularly nasty dislocation and although I had managed to return it to its correct position myself again, I was left with a huge amount of swelling and agonising pain. I was referred to an orthopaedic specialist and he stated that I had total muscle wastage down the outer aspect of my left thigh. I required surgery to attempt to improve the situation. I asked if it would fix the problem, the doctor could not give me any sort of guarantee so again, I refused treatment. I had six children at this point and a husband who was unable to work due to medical issues. I could not be out of action.

One month before the birth of my youngest child, I was in Ipswich with my husband and second youngest son, Zach, to see our eldest son, William, run his district 800m race. We were parked up on a hill that gave us a bird's eye view of the race. William had come up, after he had finished, to discuss the race. He had no sooner left us when I stepped backwards into a dip in the ground and again dislocated my patella. It was incredibly difficult for me to get it back into place this time but I finally got it. The two worst things about that day were that my poor son Zach had to hear the bloodcurdling involuntary scream that I let out when my knee went and I had to drive home from Ipswich to Sunnybank Hills.

At this point, the issue of my wayward patella was worse than ever. I did establish, through an injury incurred by Brianna, that there was a familial problem with the position in which my patella sat, making it all the easier for it to dislocate...

I do feel that I have veered away from the subject of this chapter somewhat but it is all part of my history, I guess. What I can say is that being "not natural" has caused much heartache for me and still does in many ways. It is, most definitely, not a label that I am comfortable with.

I know who I am and the fact is that all I have ever wanted is to be part of a huge loving family, and that is exactly the thing that eludes me and I fear always will.

My earliest memories may be blurry or, indeed, non-existent in most cases but one thing that is as clear to me today as it was when I was extremely young—I wanted to be a nurse, go to Canada and have 12 children. That had never changed one iota until the end of my first year of nursing training.

I did not do a university course for my training. I had a six-week orientation between the classroom and wards, then straight into it. For those six weeks, I received $30/week.

My first ward was the old TB ward at the Toowoomba General Hospital. In my very first week, I had to hold the abdominal contents of my patient in place whilst raising the alarm and I also witnessed my first death. I was hooked but by the end of year one, I needed more.

I wanted to do medicine. The problem was that I had not completed year 12 at school as all that was required to do nursing then was junior (year 10) and be 17; our family doctor had talked Mum and Dad into letting me finish after year 11 and get started on my nursing career. I had followed my parents' advice.

I decided to complete my nursing training, see how I felt and do what was required to do medicine then.

Life does have the knack of getting in your way somehow at every turn.

So, we are now back to the reason for this chapter of my book. I have always been the most open, accepting and loving person. I do know now that I was also way too naïve, too trusting... My faults are many but the worst of which were, when I was younger, the fact that I could not forgive, I could not forget and I vowed to take my revenge on those who had wronged me. I had a dreadful temper and it would show its ugly self very easily and quite regularly. It felt as if somewhere, sometime, in my life, I had to have my fight or flight mode on alert at all times. This was not the case when I was nursing, although I most certainly had a particular way of riding lazy nurses that would have them in tears by the end of the shift. This was most definitely not something that I am proud of now. In fact, I cringe to even think about that anymore but I will always be truthful, even to my own detriment. When I was working as a nurse, I knew I was good at my job, loved dealing with people who needed help and in the majority of cases truly appreciated it. I would always go the extra mile for my patients. I was very lucky to have been given a sixth sense about all things medical and I am very proud to have saved the lives of a few patients who would otherwise not be with us today if I had not, with terrier-like determination, found an error that was causing their demise.

The reason I mention all these faults, and there were many more minor ones, of course, is to question why I was so angry when I was young. What had happened to me? What was I hiding from? Would I ever know the answers to these questions?

What I did know was that all the aunts, uncles and cousins that I had thought were "my family" had seemed to drop by the wayside rather too quickly and easily for my liking. Again, we were back at the "not natural". Was it really all about blood or was it all a bit more logical than that?

My dad and I had a fantastic relationship. I have been told as an adult that from the very second that he held me in his arms, he was smitten and from that second on was a very devoted father. Mum and Dad had been married for eight years and living in Emerald in Central Queensland when I was born at the Royal Brisbane Women's Hospital.

It could be a nerve-wracking experience awaiting the letter or call to let you know that your baby for adoption was ready for you to come and take home for your new life as a family. My mother was always an exceptionally nervy type of person at the best of times and seemed to survive in the most part as long as she had access to amitriptyline. To the best of my knowledge, these had been a fairly stable medication throughout Mum's adult life. She had made me take one whilst five months pregnant to deal with Dad's funeral and despite the fact that I was a trained nurse, I was in no fit state to argue.

A very dear friend of my mother's, who lived in Brisbane, called Mum to advise that she had only today to collect her new baby girl or she would be given to the next couple on the list. The letter that had been sent to Mum and Dad had not arrived, Dad had been away on a job for Queensland Rail, so all she could do was leave a message for Dad to head to Brisbane the very moment that he arrived home, pack and get herself on a train to head towards her new daughter. She was a nervous wreck by the time she and her friend had arrived at the hospital to get me. It was then that Mum had found out that I had thrush in my mouth and the treatment at the time had been Gentian Violet, a poisonous liquid that had to be painted on the affected areas without allowing the baby to swallow any of the solution. Well, Mum and her friend set off with me to her friend's house in the western suburbs for a very long and stressful night—on my mother's part at least.

By the time my dad arrived the next day, Mum had been in a right state by all accounts. But Dad, who very regularly called Mum "Johnnie Ray", an American singer of the time, was in love with his brand-new daughter. He had long since arranged with Queensland Rail that immediately upon collecting me from the hospital, he would take three weeks holiday with immediate effect. So, the new family of Mum, Dad and me headed off for my very first train ride to Chinchilla to meet my grandparents.

No one could get anywhere near me, by all accounts, as Dad was the most devoted father of all time. That extremely special time sealed the bond between father and daughter that would never cease. Nothing and no one would ever be able to break that bond. Many have tried, as I learned the hard way. It would be 39 years in September 2016 since I had last seen my father. I did not know how I would continue without the most honourable man it had ever been my privilege to know. He had been my mentor, my best friend, the person I had looked up to more than any other in this world and he had been my dad whom I loved with every cell, strand of DNA and breath in my body. Blood meant nothing. Your real family were those that were there for you when you needed them the most. That made my dad the only REAL father I had and there was not a single day since his death that I did not talk to him and wish that he was still here to guide me.

It is my honest belief that so many things that have happened in my life since 1977 would not have occurred were he still with us. I have made my decisions and mistakes and I live with the consequences of those decisions and mistakes every day of my life and always will. I have no room in my life for blame, it is futile. The past is the past. Let it go and move on.

I sometimes think about what I would do IF I were able to go time travelling. Most people would not change anything but I truly believe that given the opportunity, I would go back to when I was 15 and tell Dad two things: the carcinoma of your kidney was a metastasis and the primary was in your spine and that I needed to complete year 12 (senior) as I was going to change my lifelong ambition of becoming a nurse to becoming a doctor. That was a silly dream to most people but I actually felt that strongly about both issues—my father and my lost career in medicine.

Moving back to the subject at hand, my childhood should have been an idyllic one given the relationship I had with my father. I must have been a cheeky little madam when small as I apparently called Dad, "Daddy Edward", and he let me do it too. The only recollections I have of my dad is adoration. So why am I unable to recall anything about Mum from an early age? Why are there so many blanks? It is only in fairly recent years, comparatively speaking, that I was informed by an aunt that Mum relentlessly flogged me as a toddler and young child to the point it sounded to me to be abusive, excessive and completely unwarranted by the way the story was told.

It is not for me to make assumptions on another person's ideas or feelings at any given time. I have always abhorred generalisations and categorisations of any people based on blanket assumptions. I truly believe assumptions to be the mother of all fuck ups! I can, however, based on the facts to hand, make an educated guess. Actually, that is all that can really be done when one is no longer alive and others are trying to fathom the reasons for seemingly unreasonable behaviour.

My brother, Jonathon, was born two years and eight months after me and also adopted by Mum and Dad. As already stated, Emma was a "fluke" pregnancy and was born two years and eight months after Jonathon. Dad had had an incredibly low sperm count, which was the reason it had been suggested that he would never be able to have children naturally.

I have already explained the type of baby/toddler/child Emma was and how Jonathon and I dealt with her in the best way we could. Jonathon and I were very close when young but as I moved off to start school, it had been he and Emma who had spent more time together and they certainly developed a bond that would stand the test of time, although it did involve a heck of a lot of "sitting on the fence" where Jonathon was concerned. A practice that to me must surely have resulted in more than one's fair share of splinters in your bollocks!

Jonathon had been a much smaller build and I had always been quite tall for my age so the size difference had been quite extensive, whereas he had been very much closer in size to Emma and it was perfectly natural that he would associate more with her. Also, complicating issues was the fact that Jonathon developed nephritis when he had been five years old and had spent three months in hospital. At that stage, I was already in school and Mum and Emma were his most frequent visitors. Children did not forget such things even though, again, their perception of events is never as romantic as the actual reasons that things may or may not have occurred in a certain manner.

So, with Jonathon and Emma so close, Dad and I so close and Mum very close to both Jonathon and Emma, there seemed to be a three versus two type division within the family. I personally did not really see this until many years later. As far as I was concerned, as a child, we were all one incredibly happy family with an enormous extended family, which was all I could have dreamed of. I had older female cousins I looked up to and also older male cousins that taught me the ins and outs of life. There was definitely a major difference between the cousins on my maternal side and the cousins on my paternal side. All from Dad's side had been funny, caring, loving and helpful. I had felt totally at ease with each and every one of them. But on Mum's side, they had been shallow, nasty at times and vindictive. They had definitely thought they were far superior to Jonathon and I. Not so Emma, of course. You didn't actually see the reality until you were much older.

It was completely natural for every little girl to want to be a "Daddy's Girl"! In Emma's mind, that position was well and truly filled in her perception. There was plenty of room in Dad's heart but Emma had been unable to see what was at the end of her nose. Her way of dealing with what she perceived to be rejection was to lie and misbehave. This manifested itself in some very strange ways with Emma. I must be honest and say that I really don't recall too many issues until we moved to Toowoomba. Perhaps with the family reunited and living a normal life, Emma had the time to see the family unit as a whole for the first time and did not like what she saw. I know that I was told things about myself by a friend when I was living in Chinchilla, was Emma as well? Perhaps after we moved to Toowoomba, she had been told by any member of families of Mum's two sisters who also lived in Toowoomba. Emma certainly developed a very strong link with Phil, a cousin, who was her age. He had a younger brother, Michael. In the other family had been Chris, Janet and Mike. Janet was constantly sporting gifts from Nanna (Mum's mother), which neither Emma nor I would receive. Although it hurt me deeply to be classed as "not natural", I can only wonder at how deep the cuts were when you were indeed "natural" but ostracised because your sister was not.

Because Emma and I shared a bedroom in Toowoomba, it was mostly me who found what she had done wrong. There had been a scenario where Emma was required to get sponsors and, for all intents and purposes, that was exactly what she had done but after she had collected the money, if memory serves, Mum had found out that she had lied and was then forced to return all the money to the respective sponsors. Dad's way to deal with this had been to give Emma a belting. Our bedroom had one wall full of floor-to-ceiling built-in cupboards. They were fantastic but one day, I had gone to get something from the shelf section and there was the most horrific smell emanating from somewhere in there. We had a situation once in Chinchilla when we had gone to visit Dad in Cloncurry where our cat had given birth to kittens and they had died. She had brought them into the house on our return and placed them well hidden in boxes in the bedrooms. The smell I was sensing in the shelves in Toowoomba was almost identical to the smell of the poor little decomposing kittens. I thought a mouse or something had gotten in and hidden itself. I asked Mum to give me her opinion. I had to empty a good portion of the cupboard but what I found was a collection of mouldy lunches that had been hidden by Emma. I cleaned it all up but Mum knew and she told Dad; yes, Emma got another belting.

From that second on, I vowed to do everything I could to protect Emma from herself and from future beltings. At the age of 12, it seemed to me that Emma longed for attention from Dad, the attention that she must obviously have felt he expended on me rather than her. It was my duty, in my mind, as the older sister to look out for her in every way I could. Emma did not stop accruing smelly food or doing any of the many things that would bring the wrath of any parent down on the child. In many ways, the way I have explained this situation makes Dad seem somewhat punishment happy. Nothing could have been further from the truth, in fact. He was the most "gentle giant", standing six foot tall. We were living in the 60s and a certain standard of behaviour was expected from children. If that standard was not met and after discussions by Dad to try to ascertain reasons, what was there left to do to try to bring your children up to be well-adjusted members of any community when they were adults? One needed to remember just how difficult Emma had been since her birth. I can clearly see now that Dad may have well considered himself a failure and maybe more so because she was a natural child. Again, I reiterate, it is impossible for me to get an insight from someone who has been gone so long. But between nurse training, midwifery, three stepchildren, nine children of my own and a very large dose of logic, I do feel reasonably well armed to take an educated guess. Plus, I lived through it, alongside Emma. There were things I did not understand either. For example, I was a teenager and in high school. We were all sitting at the dinner table enjoying our meal, which was, nine times out of ten, meat and three vegetables as was the custom then. For whatever reason, it fails me now, but I swore at the dinner table and Dad got the electric cord and I was given a sound swishing around my legs and wore those bruises for the next two weeks. I stated then and have always stated since 'that I deserved that belting'. I most certainly deserved to be punished and those times were the times they were. Was that particular punishment too heavy? I can't answer that. I broke the rules and paid the price. Action and consequences. But I still continued with all of my ability to protect my little sister. And at the end of the day, I felt certain that would be one less belting my sister would have had to endure!

But it seemed that nothing I did would ever bring Emma and I closer together. If anything, the chasm between us was growing ever wider and deeper. On weekends, I would be in charge of all three of us when we went out to something like the movies or the Carnival of Flowers, etc. We played tennis together on the road outside our house, Barbie dolls when Jonathon was otherwise engaged. Jonathon joined the Army Cadets, which gave him a different outlook on life. It wasn't really him though, I don't think. Jonathon was more of a dreamer. The Brothers at his high school always felt he was on some far-flung planet and not in the classroom where he should have been. But it was always Jonathon and Emma who were the team and I was the supervisor as I was the taller, more mature-looking of the three. I have been the height I am today, 165cm, since I was 12. That was quite tall for a girl then. In fact, the driver on the bus we got to school from outside our front door tried to charge me adult fare due to my height. He would not be convinced until told by my parents. As the years progressed, I did not change in height at all. Jonathon and Emma did not grow to be very tall either but most of my peers grew to equal or surpass me in height as we journeyed through high school.

Emma definitely gave me the impression all along that she was a nasty bit of goods, as the saying went. 'Mum, she is doing this', 'Mum, she is doing that'! She was what everyone would call a dobber but I always put that down to jealousy over her perceived unjust treatment by Dad even though she was the rightful daughter. I tried even harder. I started work after completing year 11 on Friday at a motel on the range, my first foray into very early morning starts. Very good training for what was to become a way of life for many decades of my life.

I started my general nurses training on 4 March 1974 at the Toowoomba General Hospital. There was a six-week orientation course for which I earned the princely sum of $30 per week. We had no option but to be live-in students those days. The nurses' quarters for the newest nurses were a very old and cold building with walls that only went three quarters of the way up to the ceiling so when the Toowoomba winds kicked in, it howled through the building. I felt somewhat like I had been taken from a palace and dumped into a concentration camp in WWII. I became a very frequent visitor to the matron's office, begging to be allowed to move home. We eventually were moved to the other side of the compound (no pun intended but if the cap fits!) to a far more modern building that had not run out of the obligatory building supplies before the walls were full height at least. This occurred after six months of wind tunnel alley! Dad bought me my first car, a Holden Premier sedan, for $1,000. I paid him and Mum back in instalments directly into their mortgage account every payday. From that moment on, I was in the matron's office on a weekly basis and although the rules stated that trainee nurses must live in for the first 12 months, she finally allowed me to move home just to be free of my constant annoyance. How do you put into words just how much your family means to you and that you are willing to suffer any amount of wrath just to be allowed to live with them!

The relationship between Emma and I had only improved to the point that I now had some money and there were things that she wanted. Over the ensuing years, I was very good for driving her to friends' places, taking her and her friends out, buying her treats, etc.

I even suffered a trip to Brisbane with Emma and her friend all done up in their tartan suits to see the Bay City Rollers at Festival Hall. Now if that is not love, what is, I ask you…

I would not learn for many years that no matter what I did to try to improve the relationship between Emma and I, I had never stood a chance. In her mind, I was foreign and she had all of the "natural" relatives to tell tales to. Her first huge opportunity to really hurt me deeply was when our beloved father died in 1977. Emma was only 15 and already rather artful at "sticking the knife in". She was still a child but boy, was she vindictive! The belief system installed in her by our parents seemed so totally different to the one that I had. For the first time, I truly did feel like I was "not natural"! It seemed that the penny had finally dropped; without Dad, I was a fish out of water, totally alone.

At the time of Dad's death, I was five months pregnant and single. Mum had gone absolutely berserk when she had found out. She could not get from me to Dad quick enough to tell him, as he lay flat on his back following a laminectomy of seven vertebrae and slowly dying from cancer, how I had so badly let them down. Mum had always had this theory that by raising adopted children, they would turn out to be 70% their upbringing and only 30% their hereditary. From that point in my life, she decided that she had got it all wrong and in fact it was only 30% upbringing and 70% hereditary. So, in her mind, the strict Catholic and private school upbringing had been a waste as I had fallen at the first hurdle, as had my biological mother. Dad, as always, had been rather pragmatic about the whole thing, although blatantly terribly upset. It is my greatest regret that I lied to Dad about who the father of my child was as I can never take that back. I had felt that he would take it better if he thought it was the guy I had been engaged to for some time.

The truth, which I had finally told my mother some 20 years later, I am still not certain was any easier for her to handle. I had been a very headstrong person when I was younger and even then, had held some very strong opinions and ideas. I had been working a late shift one evening when a friend and I had finished dinner and gone to the corridor to have our coffees and a cigarette. Out of the blue, she had asked me, 'What would be the first thing you would do if your father's cancer returned?'

Without even a second's hesitation, I had said, 'Get pregnant.'

She had not understood but I explained that I had observed my father for many years with my cousins' babies and it suited him so much that I felt the most precious thing I could give him would be a grandchild. I was engaged at the time so it was not a huge leap to have a child but I added that Dad was going to remain well so it was all just talk.

It had actually been on the day of my engagement party, 19 October 1976; Dad had debilitating and acute pain in his knee. All of my thoughts had been on ensuring that Dad was going to be okay. I had given him painkillers, elevated the leg, bought liniment and a ray lamp and worked on Dad for the better part of the day by massaging, strapping, elevation and providing pain relief. Although he was in absolute agony, the engagement party proceeded and went really well. Dad went to our GP and they could not work out what the issue was. They were X-raying the legs, knees and hips. I begged him to ask to be X-rayed up higher as I felt certain it was radiating pain. Dad would say to me, "Love, Keith knows what he is doing, he is a doctor.'

I only wish I had shared his optimism. Dad had continued to work and had even saved a train by running to uncouple some carriages so that the whole train did not burn. He was a hero but was in agonising pain. He had received a commendation for his efforts.

It had been Sunday mass at St Patrick's Cathedral in Toowoomba that our GP, Keith, came to Dad and said, 'I had honestly begun to think you were a malingerer but I apologise for that and want to see you in my office first thing tomorrow morning.' He had been sitting behind us in the church and had seen just how difficult the most minor movement had been for Dad.

There was now an appointment organised with the orthopaedic surgeon, Bruce Meibush. Dad had been preparing for the appointment and had just come out of the shower and started to get dressed when he lost all sensation in the lower half of his body. It had been extremely lucky that Mum and Dad had always kept a chair in our bathroom and Dad was able to fall onto the chair. I called the ambulance and they got Dad onto the stretcher and headed for the office of Dr Meibush. He came out to the ambulance and made a quick assessment that Dad needed to be admitted to hospital immediately. Bruce did not operate at St Vincent's Hospital so Dad went to the General, my place of work.

After the laminectomy was complete, Dr Meibush stated that he would stake his career on the fact that the spine was the primary carcinoma and the kidney had been a secondary carcinoma. The only way my father would ever stand again would be with a body brace and a walking frame. This had been in January 1977. I had gone to Dad whilst he was still in hospital recovering from surgery to let him know that I was not sure about whether I loved my fiancé and wanted to break the engagement off. Dad, as always, talked me through everything and said that I had to make a decision as it was not fair to him to be left dangling. In truth, my only goal at that point was to give my father a grandchild. But I was not about to try to explain that one.

I had discovered that my fiancé would not be able to father children and I was already seeing someone else, which had been such a low thing to do and I deeply regretted it. Not that my fiancé ever knew, although he had no idea how many times he had nearly caught me out. My mind had solely been on my father and my desire to give him a grandchild. I broke off the engagement, it did not go well. I then set out to locate a suitable father for my child. And I found someone and I did get pregnant. It was not my proudest time but I was completely focussed on the outcome and I really didn't mind who I stepped on in the meantime!

Mum had told me at one stage that my fiancé had been "below my station in life". Just because there had been what were called "Black Mammies" in my mother's early life, this did not give her the right to cast aspersions on her fellow human beings. He had been a wards man at the Toowoomba General Hospital where I trained. I think, truthfully, that it had been her comments that pushed me more towards a relationship with him. In June of 1976, I had gone on my holiday to Canada and the USA. I absolutely fell in love with Canada, as I had always known I would. I did not want to come home, seriously. I decided that I would complete what was left of my training and return to Canada as a trained nurse. On my return from Canada, I had little to no interest in my then boyfriend. I had made other life plans but ironically, it had been Mum who had pushed us back together! Go figure.

I had been working at a nursing home in Toowoomba whilst assisting Mum and my siblings to nurse Dad at home. He was dying and it was killing me. I was sending myself mad reading, researching and determined to find what no one else could find—the cure for my father's disease. All my colleagues thought I had lost the plot. I had long since given up on religion as any sort of assistance but as I lived under Mum's roof, I had no choice but to attend all church services, as mandated by her. It was over Easter of that year when

I was in attendance at Stations of the Cross that someone spoke to me and said that there was no cure for Dad and that I had to let it go and just enjoy the time we had left together. Had it been God? Had it been an angel? I had no idea where my message had come from but I choose to believe now, as I did then, that it had been a divine message specifically for me. I remember it as clearly today as if it was happening right now. (More on what it is I actually believe in later chapters.) I did exactly as I was advised and just tried to make Dad more comfortable. I spent every waking moment cooking all manner of things for him to keep it interesting for him. I had nursed so many dying patients by this stage but the one being looked after to be my own father was almost unbearable. I was, however, determined to hold it together. To put my grief into one of my many thousands of little boxes and store it away with the rest that were already well and truly compartmentalised. I had a duty to work, care for my father, do as much as I could to help Mum and my siblings and make sure that the grandchild that I was carrying was safe.

It became quite apparent to me that my attempt to make my dad a proud grandparent had been left too late and that he would not be around to see my beautiful little girl. Our GP, Keith, made regular home visits to check on Dad and prescribe his morphine and any other medications that were deemed necessary. Every single time he came, he would pull me aside and ask if I had told Mum and my siblings yet how Dad's disease would progress and how he would be at the end. My reply had always been the same. I would tell them what I felt they needed to know as and when they needed to know it. He had always left that decision in my hands and I was so grateful that I had stuck to my principles and held off because Dad did not suffer in the same way as dictated in the medical textbooks, which, sadly, for most sufferers of spinal carcinoma was their fate.

I, of course, wanted my father to die at home with us, his family. Surrounded by those who loved him the most. Dad knew this and he asked me to respect his wishes to go to the hospital for the end as he did not feel that Jonathon and Emma would be able to handle his death at home. They were not trained for and accustomed to it as I was. I would never disagree with Dad but I told him that I could not witness him leaving the house for the final time. He stated that he would let us know when he was ready to go.

It was to be Tuesday morning, 13 September 1977, when the ambulance was arranged to come and take Dad to St Vincent's Hospital in Toowoomba. Mum was not alone; she had my father's sister, Margaret, with her. I had said my goodbyes to Dad and promised to go straight to the hospital from work that afternoon. But by the time I had arrived at the hospital, Dad had already been in a coma. I was devastated that I had not been there for him. Once I was told that the ambos had taken Dad out of the house feet first, I was mortified. It was just not the way you did things. I have always and will always be extremely superstitious. I have absolutely no idea where that ever came from.

On Wednesday, 14 September 1977, we were all called to the hospital as Dad had deteriorated considerably. I called Jonathon at work and told him to get to the hospital and I went and collected Emma from school and made our way to the hospital. Dad had been moved to a private room by this stage. He was being well cared for but nothing was ever going to be good enough for Dad. He suffered very severe acute pain when laid on his left side; he would involuntarily groan in pain. The only thing that helped him was me playing with his hair as I had done all my life. I ended up losing the plot, seeing my father in such pain, and went and told the nurses to come and help me turn him over. They tried to insist that he needed to be rotated to prevent pressure sores on his body. I really lost it then, insisting that he was dying anyway so what did it matter. He deserved to die with dignity.

The day became the evening and Mum wanted me to take Jonathon and Emma home. I did not want to leave Dad as I knew, and I tried to tell Mum, that Dad would not be alive very much longer. His breathing had been Cheyne-stoking for some time already. Mum insisted though and I was not about to create another scene but I found it so hard to walk away that night, knowing that I would be back but that dad would be dead.

And indeed, that is exactly how it happened. My beloved father had left this world. I was totally alone and I had failed in my mission to give Dad a grandchild. I do not think that I have ever felt more alone in my life. I have most certainly had that horrid, empty feeling again for different reasons and it proved that my life choices have not always been right for me. The decisions that I have made without having discussed them with my father or having the opportunity to do so since his death have all been wrong. There have been very few days that have passed since that Wednesday evening in 1977 that I do not speak to Dad and ask his advice. Perhaps I just don't have the ability to hear him anymore. Maybe I truly am "not natural" and that is why I cannot hear his replies. What I do know for a fact is that no one could have been more blessed than I was to have had the most perfect father it was possible to have. Dad had been a true gentleman and an honourable man and I was the luckiest girl in the universe to have been able to call him "My Daddy Edward".

I cannot tell you the key to success,
But the key to failure is trying to please everyone.

-ED SHEERAN

CHAPTER 2

LITTLE GINGE

Waking up the morning after my father's death was just so surreal. Had I even slept? I most certainly felt as if I was in the realm of "never-never" land. Neither awake nor asleep but definitely hovering somewhere in between the two.

There was, however, no time for hovering in my own enormous sense of loss. Mum was up and raring to go. As I was the "one" who was responsible for the housework in its entirety, I was expected to get to it without delay as there was a funeral to plan for Dad, visitors to prepare for and standards to be maintained. No matter the circumstances that life threw at you, those standards of Mum always had to be met but the trouble was that it was me who had to do the donkey work to achieve those standards! That Thursday went by for me in a total blur. Visitors came and went, offering their condolences, but still I needed to keep moving forward with the house-cleaning. And as the ever obedient and grateful daughter, I just kept on keeping on.

My cousin Janet asked how I was going to manage financially whilst still having to pay off my car and having a baby in a few short months. I told her that I had been making extra payments on my car loan and currently had the repayments six months ahead and did not intend to finish work for some time yet so I felt that I would be able to get it even further ahead by the time I stopped working. I had also been furiously saving money in order to give my child the life that he/she deserved. I had established an investment account that would accrue considerable interest and I was working extremely hard to make as many of the baby clothes as I could to reduce costs. I was able to sew, knit and crochet, which came in very handy. We were standing in the back sunroom when Mum came out behind me after having listened to my conversation with Janet and announced that my car had been fully paid for as of the death of my father the previous evening. At first, I did not understand what she was saying to me and I most certainly did not understand her resentful tone whilst telling me. It appeared that Dad, as guarantor on the original car loan, had taken out CCI insurance. Mum had known this fact for every day I had been asking her advice and telling her how far ahead I was with the car payments. Was I wrong to feel that perhaps she could have advised me that it may have been more prudent to put the extra savings into the investment account and allow the interest to help pay off the car? I would never have expected her to actually tell me about the insurance but to allow me to just throw money away like that when there were so many better ways to handle it. I showed just how grateful I was, and I truly was—to Dad, and then stored it into yet another of my little boxes to be dealt with at some future time.

The funeral was held on Friday. It was a day I would never forget but at the same time was sometimes a complete blur. The funeral was held in St Patrick's Cathedral in Toowoomba and I would never forget when it was time for us, as a family, to follow the coffin out of the church. I had held myself and my emotions together, purposefully, but the second I turned and saw that enormous cathedral full to the brim with relatives, friends and well-wishers for Dad, I almost collapsed on the spot. The one and only thing that kept me going, that had been my reason for existing in those dark days, was my unborn child. I had heard talk from Mum with other relatives that I would probably lose the baby with the grief as Dad and I had been so close. I was determined to prove them all wrong, especially Mum. Again, I had to put it in a box, take a deep breath and move down the aisle behind the coffin holding my beloved father.

Dad was buried at the Garden of Remembrance in Toowoomba. It is a truly peaceful and tranquil setting. Or at least, it was in 1977. After the burial, it was back to our house for the wake. The outstanding thing for me was the number of relatives that pulled me aside to tell me all about "the skeletons that they had in their closets". And boy, with some, it was enough to curl your toes! I was made to feel that falling pregnant out of marriage was nothing to worry about. And yes, they fully understood 'what Flo was like' and that it would not be easy for me but I was strong enough to deal with that. The relatives' mistake, in my eyes, was to totally empty Dad's beer fridge during his wake. This had been, by and large, filled with Tasmanian beer that I had bought for him. Dad had an IDC when he was dying and beer was fantastic for keeping the urine clear so it was just one of my many missions to ensure that Dad not only got the best but also that he got variety so he would be less likely to tire of it. When I saw the fridge in the pool room empty, I almost lost the plot! I went to bed and all the relatives, knowing how much they had upset me, were up extremely early the next morning, taking all the empties to the dump. There was no such thing as a recycling bin in those days and they would most certainly have required a good many of them to clear the empties!

The rest of the weekend was spent with relatives surrounding us but by early afternoon on Sunday, Mum, Jonathon, Emma and I were standing on the front footpath, waving goodbye to the last of them.

There we stood, alone, with only our grief and each other. That was when the real fun started.

Slowly, one day became another and then it was a week since Dad had died. 25 September was my mother's birthday and it was going to be extremely difficult for her to deal with. One of her great loves was China and her favourite was the Royal Albert old country roses set. I purchased the tea set for Mum for her birthday to try to make it special as her first one without Dad. Nanna, Mum's mother, asked me what I was giving Mum. I told her what I had bought and she asked how much it had cost. I told her $85 and she then asked if she could give me $20 and have me give it to Mum from the both of us. I agreed to this and that is what we did. Mum really loved it but of course, no matter what she thought of any present, it had only been such a short time since Mum had lost the love of her life.

When Mum had collected all the most precious documents from the bank vault and Dad's will had been read, Mum marched Jonathon and I to the Public Trustees Office for a meeting regarding insurance policies. It appeared there had been four, two of which Mum knew nothing about. These two policies had Jonathon and I named as the beneficiaries. They had been taken out when we were babies. Well, Mum was having none of that and she told Jonathon and I that we had to sign them over to her. Of course, we both did exactly as we were told and signed the paperwork over to Mum claiming that we were in agreeance. I, for one, knew my father was no fool and could have predicted as accurately as Nostradamus what would occur after his demise. I have had a will stating my express wishes for what is to occur with my six bobby pins once I am dead ever since that day. The Public Trustee had advised Jonathon and I that we needed to have a will as, even if you only possessed six bobby pins at the time of your death, without a will, the government would take the lot. Having been forced to hand over what was legally mine had a major effect on the future relationship with my mother. I was single, pregnant and being forced to leave my home after the birth of my baby. How much more cruelty was to be bestowed upon me?

Time slowly moved forwards and we began to live an assemblance of a life without Dad. It was very clear that I was on fragile ground with it being a three to one relationship within the home—Mum, Jonathon and Emma versus the unmarried pregnant Daddy's girl. One evening whilst we were eating dinner, the topic of my unborn child came up as it often did. This time, the conversation turned to adoption and why I did not consider that a viable option for myself. It was made extremely clear that neither my mother, brother nor sister had any intentions of tolerating a screaming baby under their roof, disturbing their peace. The discussion was aimed, as they all were, to ensure that I knew that I was "out in the cold" where the baby was concerned, I was to be given only a couple of weeks grace to recover from the birth and adjust to motherhood before I had to find our own place to live. My sister ensured that I knew that 'Dad wasn't here to protect me now!' Emma asked Jonathon, 'How do you feel about being adopted?'

Jonathon replied, 'But I am not though.' It was that night that Jonathon's world imploded as he found out at 18 what I had found out at 10 years of age. It was much harder for Jonathon to fathom and it changed him on a very deep level. He commenced doing martial arts, which, of course, Mum could not understand in any way, shape or form. Because Jonathon would bring home books on Buddhism, etc., Mum assumed that he was "going off the rails". There seemed to be a lot of arguments between Mum and Jonathon in the ensuing 18 months to 2 years.

Having made their decision on the future of me and my baby, I had to accept that I was not wanted and tried to accept the fact that once I had given birth, I truly would be on my own. At that point in my life, I felt more alone than I had ever felt but I was never going to allow my so-called family to see that. Mum and Emma went on a holiday to North Queensland to visit relatives not too long before the Christmas of 1977. Jonathon was working and Aunty Kate(my mother's sister) had come to stay with me whilst they were away. I never could work out why. It was not as if they cared about my wellbeing in any way. I was checking out the specials in the Sunday papers and found that the dinner set, Royal Albert old country roses, which matched the tea set I had bought Mum for her birthday, was on sale in Myers for $140. On Monday morning, I was up at the crack of dawn and on the doorstep of Myers, waiting for the doors to open. I bought the dinner set for my mother for Christmas and also bought myself the one that I loved. I very proudly took them home, extremely happy that I had sorted a present for Mum that I knew she would love. In the ensuing days, I started to worry. I was being forced to leave the family home in roughly 6-8 weeks, had I spent too much, would Mum be angry? Everything I have ever done in my entire life had been to please other people. It gave me so much pleasure to give to others. I had never worried about receiving. Love, to me, had always been about giving, seeing the joy that the perfect gift or the perfect card could provide to someone.

I apparently worried myself into a bit of a frenzy as I ended up in St Vincent's Hospital with the most severe frontal headache and a diagnosis of pre-eclampsia. I was, from then on until the birth, to be on total bed rest with only toilet privileges. Mum and Emma had arrived home and Mum was none too pleased that her slave/housekeeper was out of action. Christmas came and went. It was held at the home of Aunty May, one of my mother's sisters. It was very difficult without Dad. Mum loved her dinner set that Jonathon had offered me $40 towards and asked if I would give it to Mum from him and Emma as well.

Mum truly was becoming quite weary of the doctor-imposed strict bed rest regime for me and the week before I was due to give birth, Mum loaded me into the car and off to town in Toowoomba. We pounded the pavements in and out of shops until I now possessed enough, in my mother's opinion, to be able to move into my own accommodation within two weeks of giving birth. Forgive me, but that day, I truly wondered exactly what the hell my biological mother had landed me into. Was this the way normal families acted towards each other? But it was my solemn belief that it was my duty to be grateful to Mum and Dad for having raised me as their own. If not for the attitude of my mother and sister every step of the way, I may well have totally forgotten that I was "not natural", as being adopted was never an issue to me. My issue was and still is with the one who gave me away, thrown into the too hard basket.

According to my dates, my due date was 11 January, so when that had come and gone along with many more days, I was more than a little over it. On 14 January 1978, Saturday, I got up, had breakfast, put a scarf around my hair and set about cleaning the house from top to bottom. I worked until I was exhausted. By about 17:30, I had started having slight pains in my lower abdomen. We all went off to 18:00 mass at St Patrick's. The pains continued and it was during mass that Mum noticed me flinch a few times. She knew that I was in labour. We went home and when the contractions started to become troublesome, in my mother's eyes, she took me to the hospital and went home, having left instructions to be notified once the deed was done! It was a long night, dozing in between contractions, feeling desperately alone. My doctor had told me that he would have to use forceps for the delivery as I had very prominent spines* and I had told him to absolutely forget bringing them anywhere near me as I would not need them!

*The ischial spines can be palpated at about a finger-length into the vagina, at 4 and 8 o'clock. They are felt as bony prominences. It can be uncomfortable for the woman when you press on the spines.

Why is it important to identify the ischial spines during labour?

1) The station of the foetal head is measured above or below the ischial spines:

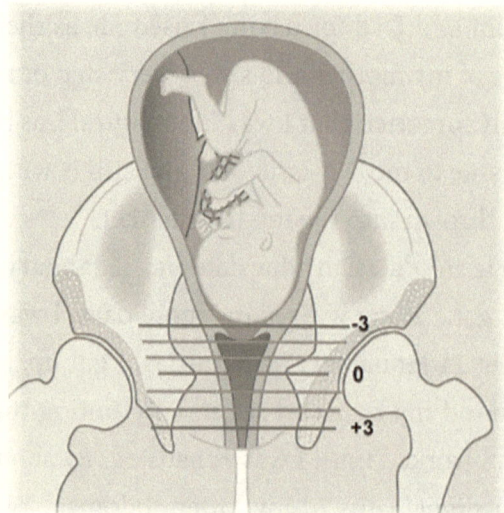

By all accounts, my ischial spines were extremely prominent and my doctor did not believe that I would be able to force my baby through the birth canal without the assistance of forceps.

When the time came for my baby to be born, Dr Keith was standing at the foot of the labour ward bed, leaning against the wall with his pyjama top on under his suit coat, arms folded and smiling as I determinedly pushed my baby out to greet the world with no forceps in sight. Once she was born, Keith said, 'Well, I'll be buggered, I was absolutely certain that you would not be able to do that alone.' My beautiful new baby daughter had quite a misshapen head but I had done it all on my own. It meant the world to me. Brianna Mary was born on 15 January 1978 at 05:45. She was very long and skinny and had red hair and was truly the most gorgeous little thing I had ever seen in my life. It was her and I together against the world. My family had made that perfectly clear.

Of course, it was not terribly long before they showed up to check out my illegitimate daughter. Mum was all over her. Emma was too busy almost fainting from the sight of blood to do anything but sit on the stairs with her head between her knees. Jonathon was an uncle and seemed to be quite smitten by the idea. I, however, had not forgotten every single barb that had been thrown at me for month after month. From now on, it would be Brianna and I against the world.

I actually called Brianna's father late that afternoon to advise him about his daughter. I had not told him I was pregnant once we had broken up. I had what I wanted from the arrangement and had not seen the need to complicate things. But having my daughter in my arms changed things and I knew he at least had the right to know she existed. He said next to nothing to me but I had, at last, done the right thing.

Later that Sunday night, I started to develop a thrombophlebitis* in my left leg caused from having been placed in stirrups to have my episiotomy** sutured following the birth. The treatment at the time was to paint it with iodine and bandage it for support. I was due to graduate from my three years of nurses training the following Friday night but I was not going to make it as my doctor kept me in hospital until Saturday morning.

*Noun: **thrombophlebitis**

1) Inflammation of the wall of a vein with associated thrombosis, often occurring in the legs during pregnancy.

An **episiotomy (/əˌpiːziːˈɒtəmiː/ or /ɛˌpəsaɪˈɒtəmiː/), also known as perineotomy, is a surgical incision of the perineum and the posterior vaginal wall generally done by a midwife or obstetrician during the second stage of labour to quickly enlarge the opening for the baby to pass through.

My dear friend Angela came to visit on Monday morning just 24 hours after Brianna had been born. Angela and her husband James had been trying for so long to conceive a baby and I felt so sorry for her. I had been so convinced that I would have a girl and it never entered my head that I could have a redhead. So, I had quite confidently said to Angela that if I had a boy or it was a redhead, she could have the baby! She came into my room with the biggest grin on her face and said, 'Well, I have come to collect my baby.' We laughed at just how silly I had been; my daughter was going nowhere but with me. Angela did have a son some years later.

I was extremely pleased to arrive home on that Saturday morning. Brianna was now on a bottle as, due to the strict four-hourly feeding regime at the hospital, I had been told to put her on a bottle or stay in hospital even longer. I was determined to breastfeed but it was a vicious cycle. When I had done my training, you were given the choice to do either midwifery or psychiatry as your elective subject. I had always chosen psychiatry. I knew all but nothing about midwifery and absolutely nothing about breastfeeding. The baby was brought to you every four hours in a strict time order. 6, 10, 2, 6, 10, 2… I would struggle for ages trying to get Brianna to latch on to the breast but having been comped with the bottle maybe two hours earlier, she had no interest in breastfeeding. Never once did any of the nurses try to help me with breastfeeding Brianna or even ask if I required any assistance. So many of them knew me from when we had worked together that they assumed that I knew what I was doing. Nothing could have been further from the truth. And as one day became the next, my breasts became more engorged and painful and it was impossible to sleep between the pain of my leg and my breasts. When I did manage to doze off, I would wake up with a fright, absolutely saturated with breast milk and would have to go and shower and change. And start all over again.

I had settled Brianna into her bassinet and was in the kitchen preparing the sterilising unit and sorting and making formula. Next thing, I heard Mum speaking to someone who was not Jonathon or Emma. She had brought one of the neighbours in and was leading them down the hall to my bedroom where Brianna was. The neighbour was asking who she was and Mum was replying that she was ours. The neighbour then wanted to know who the mother was and Mum replied, 'Ellie.' She then said that was not possible as she had spoken to me over the fence only the week before and I had not looked pregnant then. She was eventually convinced that Brianna was indeed my daughter and the doting grandmother was in her element.

That had just been the beginning of the "love affair" between Brianna and her grandma. Funnily enough, there was never any further mention of me having to leave home again. In fact, there would come a time that Mum would try extremely hard to keep Brianna living in her house with her. More on that later.

Days became weeks and Brianna and I were falling into our routine and I knew that motherhood was my life's purpose. Brianna was not to have an easy time of it though. Breastfeeding would have been so beneficial for her as she had a severe lactose/sucrose/fructose intolerance. She had to be fed with a product called Isomil. It was a soy milk substitute for babies with a milk allergy. It truly was the most feral-smelling liquid and the taste was twice as bad as the smell. It came in cans and was an authority prescription in those days. You would get five cans per script and it was made up with a ratio of equal parts Isomil and boiled water. It came at a cost of $5 per script or $2.50 for those on government benefits.

Brianna was also allergic to Napisan (the nappy soaking product) so I would have to boil her nappies every morning in order to keep them bright and white. By three months of age, Brianna had developed asthma rather severely and was on liquid Ventolin and several other medications. Of course, it would not be until she turned two that they would officially label her an asthmatic and it was, in fact, when she was just over two that she was in St Vincent's Hospital children's unit in an oxygen tent for severe asthma.

Mum may well have been totally smitten with her granddaughter, but her feelings had not changed where I was concerned. Brianna was six weeks old and I had been up early as usual, fed Brianna, had the nappies on to boil by 06:00, put Brianna back to sleep and had prepared breakfast for Mum, Jonathon and Emma as was my responsibility. All this while feeling very much less than well. It came time for Brianna's 10:00 feed, at which time I bathed her first. I did this on the kitchen table. As I lifted the bath full of water from the sink to the table, I came over all dizzy and almost lost the lot onto the floor. I went to Mum and asked if she could bathe Brianna as I was scared that I might drop her as I felt so unwell. Her answer was, 'No, now that you are a mother, you just have to keep going, no matter if you are dying. That's just how it is!'

I said, 'Thanks for nothing, Mum,' and proceeded to bathe my beautiful daughter, repeatedly apologising to Brianna for the grandmother I had landed her with and so determined not to harm this precious bundle I was fully responsible for!

I may not be able to remember very much from my childhood but I have extremely clear visions of Dad cooking us dinner on the many occasions that Mum had "taken to her bed" because she had been sick from one thing or another. Dad had two specialities that I had just adored. One had been his mince and toast dish but my very favourite had been his sausages, baked beans and tomato soup. We always had what I call vaco-sausages (these were purchased from our butcher on Ruthven Street in Toowoomba in a white box), which were nothing like the fatty greasy sausages that I have so much trouble eating these days. They were more like the American hot dog of today than the traditional Aussie snag! Dad would cook them and chop them up, then add them to the beans and soup and heat it all up. I used to love dinner when Mum was sick. Perhaps it was because I was "not natural" that the rules that applied to Mum as a mother were totally different from the rules that applied to me as a mother. As far as I was concerned, then and still today, Mum was being totally hypocritical! And I know as sure as I am sitting here typing these words, that had Dad been alive, things would have been so very different.

Brianna also suffered from severe reflux and colic for which she was prescribed Merbentyl. It had little effect at the time. In fact, the product, Infants' Friend*, proved to be of greater value in settling Brianna when she was in pain. In 1985, the health department of Western Australia issued a statement that Merbentyl caused respiratory issues and should not be given to children under six months of age!

Infants' Friend Oral Liquid is Australia's number one colic and wind medicine for baby colic relief. Distributed Australia-wide, *Infants' Friend Oral Liquid* has been a household name for more than eighty years and has been used with great success.

My poor little baby was plagued with problems. As the months had progressed, so had Brianna's need for more substantial food, as with all children. She loved her food and the time came when I thought that I would trial Brianna with scrambled egg. It was not something that she especially enjoyed, thankfully, and she had only eaten about one teaspoon full. I had settled her in her cot so that I could clean up the kitchen from her bath and feeding and she was exceptionally quiet, unusually. I went down the hall and as soon as I walked around the door, I could see that she was not well. She was as pale as a ghost, had vomit and diarrhoea everywhere, her tiny buttocks were red raw, covered with a second pink skin that had dots of blood all over it. I cleaned her up and made her comfortable and we were off to the doctor. She had a gross allergy to eggs. It was, in fact, so severe that to just touch the inside of an eggshell and touch her face or put it in her mouth would have her very quickly into anaphylaxis and me rushing her to the hospital.

Life as Brianna's mum was full on but I revelled in it. As a nurse, organisation was part of who I was but it was not only my daughter I had responsibility for. I was expected to do all the housework, prepare all meals for the family to be on the table by my mother's predetermined time every day, and anything else that my mother saw fit to throw at me. Brianna had been five months old and teething when Emma's birthday was fast approaching. She wanted a birthday cake the same as her cousin had for his birthday but Mum could not afford to buy it so it was decided that I would make one from scratch.

I had offered to try. The day came and Brianna was screaming all day and nothing would calm her or her gums. I made the sponge and iced the birthday cake to Emma's specifications whilst holding and rocking Brianna in one arm all day. The expectations placed on me were always extremely high. Even the Christmas prior to Brianna's birth, when I was meant to be on strict bed rest, I had to make the coleslaw for the family Christmas get-together.

It was very rare that I got or took a break from my never-ending duties or my gorgeous baby girl. Emma was raising money for something or other and I spent many, many weeks cooking and crocheting for the stall she was to hold in town in Toowoomba. It was not as if I was already overwhelmed or anything. Brianna would sit with Mum every evening whilst I would crochet a full 30 cm doily, start to finish, or cushion covers, etc. All that precious time spent with my daughter whilst I helped a sister who could really care less that I breathed the same air that she did! There was one time that I had organised to go to the shops with my dear friend, Angela. To understand the importance of this outing to me, I will lay down some groundwork first. In 1978, when you were a single mother, you were paid by the state government for the first six months of your baby's life. When the end of the first six months was approaching, you had to apply to the federal government for continuing support. I had done this and been told that as I had an investment account, and a reasonably healthy one in their eyes, I would have to wait six weeks before receiving any further support and I also had to seek the assistance of a lawyer to get maintenance from Brianna's father. I recall walking in a half-daze down the street after that meeting, thinking about how I could provide the life that I believed my baby girl was entitled to in this predicament. Just to clarify what we are talking about here—the most government support I ever received from DHS was $129/fortnight with which I had to pay board, pay ¼ of all household bills, private health insurance, provide all of Brianna's special requirements re medications, creams for severe eczema, her prescription milk, food for us both and also try to keep us clothed as well. The only other monies that had been paid to me had been $40 maternity allowance when Brianna was born and $21/month child endowment.

I had found a solicitor and it was a lengthy process of writing down everything that I had provided for Brianna thus far in her life and how much we were going to claim from her father. The solicitor decided to make a claim for $1,000 initial costs and $100 per month. This was passed to the opposing solicitor and a court date was set. It was to be a Monday and by Friday, I was a nervous wreck as I had absolutely no knowledge of or experience in dealing with courts and I had no intention of attending. I would withdraw my claim and try to get a job, anything to avoid having to go so far out of my comfort zone. I was in such a state all day, I had rung the solicitor several times who kept telling me to be patient, we would hear from them. Mum sat at her sewing table in the front room just letting me get more and more upset. Not a single consoling word. It was rather too close to COB for the week but the solicitor did ring, they had offered $200 and $40/month. I accepted before he had finished speaking, I think. I was so relieved.

So, after all the processes were complete and I had received my first payments, I wanted to go out and treat myself and buy something special for Brianna. I had pre-organised with Mum for her to babysit Brianna for me. I had been up early and done everything that I could, including Brianna's bath and feed and settled back down for a sleep in the hope that Mum would not find anything amiss that would affect my day out. Angela arrived and headed straight in to see Brianna and say hello to Mum. A small chat ensued and then Angela said, 'Are you ready to go?'

I said that I was and turned to go. Mum, from her position on her sewing chair in the front room, said, 'I am afraid Ellie can't go anywhere until the vacuuming is done!'

I was flabbergasted. I said to Mum, 'Why didn't you ask me before Angela arrived?'

Mum's reply, 'You should have known that it needed doing.'

Now I had options here. Well, no, I kid myself that I did. I was already getting out of having Jonathon's and Mum's lunch on the table for 12md. If I argued too much, I would hear about it non-stop and life would be so difficult for me for weeks to come. 'Do you mind if I run the vacuum through first, Angela?'

'No, that is fine, Ellie, I will wait.'

I was extremely close to the end of my tether. How was I meant to tolerate being nothing more to Mum than her personal Cinderella, chef and general handyman? Something had to give, soon. My brother had always been exceptionally fast to remind me of just how quickly I would "go off" and "fly into a rage". I wonder if Jonathon had ever once stopped to consider why I may have been forced into the actions that I took.

All that I had ever wanted in my life, especially as I was growing up, had been to be part of a great big loving family that gathered together in good times and bad, were always there for each other without question or hesitation, who helped each other out without the need to be recompensed or acknowledged and who truly loved because that was what "real families" did! I was destined to never achieve that feeling of warmth that came from true love, compassion and loyalty. I spent a lifetime giving love, compassion, loyalty and so much more, which enabled me to look at myself in the mirror and know that I was good enough and I was loved.

A mother is she who can take the place of all others
But whose place, no-one else can take.

-CARDINAL MERMILLOD

CHAPTER 3

MIDWIFERY

As if a gift directly from Dad, I received a letter from the Mater Mothers' Hospital in South Brisbane to see if I was interested in joining the September intake of midwives. I had completely forgotten that I had deferred midwifery for a year. It was an incredible gift that had arrived just in time to save my sanity. Yes! Yes! Yes! was my immediate reply but I was no longer on my own. I had to consider what would be the best thing I could do for the welfare of my gorgeous daughter, Brianna.

If I went ahead and completed midwifery, I would then be a Double Certificate Nurse (DC), which, of course, meant greater earning capacity and a better life for Brianna and myself. However, we lived in Toowoomba and the Mater was in Brisbane. I would require a babysitter that was prepared to care for a child whilst I did shift work, including overnight stays when I was on night duty.

Without the benefit of the Internet, I did as much research as I could into babysitters in Brisbane but I did not like what I was finding out. Brianna had so many health issues that it could not be just anyone that I left in charge of the most precious cargo I had ever had in my life. It was tearing me apart when Mum said that she would "babysit" Brianna, as long as I paid her! At the time, it seemed the answer to all my prayers. Mum loved Brianna, had complete and total knowledge of all her ailments, how she reacted to everything and Brianna adored her grandma. It would mean that I would only be able to see Brianna two days a week and I had to decide if this sacrifice to advance my career was worth that loss. Hindsight is a truly beautiful thing but also, in my opinion, an absolute waste of time. We make the decisions we make, based on all the facts that we have to hand at any given time and must proceed as long as our gut instinct thinks we are correct. I knew without a shadow of a doubt that leaving Brianna with Mum was the very best thing that I could do for my baby girl. And I also knew that getting away from Mum was the very best thing that I could do for me. But, as always, where Mum was concerned, there would always be something that would come back and bite me squarely on the arse! My gut was telling me that all would not be well.

After much ado and many tears, I set off for my start in midwifery training in the big smoke. I had put all new tyres on my car, it was all serviced and ready to take on the travel backwards and forwards between Toowoomba and Brisbane. I was to live in the nurses' quarters on the hospital grounds and all the other trainee midwives were great. But it was the hardest thing I had ever done in my life. I was more often on the phone outside my room to Brianna than not. She was eight months old and I like to think that she was listening intently to my every word. Oh, how awesome mobiles, Skype, etc. would have been back then. The days turned into weeks and I went home to Toowoomba for my two days off each week, leaving to head back to Brisbane with every stretch of the trip mapped out in time increments that, as long as the road was flowing, would allow me just enough time to run into the quarters and drop off my belongings and run to work. Every time I left Brianna, I felt another piece of my heart tear apart but I had to keep going to improve our lives in the long term.

I had developed a fair degree of paranoia where the ability of my car to keep me travelling between Brisbane and Toowoomba was concerned. I had each leg of the journey down to minutes and if one thing was to go wrong, I may not get to see my baby girl or I may have to leave her sooner than I felt that I wanted to. On a visit back to Toowoomba, I had heard a noise under the bonnet whilst travelling along. I mentioned the noise to Jonathon when I got home and asked what he thought it could be. Should I take it to a mechanic? Jonathon stated that he knew what the issue was when he had a look the following morning and proceeded to "fix the tappets". I did not drive my car again until it was time for me to leave to return to Brisbane for my late shift. I had, as always, only left the exact amount of time required to arrive for the commencement of my shift. I knew from the off that there was something amiss but it was during my descent of the Toowoomba Range that I knew I was in real trouble. Once at the bottom of the range, I could not get the car to do any more than 80k/hour and it was shuddering the whole time. It did not give up though, so neither did I. I actually arrived at the nurses' quarters only minimally late and dumped my belongings in my room and ran to work. No time to think about the car now.

I had two late shifts in a row so I got in the car the following morning and it started, which was a miracle, and I drove it out onto Annerley Road and straight across to a garage that was immediately on the opposite side of the road. I explained what had occurred the previous day, gave them my work number and asked that they let me know what was wrong and what was required to repair it. I was working in the Special Care Unit at the time and was so engaged with caring for the neonates that when one of the other nurses called me to the phone, I had completely forgotten I was expecting a call. Jonathon had definitely "fiddled with the tappets" all right; he had the car running on two cylinders instead of six all the way from Toowoomba to Brisbane. He went on to explain that someone must have been watching over me as I drove not only all the way from Toowoomba but also the fact that it had restarted and driven across the road to where I had parked it at the service station, as none of them had been able to get it to restart and they had to push it into the service bay. The head gasket was blown. I gave approval for them to repair it.

As arranged with the mechanic, I went to pay for and collect my car. I went for a drive along Annerley Road past Boggo Road Jail and it was apparent that the gearbox was not functional as it would not move out of first gear. I turned around and went straight back to the mechanic. He had suspected that the gearbox might have needed replacing so again I had to walk away and leave my car to spend another several hundred dollars on it. It was eventually repaired. I had needed to borrow some of the money from Mum as the first repair had almost cleaned me out. She had a neighbour bring me down the money. Once the car had been sorted and safely back in front of the nurses' quarters, he drove me down to the Gold Coast for dinner and then, after seeing me safely home, drove all the way back to Toowoomba. Moral of this story, never let your brother anywhere near your car!

Second moral—never borrow money from my mother! All the details were written in her "little black book", which was in point of actual fact, *my* little red and black book that I had purchased and used when Dad had bought me my very first car in 1974, to record all the repayments and attach the receipts to as proof of payment. It transpired that after I had given her the notebook, as I had no real need of it, she had all different sections for all three of her children and anyone else who owed her money. She was the type of lender who nagged you until your debt was cleared. I so very often wanted to remind her of the insurance policies that she had stolen from Jonathon and I. I just paid up like the dutiful daughter.

Not long after that, and in the interests of safety, I looked into buying a brand-new Datsun 180B. I took it for a test drive and was very impressed. It was only $5,000 on road. It was only a 4-cylinder as opposed to the 6-cylinder that I was currently driving, so also cheaper to run. I spoke to Mum about all the reasons I thought this was the best thing I could do for Brianna and I. When would I learn! Mum had found out the hourly rate for babysitting at the time. She then added up every single hour, 24 hours a day, 7 days a week and announced that I had better not buy this car or she would be charging me what her babysitting should really cost me… This was despite the fact that she had paid absolutely nothing out for Brianna. I had provided every single article of food, clothing, footwear, bathing products, washing products, etc. I stopped at Plainland on my way home to Toowoomba every single time I had days off and purchased the meat, vegetables and fruit that I then made up into all of the meals required by Brianna. All Mum had to do was take them out of the freezer each day and heat them and feed her. Mum could not decide to give Brianna anything due to her allergies so everything she required was provided by me. I was also still expected to pay ¼ of all the bills coming into the household in Toowoomba as well as survive in Brisbane. I thought Mum's treatment of me and the money for which I worked extremely hard to be quite callous! But Mum's only true motivation was money. I did not buy the car!

Two of the other trainees and I decided to move out of the nurses' quarters to a two-story townhouse in Petrie Terrace. It overlooked what was then known as Lang Park. This was great IF you were off duty at the time of the game but if you were unfortunate enough to have scored a late shift that day, you would have to double park and wait for the crowds to come and collect their cars before you could park your car and go to bed and get some sleep before starting the early shift the following day. There was no off-street parking with these terraces and it was a bit of a drawback but it was just a quick trip across William Jolly Bridge and you were at work.

I had brought Brianna to Brisbane on my days off to move into the townhouse. I had needed to go to the Mater Mothers to see one of my flatmates-to-be and I had asked a dear friend in the nursing quarters if she would watch Brianna whilst I rushed over to do what I needed to do. Agnes thought it was a wonderful idea so off I set. On my return, I found Agnes making her authentic Chinese fried rice with Brianna hanging on her every word. Agnes said that Brianna had touched the inside of an eggshell that was sitting in the bin but that she had cleaned her hands immediately. All seemed okay so we set off to the townhouse. By the time we arrived, Brianna was very tired so I got her to lay on the couch whilst I carried belongings up the stairs to my room. When I came back downstairs, Brianna was gasping for breath, looking very cyanosed (bluish around the lips) and quite swollen. I scooped her up and raced back to the Mater and into the children's hospital. One little touch of an egg had set off a massive anaphylactic reaction. The rest of the day was spent getting Brianna right to travel back to Toowoomba where Mum was waiting to let me know, in no uncertain terms, how stupid and careless I had been! Maybe so but she had been in the best of hands for this eventuality with me a trained nurse and the doctor in charge at the children's that day a friend I had worked with for a long time. It was always the same with Mum, and for that matter, her mother—Nanna; it made not a single ounce of difference how much nursing training I did or how highly I was regarded. As far as they were both concerned, their years of life experience ran rings around any training that I had done and their knowledge would always remain greater by the sheer fact that they were older than I. How could anyone compete with that! I had tried to politely point out when they were completely wrong but Nanna had been so bloody nasty to me one evening whilst staying for a visit that I had let her have it with both barrels. I had been in bed asleep for hours when Mum came in at 02:00 to tell me to come and apologise to Nanna for what I had said. I told Mum that I had nothing to apologise for as everything I had said to Nanna was factual. She then laid on the usual guilt trip, 'Then just do it for me so I can get some sleep tonight.' I always gave in and did as I was told, but never happily.

The townhouse was good for a while but I really was enjoying "the single life" whilst I was in Brisbane and the girls that I shared with made no bones about the fact that they were not entirely happy about my goings on. Things became a little tense and a friend had offered me a room with her in her Holland Park house. I jumped at the chance. I had my car loaded to the hilt when I went in to do an early shift before heading back to Toowoomba that afternoon for days off and take back a load of belongings that I would not require living with Pattie. When I came out and was heading to my car, one of the girls I had shared the townhouse with was standing by my passenger front door. She had been heading to her car and had seen St Lawrence students breaking into my car. She had yelled at them and they had scarpered so she was unable to stop them. They had rummaged through my belongings, leaving them in a dishevelled state, until they found a purse that only had $7 in it but otherwise had not disturbed the overloaded car. I thanked her profusely and started the long drive home to Toowoomba. I was in heavy traffic on Fairfield Road and was stuck waiting through several light changes at Muriel Avenue when my mind began to wonder as to why the boys who had broken into my car had not taken the TV, radio and a car full of things that could have been sold for money. I unconsciously must have lifted my foot from the brake as the next thing I knew, my bonnet was buckling up in front of me. I had run into the end loader in front of me. I drove straight over to the service station and they repaired the damage as best they could. I continued home rather slowly and had to get a second-hand bonnet and the radiator replaced the next morning.

Living with Pattie was a load of fun. Life was pretty good actually. When Mum wasn't breathing down my throat, that is. I was living the life of a "single chic" whilst in Brisbane and the "respectable mother" whilst in Toowoomba. I really did have the best of both worlds. Pattie and I were sitting after work one day talking about life whilst having a coffee and I said that if I were to be pregnant at that moment, I would have no idea whether it would be black or white! I was not bragging in any way but after the restrictive, almost suffocating life I had led up until this time, I was enjoying life. Midwifery had turned out to be a great love that I never knew I had. I fell into it naturally and, with very few exceptions, mostly self-inflicted, I always enjoyed work. It was the hardest thing I had ever done having left Brianna with Mum but, at the same time, it was the best thing I had ever done. I was able to be an individual, not just Cinderella to a family that could care less. I had been an adult for quite a while at this stage but every aspect of the life I had led had been scrutinised by Mum and if she did not approve of your actions, you heard about it forever more. Her favourite cry was how much I had let her and Dad down after everything they had done for me. She would then coerce what she considered to be acceptable behaviour from me by stating that I had 'to do it for her sake' as I owed her that. I realised that I should have taken the initiative and left after Brianna had been born, if only to live a peaceful life. Brianna and I would be moving into our own home when I finished my midwifery training.

The sense of euphoria I had developed about my "single" life in Brisbane was to be very short-lived. I arrived home late one afternoon for my days off and there was something blatantly amiss. I established very rapidly that there was nothing wrong with Brianna and it turned out that it was Emma who had an issue. It took long enough for her to fess up and I swear she almost choked on the words—I am pregnant! Well, well, well, how the tides had turned. Pot, kettle, black sprung to mind. Did I say everything that I had kept pent up since I was pregnant with Brianna? Sometimes I wondered what use my spine was to me other than to cause me pain! Oh no, the gutless wonder that I was, I went straight into protective big sister mode—I will get us a flat in Brisbane, she can stay with me, have the baby at the Mater, I would speak to my boss, Sister Jill Stringer, but Brianna would have to come and live with us and Emma would need to babysit, as I would not be able to afford to pay Mum and get a flat for Emma and I. What was I doing? At least I would have Brianna with me. This is who I was, I was a carer, I looked after people even if they were only using and abusing me. That was what I did.

I came back to Brisbane after my days off and my head was spinning from the fact that life was quintessentially about to return to what was effectively its norm but just in a different city. I immediately set the wheels in motion for the big move. I started looking at flats and ended up getting one in Holland Park not far from Pattie and right in the middle of all the amenities so very handy for Emma when I was at work. Not quite so handy, as it turned out, for a toddler under the age of two who loved to go exploring! When Brianna said she was "going shops", that was exactly what she meant. She would put Dolly in her stroller, collect her handbag and off she would go. It seemed to take me an inordinately long amount of time saying 'have a lovely time' to realising that I had better run. Brianna's love of the shops never waned and she is now 38 ½ years old!

Being so desperate for a proper "family relationship", I saw this upcoming experience yet another opportunity for Emma and I to become closer as sisters. It was the one thing that I had always wanted—a loving sister. I had hoped that now that Emma was in the same position that I had been less than 18 months previously, perhaps she would have a greater understanding of the trauma she, Jonathon and Mum had put me through and that we may at last find some common ground. I was determined to make every effort to achieve this goal.

Oh, how naïve can one person be! Emma had: A. absolutely no interest in the foetus growing inside of her and B. had even less interest in being closer to me. I, as always, was a means to an end for Emma. She was the coldest, most callous person I think it had ever been my misfortune to encounter in this life! But would I give up trying? Not for more than another 20 years!

Emma was giving the baby up for adoption, no questions asked, no answers given. She would not even acknowledge that there was a baby growing inside of her. She had a particularly unhealthy attitude towards her unborn child. She also seemed unable to decide who the father was as well. Some, even today, stated he was from North Queensland whilst others stated he was from Toowoomba. Whether he was ever even informed of his impending child was anyone's guess! I offered, over and over again, to raise her baby as my own so at least it would grow up in its "natural" family. I had honestly thought that this would mean something to Emma after the way she had made me feel for being "unnatural"; I could not even contemplate that she would have her own child put through the same trauma at the hands of some other spiteful sibling. No one would look twice if I appeared with a second baby having already had Brianna. Emma would not even entertain the idea as if the very thought of it repulsed her. She had definitely not been backwards in having her fun but had no concept of how to take responsibility for her own actions. I would continue to ask to be allowed to bring the baby up as he had Dad in his DNA and I would get to keep just a little bit of the most important man that had ever or would ever be in my life. It would not eventuate.

I truly enjoyed having Brianna with me and to know that at the end of a shift, she would be at home when I got there. I was able to take her on outings and simply enjoy being her Mum, my favourite role in this life. Mum and Jonathon were down rather frequently, which did not help Emma to even attempt to stand on her own two feet or help Brianna realise that I was her mother, not Mum. My mother allowed my baby girl to call her Mum so Brianna was totally confused. She never had to ask for anything, she merely had to point. So her speech was not developing at the expected intervals and I was extremely upset.

When visitors came to see Emma, we all had to pretend that she was sick and in bed—my bed. The visitor would be allowed to see her whilst she lay on her side with a cushion disguising her ever-growing bump. I was giving my sister the easiest ride through this pregnancy unlike the hell that she had put me through. Mum most certainly did not have the same bitterness towards Emma that she had when I was pregnant. She also did not seem too worried about her grandchild being given away. I wondered if she ever considered their fate. Would they be treated as harshly as I had been?

My attempt at "doing the right thing" was turning into a circus and I was very clearly the clown. I had thought that I was doing something to help my sister but they—Emma and Mum—were both just using me again. I must have had an awful childhood, except for

Dad's presence, during which the gratitude that I owed my mother for saving me was expected to be repaid a million-fold. Every single time I thought I could make headway with Mum or Emma, their agenda would show itself and I would just have to play along out of respect for all that Mum had done to save me from a fate worse than death. And to think that if Mum had not received that message from her friend telling her that she only had that very day to get to Brisbane to collect me, I would have been given to the next family on the adoption waiting list. I have to wonder just how much worse that could have turned out for me.

We are never so defenceless against
suffering as when we love.

-SIGMUND FREUD

CHAPTER 4

MY DESCENT TOWARDS HELL

I considered that the best way to deal with my feelings was to totally throw myself into work. I was working on a public floor at this time and had a patient that I thought was lovely. We hit it off immediately. She was about a decade older than me, which did not seem to be of any consequence as we shared a sense of humour, and work really was my refuge from the pain that was occurring in my home and life. This patient was English and was a long-term patient due to her gestational diabetes. As a midwife, we were trained to take in the whole family dynamic in our treatment of our patients, as to the effect their interactions would have on the health of our patient. Stress was not something that was conducive to good health at the best of times and could have a catastrophic effect on both the mother and unborn child in pregnancy, especially when there were extra pressures on the pregnancy, such as Angela had.

This particular family had quite a few peculiarities that seemed to cause Angela considerable stress. Her parents, who had also emigrated from England, absolutely hated her husband, William, with a passion. It was rather normal for a girl's parents to dislike her choice in men but this was a good bit stronger than I have witnessed in many other families. The parents and the husband visited Angela at different times so that they did not need to run into each other. Even with my weird experiences, to me this did seem a step too far.

Things were travelling along reasonably well and, at least, I knew I could have a good natter and a laugh with a like-minded spirit at work. Angela had had two children already, Tracey—11 and Clayton—8. The discussions held in handovers and with attending doctors showed that Tracey could benefit from some psychological help as she seemed to be carrying more worries than a child of that age should. Clayton was very blatantly Mummy's boy and very spoiled. Her husband, William, had had a vasectomy after Clayton had been born in UK. After having arrived in Australia from England, via a four-year residence in New Zealand, he had a reversal performed so that they could have another child.

On one occasion, I arrived at work to find Angela in a dreadful state. She was inconsolable after having found out that William had cheated on her. He had blamed her parents for him straying as, when they had first come to Australia, they had lived with William and Angela. He had apparently found the pressure too much and had gone in search of some relief.

Angela desperately wanted to end her marriage to William. To her, his actions were unforgiveable and I counselled her as best I could. Of course, this was a stress Angela had not needed so all the staff had to be informed. After much soul-searching, she decided not to end her marriage due to her current predicament. She made it perfectly clear to me and others that, had she not been pregnant, her marriage would have been over.

This event in Angela's life brought us closer due to my own feelings of utter contempt for men who found any reason to break their marriage vows. I would find the time to shave Angela's legs and assist with all manner of personal treatments for her. It was my duty to give my patient the sounding board she needed to vent any anger, frustration or feelings of loss. It was also my duty to make my patients feel relaxed, comfortable and as happy as possible to ensure that the best possible outcome be achieved for both Mother and Baby.

I was an excellent midwife and I loved my job with a passion so bringing the full package to my patients was an absolute joy that all empaths felt; that was what we were about. But we could also take on too much of the pain of our patients if we were not careful. Most of my nursing career, I had been able to offer the best of me as an empath without becoming so involved with patients that it would be to my detriment. This was not going to be one of those times. This patient would determine how the rest of my life would unfold. I, of course, could not see it coming.

When doing midwifery, a trainee spent small parcels of time in each section of the hospital and my time had come to move on to my next placement. I really dreaded the thought of no longer having Angela as my patient as it would mean that I would not be able to see as much of her. I said to her before I moved, 'Why couldn't we have met years earlier, Angela, we would have been the best of friends.' Angela agreed and I promised to continue to visit her as often as I could. She also knew everything about my life and troubles so assured me she would appreciate however often she could see me.

My working life continued in a new ward and I visited as often as I could, which was nowhere near as often as I would have liked. Life at home had not improved and was edging ever closer to when Emma's baby was due to be born. Mum was an even more frequent visitor. I had incurred one too many issues with my car and had made the decision to purchase another second-hand car. Yes, if I had been allowed to purchase the brand new car all those months prior, this would not have been an issue now. I bought a coupe, second-hand, and drove out of Zupps car yard at Mt Gravatt in Brisbane and rushed home to collect Mum, Emma and Brianna to get Emma to her antenatal clinic to which we were already running late. I wanted Brianna's car seat put in the back seat but it was considered there was not enough time and she could be held in the back seat. I got up onto the freeway and came off at the Stanley Street Exit and pulled up behind a car as we waited for the traffic to clear. I had what I called a Bedford truck behind me as we waited. I looked in the rear-view mirror and just managed to say, 'Isn't that truck too close to us?' when we were being concertinaed between the truck behind me and the car in front of me.

I lost the plot. I had not even given a moment's thought as to how Brianna was in the back seat. I was on a rampage and was not able to control myself. I had driven out of Zupps 20 minutes previously, having just bought this car, and now it was smashed at both ends and unable to be driven. I yelled and screamed and swore and Mum hit me across the face to bring me back to reality. I then checked Brianna and found that all was well. I most certainly was not proud of my actions, then or now, but when one lived an extremely stressful life, it had to emerge somewhere. Why could I not tell the people that caused that stress how I felt instead of bottling it all up and compartmentalising? And the even bigger question was why I kept helping these people, putting myself in harm's way. I would never receive any appreciation for all that I did, spent and put myself through. The cover note on the comprehensive insurance had not officially gone through yet but Zupps organised for my car to be collected from the tow truck that had taken it and have it taken to their preferred repairers and for the next month+, I had to use buses and taxis for everything I required in life or, when close enough, Shanks' Pony.

I was busy during a shift dealing with a patient when I overheard two other staff members talking about how sad it was that a patient within the hospital had been diagnosed with acute myeloid leukaemia and no one really knew what to do next. I went cold all over. I had been on four days leave and had not had the time to check in with Angela. I interrupted the other staff members and found out that it was indeed Angela. I was shell-shocked; I could not believe the hand that fate had dealt her. It was just so completely unfair and cruel. The empath in me had always felt such injustices, as I saw them, very deeply. As soon as I was able, I flew straight down to see Angela.

A new doctor had started on the ward and felt that Angela looked way too pale and anaemic and had ordered immediate blood tests. Once the results were received, it had been a whirlwind of tests, doctors and emotions. A bone marrow test had been performed and it had confirmed the diagnosis. It was an aggressive form of leukaemia and also had the added complication of the pregnancy. Knowledge was sought from around the globe but before anyone had the opportunity to make a definite treatment regime, Angela went into premature labour and delivered Jack at 34 weeks gestation via a normal delivery on 18 October 1979. He went to NICU as a diabetic baby but was doing rather well under the circumstances. Angela was transferred to the Mater Adults to commence chemotherapy.

It is said that it never rains but pours. On 20 October 1979, Emma delivered a healthy baby boy via a normal delivery. I had, through the kindness of Sister Stringer, been moved to the private ward at the Mater Mothers to work over the period of time that Emma and her baby would be in the hospital so as not to place any undue stress on me. Sister Stringer knew every piece of information that I did and knew how I felt about everything. I was working that day and was constantly ringing the labour ward to check how Emma was progressing and asking her if I could see her or be with her. She had no intention of allowing me to show my love, compassion and kindness to her even in childbirth. I am, to this day, unable to fathom why I even cared. I cannot turn off being an empath; it is part of the fabric of who I am along with integrity, loyalty, respect and honesty. My life could have been so much easier if I had just not cared.

Emma was done with Brisbane and the flat I was renting for us, but most of all, she was done with me. She had gotten what she wanted from me and I was no longer of use to her and was to be discarded like an old rag. Unfortunately, through Emma's own rather heightened sense of herself, she had managed to get her episiotomy scar well and truly infected and required a return to the hospital. It was soon sorted and Mum, Emma and my precious Brianna were back off to Toowoomba as if the entire episode had been a very long dream. I felt worse now than I had when I had first come to Brisbane over a year earlier. There has never been a single word spoken between Emma and I about her pregnancy or her son ever since.

I again threw myself into my work and did everything I could to help Angela. Several other midwifes and me would take Jack over to visit his mum in the Adults. It was the very least we could do. Once Jack was able to go home, me and others would go to the house, bathe and feed Jack, cook for the children, do housework and anything else we could do. Angela was allowed day passes from the hospital and on one such occasion, I had them over to my flat for dinner. I cut Angela's hair for her and we enjoyed a very happy evening. I did the washing up and William did the drying up. We talked and laughed whilst Angela rested with the children in the lounge. It had been a great evening but as I washed more and more, something happened inside me. I wasn't certain what it was but I had a pretty good idea. I had fallen in love with a married man!

I could not sleep that night at all. I tossed and turned. This was a totally unacceptable predicament for me to be in. I did not believe in all this love stuff. It had not served me up to this stage and I was totally confused but equally positive that I would not be able to go against my own principles, morals and ethics. The first thing the following morning, I went and got the Toowoomba Chronicle and wrote a letter of application for four jobs and posted them before I had even left for work.

It was rather prestigious to be asked to remain on at the Mater Mothers' as trained staff and it was offered to very few. All through the year, the other trainee midwives had been quite blasé about the fancy cars they drove and the fancy houses they lived in but they really showed their true colours as our time at the Mater drew to a close. Those self-same people were now in a state of complete panic as they had been applying everywhere and if they were not asked to stay on at the Mater, their lives would be in tatters. It was a shock to see such a total turnaround in their character. They were not offered the opportunity to stay on at the Mater, I was.

I arrived at my ward one weekend to commence my shift and was advised that Sister Stringer needed to see me. It transpired that there were a lot of the senior staff off sick and they needed me, if I was willing, to work in the nursery where my nephew was. I had managed to stay away from him for so long. I had requested that his hospital name be Michael. Mum had chosen that name for Jonathon but an aunt had had her son just before Mum and Dad had gotten Jonathon and had called him Michael. I had considered that was the least I could do for him. I agreed to do the shift in the nursery and set off.

After handover, I checked all the babies and their feeding. The adoption babies were kept in a section at the back of the nursery as they were older and slept better than the new-born babies. It took me a while and many deep breaths but I finally summoned up the courage to go and see Michael. I almost collapsed when I saw that he was the spitting image of my father. He even had the gorgeous curly hair, although Dad's had been blond at this age and Michael's was dark.

It was not very long after that day that Michael went to live with his new parents. I was told where he had gone to live and he still lives there today and is still the spitting image of my dad. If he is even 1/10th the man Dad was, he will be a very fine adult.

I actually managed to land all four of the jobs that I had applied for. One was a matron at a small country hospital, which would have been nice, but one was my old training hospital, the Toowoomba General Hospital, and I chose to go home in more ways than one. I disappointed the Mater and the other three jobs that I had applied for. I decided to take two weeks off to spend with Brianna and find us our own place to live.

I was certain that I was walking away from the frying pan and straight back into the original fire but I was so desperate to get away from Brisbane and William that I was willing to put myself back into the middle of hell.

Much suffering, much unhappiness arises
When you take each thought that comes into your head
For the Truth

-ECKHART TOLLE

CHAPTER 5

WHERE THERE IS SMOKE, THERE IS FIRE

I found Brianna and I what was considered to be a rather expensive flat at the time. The rent was $50 per week. I had fallen in love with it the moment I had seen it. The lounge room had shag pile carpet and the two bedrooms and small hall had polished wood floors, all of which I adored. But to top it all off, the master bedroom had floor-to-ceiling built-in cupboards. I was sold…

The flat was furnished so there were only a few pieces of furniture that I needed to purchase—a buffet to hold my glassware, etc. I already owned a large wardrobe and a desk so it was rather easy when the time came to move into our new home.

The biggest problem was Brianna. She could not understand why I was moving all of her belongings from Mum's house to another house. This was not her home; she would scream as we drove into our new flat. 'I want to go back to my home,' she would shout. I felt absolutely dreadful but was extremely determined that this was the beginning of our lives together as a family. With enough patience, I was certain Brianna would learn to understand and accept her new life.

I took in a lodger to help with expenses and I also hired an in-home babysitter for Brianna in my attempt to create a new family home. She was a friend of a friend from New Zealand. Brianna wonders today why she has a very distinct Kiwi accent! I returned to work and from that end, at least, things were going extremely well.

My need to minimise Brianna's contact with Mum was such that even when I realised that the babysitter was not interacting with Brianna whilst I was working, instead preferring to watch television for the entirety of her employ, my response was to go and buy heaps of interactive toys and games and insist she spend her time playing with Brianna.

I was determined to win but it turned out to be a battle that I could not win, and in the end, I had to put my tail between my legs and ask Mum if she could again babysit Brianna. I was safe in the knowledge that Brianna would, at least, be safe with my mother. That did not turn out to be totally true as I returned to Mum's house to collect Brianna after having completed an early shift. It was only May but an extremely cold day in Toowoomba. I walked in to find that Mum, Brianna and visitors were all sitting around the kitchen table with everything closed up and many in attendance smoking. Brianna had been sick when I had left her with Mum and she was now quite cyanosed and having difficulty breathing. I hit the roof. I could not believe that Mum would put Brianna in such danger, especially when she herself did not smoke.

From that episode, Brianna ended up being in St Vincent's Hospital in an oxygen tent. I was devastated that the only person that I had to trust with my precious daughter had let Brianna down so badly. What a dreadful mother I was to not be able to care and provide for my daughter better than this. Again, I felt totally alone with no one to turn to.

It was whilst Brianna was in hospital that I had to see a surgeon, Dr Richard Vickers, regarding a rim of very sore lumps that I had following the bra line under my breasts. He told me that he would "stake his reputation" on the fact that they were cysts and we should continue to observe. That was, of course, a major relief but not a definitive diagnosis and something that would require careful monitoring.

That was not the only thing that required extremely careful monitoring in my life. My temper was spiralling out of control. 1980 was proving to be one of the worst of my life. I had returned to Toowoomba to escape an unthinkable situation. I could not accept that I had fallen in love with a married man. The fact that his wife, Angela, and I had started to develop a friendship through our like-minded spirits only served to make me feel all the worse for the way I felt about William.

I was more than happy when I was at work, as always. That was the one place on earth I knew I belonged. I knew I was brilliant at my job and I constantly strived to improve myself and help the junior nurses be the best that they could be. I tried to always be available to assist them but my main priority was always my patients. The nursing care I provided to my patients had to be above and beyond expectations. Then I knew they were well cared for and that I was doing my job.

There were a few patients that year that I saved. I was like a terrier—if something was not right with a patient, I would not stop until I had found the problem. In one case, it was incorrect medication. The original nurse had not been able to understand the doctor's handwriting and had inadvertently placed the wrong drug into the medicine trolley for him. No nurse since then had noticed the error. The drug prescribed would have seen him on his way home to his young family in days. But the drug he was receiving, which had the complete opposite effect to the one required, was slowly killing him, day by day.

He responded extremely well once he had the correct medications on board and was soon heading home to his lovely family.

But work was not the only thing in my life. I had a mother, sister, brother and Brianna and feelings that would not diminish no matter what I did or how hard I tried to get rid of them. I had returned to Brisbane on occasions to visit William and the children, to visit Angela and to go to Fortitude Valley to get my Chinese cooking supplies. I took Mum and Brianna with me on these trips. I did not trust myself.

In February, William had come to Toowoomba to visit me one evening. He had to be at the Mater Public first thing the following morning to give packed cells for Angela. It seemed odd to me that he was there so late in the day. The reason became apparent soon enough. He was there to try and talk me into having sex with him! I could not believe what I was hearing. 'You are married.' I said. 'Angela is laying in the hospital dying.' Once he realised that there was not a chance in hell of me giving him what he had come for, he left. But not until he had finished the steak, chips, eggs, tomatoes and beans that I had cooked for him.

It was even harder for me to cope after this visit. I decided I could not visit them again. But my feelings were stronger, if anything, and my poor little angel, Brianna, was copping the wrath of her mother's inability to cope with her own naivety. My response to the slightest thing was to go into a rage and scream profanities at the top of my lungs. My aunt May, my godmother, was so concerned that she came over to talk to me before someone reported me to Social Services. I had a great amount of respect for May and I took a long hard look at myself and decided that I needed to calm it down, immediately. It was not going to be easy as all the biggest triggers for my temper were in my life on a daily basis but I owed it to my beautiful daughter and myself to do everything I could to control my temper.

Easter was approaching and I had four days off work. I was really looking forward to spending extra time with Brianna. We were leaving the flat to head to Mum's for dinner on Saturday night. We had come out of the driveway and turned right and the accelerator cable in my car snapped and we were going nowhere. I immediately knew that Angela had died. The knowledge rolled over me in a wave of emotion.

It took some time to get the accelerator reattached, there had been ample excess to just pull it through and reattach it. We were on our way again. But by the time we got to Mum's, something equally awful had happened. My aunt Kate was being rushed to the Toowoomba General Hospital after suffering an extremely severe asthma attack and respiratory failure.

Kate was in a critical condition and went immediately to the ICU at the General. It fell on Mum and I to contact her two children who were not spending Easter with their parents. To contact her daughter, Faith, I had to contact the police and have them advise her of the situation. Mum made contact with her son, Shane. Kate's husband, Matt, was with her at the hospital.

I had also called William to pass on my condolences and he said he would advise me when the funeral was to be held. This Easter break was not turning out to be the mother/daughter time that I had so hoped it would be. The nurse in me spent my time running backwards and forwards to the hospital and trying to be there for Brianna.

Aunty Kate died a few days later. Angela's funeral was held on Wednesday. I did not attend as it was my first day back after four days off and I had another funeral that I would be attending. Aunty Kate was family, my mother's sister. I sent my apologies to William and continued with what was an incredibly difficult week.

Time moved on, my lodger moved out and I had no desire to have any other stranger living with Brianna and I in our home. I suffered glandular fever during this year. I felt awful but kept going to work. It was not until I actually collapsed at work in front of who was then called the Senior Sister, that I went straight from the hospital to my doctor who had by then received my test results. I was diagnosed with glandular fever officially and sent home to go to bed and rest! Dr Keith stated, 'Flo could look after Brianna.'

Mum was again at her absolute best and refused to keep Brianna. I just had to get on with it, as usual. 'That's what mothers have to do,' she repeated. The only issue was that she never did. She had always taken to her bed and left Dad in charge. Later that evening, Emma actually came around and got me out of my bed to see if I wanted her to look after Brianna. It was, as always, way too little a good long while too late! Brianna was already sorted and on her way to bed. Thanks for nothing. I have never understood why their actions shocked me. They were consistent in their animosity towards me yet I always hoped that they would develop a conscience and act like human beings, let alone members of a supposed family. I certainly was the eternal optimist.

My holidays were due in October and I had two weeks booked in a house in Caloundra, the property of friends. It was close to the beach and I couldn't wait to take Brianna. I was at work doing a late shift one Sunday contemplating life and our upcoming holiday. Mum and her mother, Nanna—aka Super Dragon—were coming up for the first week. Again, what was I doing to myself! Anyway, I thought of William and the children and the year they had endured and thought how nice it would be to share my holiday with the children. It would give them something to look forward to and enjoy. I procrastinated for a long while but finally, after everyone had finished their dinner breaks, I went to the hospital foyer and called William. I invited him and the children to come up to Caloundra for a few days break.

William told me about having been quite overwhelmed after Angela's death and about having to put Tracey and Clayton into temporary foster care. Jack spent a considerable amount of time visiting another midwife, Sue, who continued to help out as much as she possibly could. William also told me that he had returned to work as a merchant sailor and now had a dear friend of Angela's from New Zealand, Sandy, living with them as the babysitter/housekeeper. Things seemed to be looking up at least for this family that had been through so much. He advised that he would let me know. I felt that I was doing the right thing and was quite pleased with myself.

The time came very quickly for Brianna and I to start our holidays. It was a lovely house and we were very comfortable. It was difficult with both Mum and Nanna there but they also seemed to be enjoying themselves. It was a long week though and I was definitely on edge the day they were leaving as I was not sure if they would have left before William arrived. He had decided that it would just be him coming as the children could not be taken out of school. Jack was a baby and I am certain he would have had fun. But it was made very clear what William was after and I was too weak to resist any longer.

And so, the die was cast! My mother knew that William and the children were coming but went ballistic when she found out that he had not brought the children. She accused me of having him waiting around the corner until I gave the all-clear signal. I was 23, for heaven's sake, and rightly or wrongly, I was legally capable of making my own decisions and mistakes.

I very quickly lost all guilt about the situation, although I did consider it to be too soon after Angela's death. We travelled to Brisbane to see the children anyway. William was due to leave on his next ship in a few days and as all Australian ships departing Brisbane and heading up the coast followed quite closely up the coast until they reached the top of Bribie Island and then headed out to sea at Caloundra, we should have been able to see the ship as it took off on its travels. That day, Brianna and I set out in the car and again had travelled only a very short distance when the accelerator cable again snapped! I felt a cold shiver. What did this mean? I called RACQ and found that there was, again, enough cable remaining to be pulled further forward and reattached. I could not get rid of my strange feeling around why this had happened again. I did not allow it to upset what remained of our holiday though. Brianna, like her mother before her, turned out not to like bikinis as a toddler. Apart from that, we had a fantastic time together in Caloundra.

It was not until I was well and truly back at work and William was again home from sea that I had discovered that at the same time that my accelerator cable had snapped, William had lost Angela's wedding ring, which he wore on his little finger, in the engine room of the ship. I was actually relieved in a sense. At least, I had found a correlation between the same events occurring at seemingly random moments. And due to my never-ending optimism, I thought Angela was giving me her approval for the relationship that was developing with William.

William had decided to come and visit me in Toowoomba. I was lying in bed as I had an early shift the next day. We were talking and William was pacing. Then out of the blue, he said, 'Well, are we getting married or what?'

I did not say 'or what'!

We are addicted to our thoughts.
We cannot change anything if we cannot
change our thinking.

-Santosh Kalwar

CHAPTER 6

WEDDING BELLS

Why was I not ecstatically happy and shouting my news from the rooftops? For one, I knew my mother would hit the roof and indeed she did. 'He is 15 years older than you; he is from the other side of the world and he already has three children, he lives in a housing commission house. Do you know what you are taking on?'

I did not receive any support from my brother and sister either.

I have never had any one person that I felt I could tell my deepest fears and secrets to and because of that, I had always kept everything inside, in its little boxes, all neatly compartmentalised. The truth was that no matter what stage of life I have been at, I have always been too ashamed of my life, my family and their actions, etc. to let anyone know how I feel. I have always had the feeling that what I felt truly and deeply was of absolutely no consequence to everyone else in my life. I have always been expected to "do this for my sake", my mother's favourite expression to get me to do what she knows that I did not want to do. And the ridiculous debt of gratitude that my mother made certain I knew that she considered I owed her for adopting me always saw me doing exactly as she wanted of me. Time after time, I would go above and beyond and never received any real appreciation for my efforts. As an empath, on many occasions, it was me who would instigate the extras but that was who I was at heart.

I have always had incredibly low self-esteem, no confidence at all and I just put up with whatever had been dished up to me and always came back for more. This has always been my greatest fault and everyone in my life has used and abused this dreadful quality in me to their fullest advantage. The one and only time when I had supreme confidence was when I was nursing. It was my domain and I knew my stuff and I loved it with a passion. All other areas of my life, I have been a complete failure.

Perhaps my need to get away from Toowoomba and Mum, once and for all, was so great that I would have done almost anything to achieve that end. I knew I loved William but was I absolutely certain he loved me? How could he? Angela had been dead such a short period of time, was it even possible? I fooled myself into believing that he did and went about organising my wedding for my birthday the following year—25 January 1981. I had asked Emma to be my bridesmaid and we had started shopping for clothes, although I had bought a beautiful outfit in Caloundra, which I would wear as my wedding dress. William and I had been to see the priest to organise the ceremony. It had been my wish that we only have a very small wedding and something small at Mum's place before we set off for family life in Brisbane.

William only had one aunt and uncle that lived in Australia and they were in Sydney. I had a four-day weekend and William asked if we could go to Sydney to meet his relatives. It meant a lot to him as I would not be able to meet my future parents-in-law as they lived in England. I had spoken to them on the phone, of course, and they seemed really lovely people. William 's father, also William, and I spoke as if we had known each other all our lives. I thought to myself, *If your son is even half the man you are, I am going to have a fantastic husband.*

I had asked my mum to look after Brianna for me over this long weekend. To say she lost the plot would be the understatement of the century. 'Going on a honeymoon before the marriage' and such like comments. I was almost 24, a mother, a trained nurse and midwife and yet I was still to be treated as an errant schoolchild guilty of tardiness!

We drove to Sydney, stopping in Coffs Harbour for the night. It was during a phenomenal heatwave that certainly got the better of me. But it was so lovely to meet William's aunt and uncle and one of his cousins. Our time in Sydney went way too quickly but we had to head back so that I could arrive in time for my shift on Wednesday. Mum was equally if not even less impressed with my "honeymoon" when I got back home.

I tried to broach the subject of minimisation with Mum. She was not having it. These people have to be invited 'for my sake', those people needed to be invited 'for my sake'. This was going to blow out of all proportion. I was not sure that I was strong enough to fight her. Then she sent one of my oldest girlfriends around to see me at my flat. William was there and the three of us spoke whilst her daughter and Brianna played in Brianna's bedroom. Anne was trying to make me see sense and agree to not marry William. Mum was only thinking of what was best for me and on and on.

Our two daughters were playing away until her daughter slammed the bedroom door shut and then panicked because she could not see her mother and started to scream. I jumped up and went to rescue her and bring her to Anne. The conversation went on for a short while longer but once Anne realised that I would not change my mind, she left.

What I was not aware of until later that day was that Anne had dropped in at Mum's to tell her and Emma how the visit had gone. When I went around later that day, I was confronted with a huge amount of animosity and asked how I could even consider marrying a man that would lock a scared little girl in a wardrobe! Well, that had never happened and I tried to explain this but neither Mum nor Emma were actually interested in the truth and as I walked through the garage to leave, Emma leaned over the kitchen sink to the open window and called me a "spineless bitch". I was devastated that again, lies were going to ruin what I would have liked to have happened.

I told William what had happened and he said, 'Let's go and talk to your mum without Emma there.'

Mum and William were a fair match for each other as it went. William played the part, down on his knees begging her to give him a go, but Mum was not having a bar of it. William said his piece and went to walk down the hall. I went to follow him when Mum said to me, 'You will have to choose, Ellie, him or me.'

I did not falter, I turned to her and said, 'I love you, Mum, but I am going with William.'

I left the house and was utterly devastated. What would I do now? We went back to my flat and William told me that, as a merchant marine, he was entitled to get a marriage licence that would entitle us to get married in three days. On the rebound from such a tongue-lashing by first Emma and then Mum, I agreed. William went and got the paperwork from the courthouse the following day and after I had finished work, we went to see my uncle Trevor, who worked at the courthouse and was a JP, to have the papers signed and lodged them.

I advised my family of the impending nuptials. Mum stated she would not attend but would instead go to church to pray for me.

Jonathon and Emma also refused on the grounds that they had to live with Mum and if they went, they would never hear the end of it.

We had decided that only Tracey and Clayton would attend the wedding and that Brianna and Jack would stay at the flat with Sandy. We were married at the Toowoomba Courthouse Registry Office on Friday 10 December 1980. There was no pomp and ceremony but I took the vows I made that day extremely seriously. That was it for me; whether I had chosen well or not, William would, from that moment on, be the only man I would ever allow near me for the rest of my life. My extremely strong feelings on marriage had nothing to do with religion and my very strict upbringing. It was far deeper and more personal than any of that could be. I knew that once I had made a commitment to a man, that would be it for me, for life. I have always believed that marriage is the joining together of two kindred spirits, souls that are never to be separated, ever. I would give my soul to this man, the very essence of my being and I would expect nothing less in return.

After we had left the flat with all on board bound for Brisbane, we stopped in to drop Brianna off to stay with Mum for one last time. I explained that I was married now and that when I came back to get Brianna, she would be part of a family and we would both be moving forward. I would never forget my mother's words until my last breath, 'Please let me adopt Brianna, Ellie?'

The torrent of emotions that went through my mind in that instant had been incredulous; after everything she had put us through…but I very calmly replied, 'Brianna is *my* daughter and after the next few days, she will be coming to Brisbane to join her new family!'

We continued on to Brisbane, settled everyone in, then headed back to Toowoomba to have dinner with my dear friend, Angela, and her husband, James. It was extremely late when we finally got back home to Brisbane. There had been no engagement ring and I was forced to get married with Angela's wedding ring as mine. It had only been eight months since her death, the ring barely felt cold. Had I done the right thing? There was no turning back now, at least not in my mind. I could not see any problem that would not be resolved if the parties involved were equally committed to an amicable resolution. I had committed myself to this man until my death. At this point, I only had the hope that William was true to his word and really did feel for me the way that I felt for him.

Amen.

The trust of the innocent is the liar's most useful tool.

-STEPHEN KING

CHAPTER 7

WICKED STEPCHILDREN

The first few months of my marriage most certainly did not go to plan. Whilst Tracey had loved being made a fuss of and having her new stepmother buy her a brand-new dress from Myer for the wedding and her brother Clayton a safari suit, a place neither of them were used to getting their clothes from, the reality that I was going to be around for the long haul was a bit more than either had really been prepared for. Both Tracey and Clayton were very used to getting their own way and were not prepared for that to change in any way.

I started working at the Mater Mothers soon after William and I were married and I enjoyed being back in my old stomping ground. Christmas was fast approaching and due to the fact that I had left the Toowoomba General on very short notice, I had not received my final pay. The deputy matron at the time had stated that I would forfeit my fortnight's pay in lieu of acceptable notice. I had actually handed in a resignation letter but that was for when I would be finishing in January. I would not be receiving my first fortnightly pay from the Mater until after Christmas so things were looking rather bleak.

Mum had decided that as she had Brianna early in December, they would all do a special meal and presents for an early Christmas Day for Brianna in Toowoomba.

Prior to our wedding, William had assured me that he had over $2,000 in the bank. I thought he was wonderful to have been able to save that much money as he had not been back at work for terribly long. There was a vast difference in upbringing and there were the cultural differences between us, of course, but in my world, when you tell someone that you have said number of funds in the bank, you are speaking about savings. To my mind, you do not disclose the cash flow of your everyday account. But as William was paid in cash, that was exactly what he had been speaking about and we were now down to the bones of our arse, a brilliant way to start married life!

I did manage to pull together a few very inexpensive gifts and food for the day. I had to work a late shift on Christmas Day and was very much less than impressed that William made a huge to-do of opening the box of gifts from Nanny and Grandad in England for Tracey, Clayton and Jack in front of Brianna. I considered that to be totally unfair on a 2-year-old child.

Tracey stamped her intent to make my life hell from the very outset. 'My mum would have done this or that.'

My reply, 'I am not your mum, but we had become friends and spoke a lot about many things and I am afraid I do not agree with you on this or that. I am not trying to take Mum's place, Tracey, I have too much respect for her to do that, but we can be friends and I will help you in any way that I can.'

Tracey found a far more effective way to ensure that I did what she wanted rather than use my own ideas. I had a rather large "glory box", as it had been called in my day. Basically, household items in preparation for setting up home. I had enough to set up several homes, in fact. It was not even slightly amusing when Tracey started breaking my possessions—casserole dishes, crystal vases, glasses, china and on and on she went. Oh, there was always an 'I am sorry, it was an accident'. It is an accident if it occurs across the board but when it *only* occurs to my things, it is a purposeful act.

Clayton decided from the outset that Brianna would be the cause of all the things he did not like in life. He would blame her for everything that would go wrong henceforth. I could not imagine what he perceived that a two-year-old could actually be responsible for in a 10-year-old's life! When Clayton's behaviour towards Brianna, myself or anyone else in the house became overwhelming, which was unfortunately quite regularly, I would call Jonathon and get him to take Brianna to Mum for a week. She had done nothing wrong to justify the attitude towards her, especially from Clayton. Brianna idolised both Tracey and Clayton as her big sister and brother. Brianna and Jack were incredibly close from the outset. Brianna loved him with all her heart.

With Brianna at Mum's, I could devote so much more time to trying to help Clayton come to terms with the death of his mother and work on how we could move forward together as a family. It was the duty of his father to help his children grieve but he was either incapable or unwilling. Clayton was fine being showered with attention and being made the centre of the universe but once Brianna returned to her family and Clayton was again one of four children, the whole cycle would start all over again. I tried desperately to help Tracey also but she was a completely closed book. All I could do was to make the offer constantly and hope that she would one day take the olive branch I was offering. It had been my profound medical opinion that Clayton and Tracey would both greatly benefit from counselling but William did not agree or see the need and I was left to do the very best I could for the two of them despite considerable handicaps imposed on my situation and circumstance.

One Sunday morning, we all piled into the car to take Tracey and Clayton to Mt Gravatt Cemetery to visit their mother's grave. We were all in and organised and as we set off, the accelerator cable snapped for the third and last time! I was then totally convinced that Angela was sending me her seal of approval for my marriage to William. I was extremely superstitious and everything happens in threes and it was my car that had the accelerator cable snap so what else could it mean? I was even more determined by this sign to work ever harder to help Tracey and Clayton overcome all their issues. I continued to ask if they would like to revisit their mother's grave but they always said no. In the end, I said that they just had to ask me and we would go. I found their behaviour on this a bit odd but just because I had visited my father's grave every week or two, especially in the early days, did not mean that I could force feelings onto them that they did not have. I decided that they would let me know what they needed and when.

I had become pregnant and we very excitedly told the children in the hope that it might help make for a more cohesive family unit. That was not to be. Towards the end of January, I started to bleed and went straight off to the GP. He sent me off with a script for Valium 5mg and I was to be on total bed rest. I got home, contacted work to advise them of the situation, took a pill and went to bed. I was so grateful at that point that Sandy was living with us so that I could rest as I needed to. William was at sea at the time. He returned later that week. It was not the homecoming he would have liked. Tracey had a friend over; William put some music on and wanted to show the youngsters how to disco. I obliged but was soon feeling that I should not have moved from my bed. Later that night, I had a miscarriage. As a midwife, I knew what to check for and when William rang my obstetrician, we spoke as doctor and nurse. I assured him that what I had lost seemed complete and he advised that I would not need to be hospitalised.

The following morning, my 24th birthday, we had to tell the children that there was no longer going to be a baby. It was extremely difficult for the younger ones to understand. I continued to feel absolutely dreadful with abdominal pain, which worsened through the day and into the evening. I had a craving for a hot fudge sundae from McDonalds but when William drove me to one and they did not have any left, we went for a drive. However, as we did, the abdominal pain became too intense. We went back home but were not there long before William took me to the Princess Alexandra Hospital Emergency Department. I had a D and C (dilatation and curettage) after which the doctor suggested that I had, in fact, been pregnant with twins. The first one that I had lost at home the night before had not been viable but the second one had been perfectly normal but had obviously been affected by the first twin. They were certain that I would now be fine and able to move forward and fall pregnant again.

However, I continued to bleed randomly and approximately a month later, when I lost a blood clot the size of a rugby ball, the doctors at PAH performed a second D and C on me and stated that there was now no doubt whatever that I had been pregnant with twins. I spoke to William and we decided that we should wait a while before trying again to fall pregnant as I was unsure if I could go through anything like this again.

It was not just the loss of the pregnancy that was difficult. When I had first let my mother know that I was pregnant, she had said, 'It's a shame that you are not married!'

'What do you mean by that, Mum? I was married in the Registry Office.'

'You are not married in the eyes of God and therefore, you are not married.'

I was flabbergasted by this ridiculous rubbish. 'I am married in the eyes of the law, Mum, and that is actually all that matters.' She was not listening.

To make matters worse, when I miscarried, Mum decided to believe some friend who told her—totally incorrectly, of course—that you could not have a miscarriage until you were 12 weeks pregnant. As a midwife, I had heard some real stories in my time but for my own mum to believe someone untrained over her trained midwife daughter meant that, as usual, Mum had no interest in the truth at all but needed a reason to berate me even more than she had spent my lifetime doing. She had apparently sat down with a calendar and worked out when she assumed that William and I were 'at it like rabbits. At the time she claimed that I had become pregnant, William had actually been at sea so that would have been an extremely interesting liaison!

After the first D and C, the second was a rather difficult time as well. Tracey and Clayton had returned to school for the New Year. In February, Tracey came home from school in a feral mood and I was the object of her angst. She spent several hours revving Clayton up and once she was ready, the unrelenting attack on me began verbally. I have a vicious temper but, on this evening, I held steady, barely even managing to raise my voice. It was blatantly clear that Tracey wanted me to take Brianna and leave whilst her father was at sea, and this tirade continued very late into the evening. Clayton had lost puff first and gone to bed and eventually, Tracey lost her reserve as she could not get to me in the way that she had intended. I, of course, was never going to be able to sleep that night. Sandy told me that I had every right to walk, that Tracey was way out of line, that she would never have done any of this had William not been at sea. I scooped up my car keys and my purse and paced up and down the footpath for hours in the wee small hours of the morning. I would open the door, close it again, I even got into the car several times, putting the key into the ignition and turning it until the radio came on, uncertain and in desperate need of a conversation with William. If I had allowed myself to start the car that night, I know it would have been over for good. Had I really needed to be told that William had slept with at least six women since Angela's death? Did I really need to know who she had preferred and why they were so much better than me? I had actually thought that all this time, William had been grieving for the wife he had lost. He was most certainly not grieving in the way I had anticipated but I had not slept with anyone until William since leaving Brisbane. I had thought that Tracey and Clayton had been placed into temporary care because he was so overwhelmed. Jack often went to stay with Sue so what had he actually been doing with all this alone time? He had obviously been trying to find a new wife. I was shocked and surprised at how much grieving he obviously had not done but in the end, I had to come back to the fact that I had signed my marriage vows and I believed in them and it was my job to improve our lives, all of us, and make one large happy family.

Besides, I could never allow my mother to win when she had stated that we would be lucky to last two years! She was now very squarely under the thumb of Emma and whatever stories she chose to fill Mum's head with about me. My only escape, should I have decided to leave, would be to return to Mum in Toowoomba and as far as I was concerned, that would be a fate worse than death! Never again!

Clayton had always been very easy to manipulate and Tracey always used that to her full advantage. One afternoon, Clayton did not arrive home from school. I waited, thinking the bus must be late. Then I started calling people, first the school, then his friends. He had decided to go home with one of his friends. He did not see an issue with not having informed me. Of course, as was always the case, when Tracey and Clayton decided to "try it on", Dad was at sea. I headed over and collected Clayton and explained why he should have told me. I had no issues with my children seeing their friends or having them over to our home but it was always best to be organised first. As the evening wore on and I tried harder and harder to communicate with this very angry young man, it became rather apparent that he really did not know why he was angry other than that he had been told he should be by Tracey. He did say that I was not his real mother and that there was nothing I could do to stop him doing whatever he wanted and if I tried, he would call the police. All words that had come straight from Tracey via Clayton's mouth.

So, once I was finally past the miscarriage and all its effects on my life, I tried to set up home properly. Tracey continued to make things extremely difficult. When William was at sea, she was the stepdaughter from hell but once Dad was back, she was all sugar and spice. She was in high school now and was having trouble with maths. I had done senior maths A and B and set about trying to help her. I was in shock to learn that in the time since I had finished high school seven years earlier, all of the mathematical equations had been totally changed. It was a case of going through each section and teaching myself the new curriculum and then trying to teach Tracey. It was slow progress and lessons that Tracey loathed. I was more than happy to do whatever it took to make this work but I was in a minority of one.

As the first anniversary of Angela's death approached, I sought out an Anglican church to organise to take Tracey and Clayton to the Sunday service to commemorate their mum's passing. The pastor was very kind and asked me if I remembered what the Catholic service had been like a decade earlier. I did and he said, 'Well, that is what it will be like here, we are just a bit behind.'

I took Tracey and Clayton to the Sunday service. I felt that it should have been a family outing and that William and Jack should have been there as well to pay their respects. I asked again for several years in a row but neither was interested in attending a service to pay respects to their mother. Again, I left it to them and their father to decide.

Tracey was constantly accusing other students of bullying or sexual harassment against her. I would leap to her defence. When William was at sea, I would get Jonathon to go and chat to the boys concerned but he would always return with the same old tale. They were very small lads who really had no idea what we were talking about. It did not stop despite my trying to council Tracey in ways to avoid this kind of issue. She ended up finishing school a few weeks early that year and refused to return to that same high school the following year.

William was happy for her to stay at home. I was out of my depth here. I did not have some endless pot of money to set her up in a new school but by the time Juvenile Aid Bureau Police came to the front door—of course, whilst William was at sea—I was in no doubt that I and I alone was going to have to sort out this problem. I took her to Yeronga State High School and she was enrolled, we got some second-hand uniforms to start and she was back into the school system.

The same old issues reared their ugly heads at this high school. Tracey would travel home by bus and one afternoon claimed that another female student was bullying and harassing her so I went to the girl's house immediately and berated the poor child, then left. The look on her face left me in absolutely no doubt that she had no idea whatsoever about what had just occurred or why!

I began to learn that Tracey's stories were just that. Over the years, they became more and more elaborate. I am very sorry now that I did not see what was truly going on. She was one very lazy young lady that drove me to distraction as I was a perfectionist bordering on OCD. I would be cleaning their rooms and find letters she had written to her grandparents in England. The lies astounded me and I actually felt sorry for her at the time. I did not think that she was doing any real harm to anyone wanting more than she had, despite my abhorrence of any and all lies, but felt it was not my place to try and instil basic human values in a 13/14-year-old. I did not know then just how much damage her lies would do, to me and to us as a family. Had I made that realisation early on, I would most definitely have handled the situation very differently.

I did become pregnant again in 1981 and the baby was born in March 1982; more on my children later. After a very difficult but normal delivery, I finally got home and settled into family life again when Tracey shocked me when she told me with conviction, 'That is the only baby you are allowed to have with my father, there will be no more.'

After the second baby was born in 1983, she was even more adamant and I was told to stop. She was positively ropeable after I had the third baby in 1985, 'You will not be having any more babies now. You are not allowed to have more babies with my father than my mother did.'

I had always wanted 12 children and had absolutely no intention of adhering to Tracey's decisions. Again, I believed that counselling was required, again it was rejected.

Tracey had decided that she was legally allowed to finish school at the end of year 9 as she would turn 15 in the early part of January the following year before school recommenced. She had decided to finish with school once and for all. She did not have a job though so William decided that she could assist the family and pay her way by babysitting Brianna and the baby whilst I worked with the Blue Nurses. Brianna was at school by now and attended a small Catholic school close to our home, St Elizabeth's. Tracey would walk her to school and collect her again when the school day was finished.

It was the most horrendous few months for me trying to manage to work from 07:00 and finishing at 15:00, then coming home to a sink full of dirty washing up, clothes washing and ironing to be done, cooking dinner, making Clayton's and Brianna's school lunches for the following day, vacuuming, my poor little baby's bottom full of nappy rash from not having his nappy changed all day. For what was not the first time and most definitely would not be the last, I worked full time at work and got home to have to do it all over again until I was so exhausted that I would collapse on the couch asleep whilst Tracey stole whatever cigarettes were still worth a puff or two from my ashtray and lined them up on the kitchen sink to be smoked later.

She had been telling tales to the principal at Brianna's primary school about her horrid life as Cinderella at home. Of course, nothing could have been further from the truth but as I was to learn many years later, Tracey was not actually being vindictive for its own sake. She actually had psuedologia, a liar with a problem with the logic part of the brain. That did not make an ounce of difference to children's services when the principal reported William and I to them for enslaving Tracey!

As we were already known to children's services because of Jack—more on that soon—it was Jane Wilson, our case worker, who set up an appointment with William and I. I had suspicions regarding this meeting and as I had finished my job the previous week, I had organised for Tracey and Brianna to spend some time in Toowoomba with Mum. Jennifer arrived as arranged and wanted to discuss Tracey and how we had been treating her. That fell rather flat as she was not in the house and all of the accusations were debunked by me, as it was me that Tracey wanted to get into trouble to get me out of her life.

What she had said was forever recorded with children's services and my name would be forever tarnished over the vindictive lies of a silly, jealous, bone-idle little girl. It would actually be funny if it were not so sad. That was only the beginning of her lies and the effect that it would have on my life. I did apply for and receive Freedom of Information documents regarding Tracey's lies to Jane Wilson, which I still have in my possession. Despite some redaction, there is more than ample remaining to know what lies she told them. I never believed another word she said to me after that original visit from Jennifer and the official document only served to prove my beliefs to be correct. But then, even Jane Wilson had lied to William and I. What faith could you have with that type of person in charge of the welfare of children's lives?

When Tracey was 16, I was heavily pregnant, William was on a four-and-a-half month around the world sea journey and it was the most difficult time of my life, financially. The phone was disconnected during these four months, the rent was falling behind and I have never had to feed my children such crap for such an extended period of time.

One Saturday—my major housework day—Tracey decided that she had to do nothing but entertain herself with music. I fed and cared for the children, cleaned the bathroom, did the dusting and vacuuming of all bedrooms and the lounge, washed the bathroom and kitchen floors amid doing numerous loads of washing—clothes, towels and bed linen—as well as prepared the lunch. Clayton was helping me do the mowing, which involved us unscrewing every second fence panel on the side fence where there was an empty paddock with very long grass and mowing several feet over our boundary line to prevent the long grass from growing through to our side.

When we completed the front footpath, the front yard and both the sides, I called Tracey to ask her if she would get the washing off the line for me so that we could finish the mowing. I called and called but received no response. I trudged up the stairs carrying my very pregnant belly with me to find her. She had heard me but had ignored my calls. When I asked again if she would take the clothes off the line, she starting yelling at me about how much she had to do and how hard done by she was. I snapped and slapped her across the face. I stormed back downstairs, took everything off the line myself, finished the mowing with Clayton's assistance, then back upstairs to fold and iron, cook dinner, bathe the young children, get them to bed and then die on the couch as usual.

As night became day and I found myself awake on Sunday morning, I was advised that Tracey was not at home and that a lot of her things were missing. My first thought was that she had managed to elicit the response she was aiming for and now had her excuse to prove to her father that I had to go. Remembering that I was told, in an extremely confrontational manner, that I was never to be allowed to exceed the number of children *her* mother had with *her* father and she would make sure that I did not! The fact that I was coming close to delivering my 3rd child to William, one could understand why she had orchestrated what she thought would be the perfect way to ensure that I could no longer procreate with her father.

As the telephone had already been disconnected by Telecom as the bill, which I had no way of paying, stood at more than $1,200! So I had to put all the children in the car and head off to a public phone box. I first called my uncle, an inspector of police, to get the legal viewpoint on the situation, then I called my mother to see if she had heard from her. Then it dawned on me, she was with her maternal relatives so I headed there to check what the story was. I apologised for the fact that I had hit her but she refused to come home. She would be staying there until her father was back in Australia. We went to a friend's house and I called William to advise him of the current situation. He was not concerned that she had left or why as he believed that she had deserved the response that I had given her.

Life at home was so very much more peaceful without Tracey. I coped so much better without her stress. When William arrived home in late November, he refused to go and see Tracey at her grandparents'. He said repeatedly, 'If she wants to see me, she knows where I am.'

Even Jane Wilson rang William, when the phone was reconnected, to ask him to go and see Tracey. It was at this time, when Tracey could not get William to behave like her pet monkey, that Jonathon popped over to finish a job in the laundry that he had started a few days earlier. William told me that Jonathon was here and I said I would be finished what I was doing and I would put the kettle on in a minute ready for when he came upstairs. He did not come upstairs, he returned to his car and left. This was very bizarre behaviour, even for my brother.

I learned that he did not wish to speak to me and I did not beg. I knew I had done nothing wrong but could not, for the life of me, work out what was going on. We would not speak again for six long years. Again, it was Tracey who was at the root of the issue.

Clayton and I had, to my belief, developed a reasonable relationship as the years went on. He was a normal teenage boy in a situation he did not know how to handle. His father was away at least six months of the year and he was married to someone only 11 years older than Tracey and 14 years older than him. He tried it on three times with me whilst still a teenager. The worst instance was when I woke up one morning with the most dreadful fright because someone was lifting the sheet that covered me and heading for my private parts. My response was to shout, 'What the hell do you think you are doing?'

It had the desired effect and he ran for the hills. I told his father but William's excuse was that by the time he got home from sea, it would be too late for punishment. He used the exact same excuse for every action by Tracey and Clayton and on every single return home from sea. Not my idea of great fathering, I must say; it seemed to me to be tantamount to approval if they were never chastised for wrongdoings. As the years would roll by, I would learn that this particular type of non-punishment was reserved only for Tracey and Clayton.

On the exceptionally rare occasions that Tracey or Clayton would get into any sort of bother with William, first-hand, he inevitably turned violent towards them and it would be me screaming at him to let them go. This unacceptable violence towards his children not only continued but escalated as the years progressed.

Tracey finally did speak to her father; I was not privy to the conversation but it was not terribly long after the baby had been born in late January that Tracey returned to the family home. It was a turbulent time and extremely stressful. Brianna had gone to Sydney with Mum for a holiday to see my sister and her new cousin, Erin. Brianna had turned seven whilst in Sydney and I had missed celebrating this milestone with her. I was home from hospital with the new baby when Mum brought Brianna home. Mum was in a dreadful mood and stated that she would no longer be prepared to stay with us when William was home from sea. I asked why and she refused to give a reason. I tried to push but I was exhausted having just given birth, dealing with all the stresses of a new baby, trying to prepare for the new school year and having Tracey in and out of the house again. I gave up thinking that Emma had very obviously been in her ear cooking up some new nonsense and that it would die down eventually.

I returned to work two weeks after this baby was born and I had no time to stress about what Mum may, or may not, have meant by her outburst. Tracey was busy getting drunk, coming in late and vomiting all over the shared bedroom. This was the one condition I had stipulated would see her leave the family home again. As always, no notice was taken of my requests or feelings. I carried on with working and taking over with the children when I got home.

It was the week before Mother's Day that year, that I had a call from the Frankston Hospital to advise me that William was an inpatient and had been diagnosed with left lower lobe pneumonia. He was quite ill and would be in the hospital for some time. I was stuck between a rock and a hard place. I finished work and booked a bus to Frankston. Tracey and Clayton had agreed to look after the children until I returned with Dad. The hospital had advised that they would not allow him to leave unless it was into my care. Mum certainly would not come to Brisbane to stay with the children after her barrage only a few months ago. I felt sick as I left to head to the bus. There were no mobile phones in those days but I called home at every stop the bus made. I arrived on Saturday and spent most of the day with William. I went to the motel room and again called home.

They were all doing well, or at least that is what they decided to tell me. William was to be released to me on Sunday and then we would fly home on Monday.

I got William back to our room and he went to sleep. Instead of trying to call from the room and disturb William, I went for a walk around Frankston and I think I used every public phone box as I tried to call home. There was no answer for hours, but I kept on trying. Eventually, I had to return to the motel to check on William and see if he was ready to eat. I tried again to call home from there with the same response—engaged signal. I was at my wit's end by then. Would they not want to know how their father was doing? I most certainly wanted to know how the children were, especially the baby.

When I finally got through on the phone, I was exhausted, agitated and rather fearful of what might have been occurring. It transpired that they were trying to win some competition on the radio and had been hanging on the phone all day. I never believed that story but there was nothing I could do to disprove it. I knew that because I had been so worried about my children and my husband that day, in 1985, I had not called Mum to wish her a Happy Mother's Day and the wrath I got over that was unbelievable. I often wondered if she had come down to stay with the children that weekend, she might have controlled the children's behaviour and received the Mother's Day call that she so richly deserved, according to her. I know that I was one very happy lady to cross back over the threshold of my home that Monday but what I did not yet know or understand was that my life would never be the same again.

Whoever is careless with the truth in small matters
Cannot be trusted with important matters.

-ALBERT EINSTEIN

CHAPTER 8

THE CRACKS BEGIN TO APPEAR

We moved to a new residence in February 1986. We started the move just days after I returned from hospital, having given birth by Caesarean section for the first time. It was a slightly larger house, four bedrooms instead of three, but we had barely moved in when Tracey moved out. There were several articles that went missing and William suspected that Tracey had taken them.

Tracey would still visit with friends and tell wondrous tales. She had the canny knack of being able to disrupt occasions like no other I had known, at least for a long while. She had to be the centre of the universe at all times and caused arguments at so many family gatherings and birthdays that it was fast getting to the point that they were a thing of fear, not an occasion to look forward to.

It was in November 1986 that William went to sea for the last time. From that day on, he never worked again. He was told that he could never go to sea again, that it would be best he also not mow lawns due to the flying dust and grass but he was never once told that he could not work! William decided that his life was over, he was too ill to work and that he would just wait around for the Grim Reaper to call, which he was certain would be very soon. He was most certainly wallowing in self-pity from that time onwards. I had no concept of where the extremely strong man was that I had married. I was pregnant at this time and had just stopped work again due to difficulties with the pregnancy but was determined to return to work full time and work until my retirement so as to take over the mantel of breadwinner in lieu of William 's inability and unwillingness to provide for his family. It was my place to do what he could not or would not do. That was how I had been brought up.

My current pregnancy turned out to be a marathon of endurance. Everything that could go awry did and although I had been pushing very hard for a trial of labour following the previous Caesarean, there came a point where I was unable to handle the pain and discomfort a minute longer and instead agreed to an elective Caesarean at 38 weeks. I was prepared to allow myself a month to recover from the birth before looking for work but it had become apparent very quickly that if I had thought the pregnancy was difficult, I had seen nothing yet and this baby would be the one that broke the camel's back…

I had chosen not to breastfeed so that I could return to work sooner. This little bub had no intentions of feeding, sleeping or really doing anything much other than screaming. One month became two became six, etc. William was not "well enough" to look after such a troublesome baby, or so he said. Hand on heart, I think I would have been extremely lucky to have actually had the equivalent of two full nights' sleep in the first year of her life. I had moved into the lounge room for sleeping, every night, with the bassinet. I saw all of Wimbledon for 1987 and saw Pat Cash win triumphantly that year. I also saw all of the 500cc motorbike races and watched Wayne Gardiner take out the championship. Once all of the programmes were finished, the only thing that would keep this little "bundle of joy" quiet was: A. me constantly rocking her bassinet and B. the white noise from the TV.

Life took a rather decided downhill turn from there on in. Financially, it was a real struggle once William was no longer receiving sick pay from the shipping company. The chest physicians had decided that he could no longer go to sea. William was then put onto sickness benefits from the government. His retirement/ superannuation fund paid him for a partial disablement with a view to his situation being reassessed in six months' time. Less than one month later, they again wrote to William to advise that he would not be receiving any further monies from them as the Board had met and decided that he was only entitled to the partial disablement payment, which he had already received. William went further downhill after this occurred, psychologically, but instead of seeing it for what it was—the Board had discussed his situation carefully and had considered that he was still fully capable of work as long as he did not work in air-conditioning or mow and inhale grass and dust, but just not of the kind of work he had been accustomed to performing. However, William did not see this as a new opportunity to start over, as he had planned to do for several years prior to this happening and had applied for jobs all over Australia so that he could be at home with his family more. There were endless kinds of jobs that William could so easily have undertaken to help support his family but his choice was to play the dying swan.

It was just after the birth of this child in 1987 that William decided he would take the children fishing. He was never, ever too sick for fishing and one other activity that I will discuss in a later chapter. He was, as always, speeding along when he was pulled over by the police and asked to produce his licence. He did not possess one; he had never ever possessed one. By all accounts, he had actually attempted to get his driver's licence once but when he had failed, he had made the decision that he would never try again. He had driven, unlicensed and uninsured in many different countries, in two different hemispheres and many different cities for 30 years and had never before been caught. He had most certainly been pulled up for one thing and another but he would very quickly go into his spiel of lies and semi-truths, rambling like a mad man, never giving the police a chance to think and they would always let him pass on with a polite warning to look after himself and his family. I actually would not have believed all this to be the truth had I not actually been in the car for more than one of these occasions. Once he had to go to court and pay a fine and be ordered not to drive for said period before trying to actually obtain a driver's licence; he refused to even try to get one. There were actually dozens and dozens of arguments in the ensuing years as to why he could not learn the current rules and take a test. I had an enormous amount of stress placed on me being the only driver for such a large family but William would state that I 'could not make him do anything that he did not want to do' and that he would not be getting a licence. This was also not true for me and no matter what demands were made on me re driving to or collecting from, it was *my duty as a parent* to do it all without question, according to my husband! Those rules, however, did not apply to William, only me. He was a "sick man" and I suddenly became extremely subservient to his every whim.

I was sinking lower and lower and further under his control for the sake of "keeping the peace" within the family and our relationship. (More on that soon.) When it became obvious that I was not going to be able to return to work as I had intended and planned on doing after the birth of our youngest child in June 1987,

I set about creatively trying to provide the very best I could for my family on what little money we had. There were many good times but some extremely tight periods. It was during those times and all the future tight moments in my married life that I would thank my father for having taught me how to budget as well as I did. I have also considered having done senior logic and economics to have been of a huge benefit during those times of extreme struggle.

Lay-bys were my greatest friend when it came to Christmases and birthdays in our house. It was also a major asset that I could cook, sew, knit, crochet and many other skills that I had developed along the way. I would spend an evening cutting out clothes and then sew them all during the following day so that the children always looked neat and presentable even when they were at home.

The major hiccup to my budgeting plan was William. He would decide that he wanted something, he wanted it then—that day, he had to have it, he was entitled to have what he wanted as he received money from the government in his name and he should be allowed to spend that money in the way that he saw fit, when he saw fit! My argument was that as a family, all monies—mine included—were for the upkeep and maintenance of the entire family. If he was desperate for said article/s, I was more than happy to try and budget for it/ them in the next pay cycle after the rent, bills, utilities and food had been accounted for. That is how I function. That is how I was taught to budget and I have never ever differed from that in any way. There had been a very sound reason why William had handed over the money management for our family to me and that was because he had already caused us to receive two eviction notices from the Department of Housing, Queensland, due to his lack of paying rent to the landlord. From the day that I took over being the financier of the household, all rent, bills and utilities were paid before the due date and over time we became "preferred clients" with housing and were treated accordingly. But when William got a bee in his bonnet, which was way too often for me, I had to produce the goods or feel the wrath until they appeared. (More on that soon.)

Life continued to be a struggle but I had been lulled into a cocoon of false belief by William that we were doing okay and that either 'it would all come out in the wash' or 'something would turn up'. I know now that I was under a spell of control and that I even defended William more than I already had in the many years of our marriage. I now believe that I couldn't see the forest for the trees. My lower socio-economic life continued. The very proud professional had been talked into becoming a person whose expectations were set so low but I had not even made the correlation between William's bizarre behaviours and how I was behaving and fitting in with his way of thinking.

We had another baby in 1989. I had felt all through the pregnancy that something was seriously wrong. I did not intuit that the issue was with the baby, instead thinking that the problem could be with my heath. I had the dreadfully overbearing feeling of doom and gloom for that entire pregnancy. (More on that in another chapter.) After the birth of this baby, there was no way I could return to the workplace as he required 24/7 care and as I was a nurse, the care was left entirely to me. My life became extremely busy between all the other children, my extremely errant two-year-old and a baby who needed far more care and time than any other three or four children would.

I was totally consumed with my family and my home and just trying to survive. How had I managed to arrive at this point? I loved my children with a passion, the level of which caused me to suffer physical pain when they were in pain, hurt, sick or sad. I had suffered in exactly the same way with my father. I truly believe that is why I have never really accepted his death. I was accused many times of wrapping my children in cotton wool, of trying to protect them from too much, of not being able to cut the apron strings. My policy has always been one of strictness but with so much love in their lives that they would never question my love, loyalty or integrity and would always know that I was there for and with them, no matter how hard their lives became. I tried to bring them up to be caring, honest and loving adults with integrity, ethics and morals and I truly believe with all my heart, even today, that I did manage to do that with all nine of my children. Unfortunately, I alone was too naïve and damaged by the abuse I had suffered at the hands of my husband for over three decades to counter the effects of their father's brainwashing and lies and the various psychological disorders suffered by Tracey and Clayton. I feel pity for the children that I am no longer permitted to have in my life. They have succumbed to the ego-driven society in which they falsely believe they hold such high stature. They are unable to accept the depth of the depravity of their father's actions towards myself, Brianna and others and were so ready to believe the constant volley of misperceptions that their father *created* to confirm his lies to them and thus have become the uncaring nameless faces that is society today. They cannot have the truth of their father invading their perfect lives so it is easier for them to believe the fantasy world that their father has created for them and to completely and totally abandon their mother without ever giving her any sort of explanation as to the reasons they have acted in the manner in which they did. Their actions are unforgiveable. One of Billy's best friends wrote me an email in which he stated, 'No mother should be treated the way that you are being treated!'

My days of boxing and compartmentalisation finished a good long while ago. No longer do I keep all the hurt, loss and pain to myself, instead choosing to fully inform everyone, who care to listen, to the tale of my husband and my children. To say that they are utterly appalled is a great understatement. People who had known our family for decades and had only recently found out the truth were horrified and suggested that it was 'the kind of stuff you only see in movies or criminal dramas'. I can no longer concern myself with the feelings of my criminal husband or children who "aid and abet" that criminal. It is only now that I have made the full realisation of Clayton's real involvement in all that has gone awry in my life. More on Clayton's culpability soon.

During the winter of 1989, as the three years were quickly approaching, at which point I would lose my six years of registration as a nurse and midwife—meaning then I would slip from the top pay grade down to the bottom and have to start to build up my years of service all over again—my dear friend Peta made me a brilliant offer. Peta was the matron at a nursing home on the Brisbane Northside and she desperately needed a live-in on-call acting matron for *one* weekend. I was her first call as she knew of my predicament. Peta and I were kindred spirits; we both had a very large family and shared the same values. I thanked her and said I would speak to William but was certain that all would be well and I would be able to fix my registration. In actual fact, the requirements were such that one single hour of work would have extended the time for me to re-enter the workforce by a further three years!

I very excitedly told William about Peta's offer. I very quickly became totally deflated as William stated that it was my duty to be at home caring for my children, especially the youngest child who still required and always would require so much extra care. I pleaded with him, it was only one weekend but it would mean so much to me to know that in the future, I would still have the opportunity to return to my beloved nursing without having to start at the bottom of the pile again. After everything I had sacrificed in order to get my registration, could I not be given just one weekend to ensure its continuation? All the children I currently had deserved to have their mother earn as much as she could possibly earn to help keep the family afloat. William was having none of it and I was so controlled by him that I could not defy him. He claimed to be too sick to be able to care for our two youngest children, let alone the rest. I called Peta, absolutely heartbroken, to make my excuses and to thank her profusely for the offer. It was then that I decided that I would never start from the bottom again and that my nursing career had just ended without so much as a fizz! I lost a considerable amount of respect for my husband that day. Losing respect was becoming more of a way of life as time went on.

Clayton had joined the army in 1990 and it was not long before his girlfriend, Elise, who was 18 started to board with us as she was having issues with her own parents. I found this rather inconvenient with so many children already and very little extra space but being an empath, I accepted it and did my best to move forward. By this stage, I had moved back into the bedroom to my gorgeous waterbed for sleeping and William had moved into the lounge as our youngest child often woke many times through the night due to his medical issues and lying on the warmth of the waterbed would help with his pain relief.

I started to note behaviour in William that, at the very least, was rather bizarre but tended to edge more towards suspicious. His night-time habits seemed to involve hovering outside the bedroom where Elise slept with Brianna. My door was pushed over to darken the room for the baby but I had a direct line of sight to that bedroom door. Due to the younger children not liking the dark, the hallway light would remain on all night to light their way to the bathroom and back to bed. When asked what he was doing, he had always thought he had heard a noise. Elise had a bad habit of wearing very torn t-shirts to bed, which exposed her breasts totally, and she was happy to sit around at the dining table like this for an inordinate amount of time.

On the very last day of the school year for 1990, I had a jam-packed day ahead. First was the preschool break-up party and as I had been the president of the P & C that year, I needed to be in attendance for the entirety of the proceedings. There was time to dash home for lunch and Elise chose this time to tell me quite a bit more of her adventures whilst living with Tracey. She had certainly saved the best for last in my opinion. William was playing with the children whilst Elise devastated me with the news that no mother wishes to hear. Tracey had told her that William had sexually interfered with her. There was no mention of when she claimed any of this occurred and I found that the story lacked credibility without additional information. I had long since known that Tracey was a habitual liar. I stored that information in my mind for later. As William and I travelled with our youngest son to an appointment with his paediatric surgeon, I let William in on the latest information about Tracey. I was so furious with Tracey for lying again that I was not seeing straight and not thinking at all! We rushed back home, bathed and fed all the children and then I had to take Brianna to her year 7 graduation/dance.

It was rather late by the time we got back home and Brianna was soon asleep in bed. It was MN when I could no longer control my anger and I insisted that William call Tracey and got her and her husband over to our place, immediately. I made one major mistake that night. We had a corner lounge suite at the time, which had a long three-seater couch, a coffee table and then a two-seater at right angles to the rest. William sat on the inner side of the two-seater next to the coffee table and I sat at his side. Tracey was sitting in the middle of the three-seater with her husband to her left. I could see all the micro-expressions on her face but I could not see William's face at all. At that point, I did not think that I needed to. I went for Tracey in a big way; I had years' worth of ammunition against her, this was just the icing on the cake, so to speak. There was one tiny nanosecond when my heart and my head almost believed that she was telling the truth but I brushed it away very quickly. It was when she looked at her father and said, 'But Dad, we have discussed all of this and came to an agreement.' I will never know what his expression was at that second but I am certain that I should have seen it to know the full truth.

The following morning turned out to be the beginning of a whole new phase of my life. One I neither expected nor wanted. I could not understand why my husband, from that day onwards, turned every conversation into an argument, he became violent with me for the first time and became ever more demanding day by day. I dissolved into tears as days became weeks for the lack of being able to comprehend what had changed. I tried to be supportive, believing that he was finding it too difficult to deal with Tracey's accusations. I insisted on taking her to court to clear his name in the hope that he would then feel exonerated. He absolutely forbade it. I said I had the right to clear my husband's name, he asked why I was not putting the need of all my other children first. I stated that I was as it was them as much as him that I was trying to protect. I argued the case for clearing his name for months; he just argued, with me.

Almost exactly six weeks after that Friday night, I was called to go to Toowoomba to collect Brianna who had been visiting Mum over the holidays. She had a dreadful toothache and needed to see the dentist. I travelled to Toowoomba by bus and stayed overnight and returned to Brisbane the following day. I had told Mum all about what

Tracey had said and what I had done, etc., never for one millisecond connecting the dots between Tracey's lies and Jonathon's six-year gap out of my life. I was also to learn many, many years later that on the *one* night that I was away from my home, William would have a pornographic movie playing in the lounge room and ask his son's 18-year-old girlfriend to "suck him off"!

A mother's love for her child is like
nothing else in the world.
It knows no law, no pity, it dares all things, and crushes
down remorselessly all that stand in its path.

-AGATHA CHRISTIE

CHAPTER 9

MY BEAUTIFUL BABIES

William and I decided it was silly to wait to get pregnant again despite the pain losing twins had caused me. If I did not try again, sooner rather than later, I was not certain that I ever would, despite the fact that it had been my life-long goal to have twelve children.

Once the decision was made, I fell pregnant very quickly but we had no intentions of advising any of the children after the events of the previous pregnancy. It was not overly difficult to hide the morning sickness from the children but once I developed a bump, it was clearly time that they should be informed. Tracey was none too pleased, Clayton seemed to at least pretend to be excited but was reined back in by Tracey. Brianna was ecstatic and Jack didn't really seem to understand but was full of smiles.

From the very second the baby started to move in utero, he was destined to be a sportsman. He could most certainly win gold for kicking and indeed, had actually kicked his dad out of bed one night. I was shocked his foot did not appear through my abdominal wall. It was a rather good pregnancy with the exception of the severe heartburn, which I was reliably informed that it meant this baby would be born with lots of hair.

The due date was 6 March 1982 but my father-in-law, also William, begged me to 'keep my legs closed until the 7th', his own birthday. It was not to be as I went into labour early and after an 18-hour horrifically painful labour, my son, William, was born. He had to be rushed out to resuscitation as he had been a Mec Liq (Meconium-stained Liquor, which means the baby had defecated in utero before birth). In this case, it had been considered by the obstetrician that it had been passed at least a week prior to my having gone into labour. Mec Liq is generally a sign of foetal distress, and if he hadn't been then, he most certainly was whilst I was in labour. William junior had decided that he was coming into the world looking at the skies. His foetal position was POP—Posterior on Posterior—his spine was along mine. This is the most painful position for the mother to give birth naturally. His heartrate was dipping and the doctor had to perform a "strip and stretch", where the fingers are inserted into the vagina and you literally try to open the vagina further and stretch down on the walls to efface them more quickly. This baby had to be born quickly or I would be rushed to the OT for an emergency Caesarean section for delivery.

I was in absolute agony and all I wanted was my husband to assure me that it would be okay. He was nowhere to be seen. He had brought me to the hospital in the small hours of the morning and once they decided that I could labour in the ward for a few hours, he went home to sleep. He was dealing with what turned out to be caffeine withdrawal but at that point in time, with me in so much pain, he was all that I wanted. Young William did not quite get his way in the sense of looking to the heavens as he was born as the pain was so intense that I was actually lying on my side when I delivered him. William had almost missed his son's birth but I was to learn that I would be alone for most of my children's births. That was not something that I had ever envisaged happening. My beliefs ran very deeply regarding this subject and also on how parents should act with their wives and children. As a midwife, I had seen all sorts and I had most definitely refined what I considered to be acceptable behaviour for the father, in particular, but parents in general. It takes two people to create a new life and there should be two people present to welcome that new life into this world. Gone were the days where it was acceptable for fathers to sit in the waiting room, leaving the wife to get on with the hard work and then, once presented with their cleaned, buffed and wrapped new-born, head out for the obligatory cigar and pint to "wet the baby's head"!

William made all the right noises but as soon as he could possibly leave, he was full of excuses and I was, again, totally alone. I had suffered a PPH (Post-Partum Haemorrhage), which was quite sizeable and I had to remain in the labour ward for many hours to ensure that I would not need to be rushed into the operating theatre. Young William was born on Tuesday and I had to remain in the hospital until Saturday. I had an IV infusion and many blood tests to ensure that I did not require a blood transfusion. I was very weak and light-headed for the most part of that week and was still not back to my usual self when William came to take William junior and I home on Saturday morning. We got home, I settled William junior after everyone had seen him, had a cup of coffee and was slowly starting to feel I had arrived home properly when William announced that he was off to see his ex-in-laws with the children and that I would need to do the washing that was waiting downstairs in the laundry. I was alone again but instead of being upset and kicking up a fuss, I just got on with it and did as I was told.

I was to learn just how far apart our parenting ideas were within the first couple of weeks of William junior's life. One evening, William decided that he wanted to go to the shops. I said that I would get the children ready to go. William said that no, it was just he and I that were going. I said that I could not leave such a tiny baby in the care of a 14-year-old, an 11-year-old and a 4-year-old. What I thought was *There is no way that I am leaving my firstborn son in the care of someone who does not consider that he has the right to be alive, a young boy she can so easily manipulate and my firstborn daughter whom Clayton hated with a passion and Tracey was totally indifferent about!* That is when the pressure started, it was not optional, William had decided and I was going, End Of!

Of course, it was so much more subtle than it sounds. All of his arguments to back up his rationale had a slight degree of sense about them and it seemed that, although my gut disagreed with my head, it was so much easier for me to not kick up a fuss but to just do what I had to do and make sure that it was over and done with as quickly as possible so that I could stop stressing and move forward. Having my heart in my throat was becoming not only an almost daily event but a real way of life for me.

William junior had a wonderful set of lungs, especially at 03:00 every morning. He would have a feed but be totally unsettled and crying/whinging until 07:00 when he would be out cold just as I had to get the other children up and get them sorted for school and start the day's housework. He was so predictable that, on one occasion, I assured William that I would be able to record a movie that would start at 03:00 one morning. William watched that recording many times over the ensuing years. The movie was *The Day the Earth Stood Still*.

Due to financial constraints, I returned to the workforce when William junior was just three months old. I was doing night duty at PAH and William was working on a barge out of Fisherman's Island in Brisbane. I finished work at 07:00 and William left the house for work at 07:00 so there was an overlap where the children were home alone whilst I collected the babysitter (the newly arrived pregnant girlfriend of one of William 's ex-in-laws) and got back to the house to organise them for school, sort washing, etc. and grab some sleep before taking the babysitter home and collecting Brianna from preschool, and again back home to sort meals, wash, clean and iron before being at Fisherman's wharf by 17:00 to collect William from work. It was then back home, dinner, bath and get the younger children to bed and I would attempt to grab an extra hour or two of sleep before heading back to PAH for the next night duty. William had very different ideas... More on that later!

It was probably not overly hard to guess that this lifestyle was doomed to failure. I became quite sick; I ached all over. I was listless and had no energy. I saw my GP and he referred me to a rheumatologist who diagnosed viral polyarthritis. I was left with no choice but to take a break from work again. It was so frustrating but once I began to feel a bit better, I sank all my efforts into my family and my home.

I do not believe that I ever fully recovered from that episode but I was so stubborn that I just kept moving forwards. It probably turned out for the best as I was pregnant again and William junior was quite the handful. I had always known that William junior would be an athlete but I had not figured on running. His biggest party trick, however, was escapology. He could spy an opportunity at great lengths and always seized his opportunity when you least expected it. Screaming brakes were a tell-tale sign that William junior had managed to get out of the yard and onto the road again! Even with the gates bolted closed, he would wait until I was busy and he would tunnel underneath with his bare hands. There was no obstacle too large for William junior to get out of, over or under in order to escape. The funniest of all his escapes was a day when I had both the back and front doors securely locked and I was dusting and vacuuming and stopping every few metres to check on Houdini. I could hear a faint voice calling 'Mum' and I went through every room in the house calling 'William junior, where are you?' I repeated my search of every room over and over until I was frantic. I could still hear the faint voice calling Mum and I was now running from room to room in a blind panic. It was not until he slipped up when I was in the front room and called 'Mum' once more that I looked out the windows and found him hanging on the window hook by the collar of his shirt. He was dangling there for all the world to see. I did not know whether to smack him or hug him. Thank goodness I had not put a t-shirt on him that day or he would have been off and running…

It was in December of 1982 that Emma and her boyfriend, Adam, were to be married. I had not been asked to be part of the bridal party but Brianna was asked to be the flower girl. William arrived home the day before the wedding after having been at sea for longer than expected in the Solomon Islands. William decided the night before that he didn't want to go to the wedding, we argued. My daughter was in the wedding party and I had no intention of missing it. Emma and Adam had requested there be no children at the wedding to help control costs. Mum had organised a very dear family friend to look after all the children at Mum's house whilst we all went to the wedding reception. William was livid that Tracey and Clayton were being excluded. They could not have cared less about Emma and all their food was provided for.

As we went to set off for the wedding, which everyone could attend, my cousin Faith said that her camera batteries were dead and she didn't know where to get any at this time as shops were shut at midday in Toowoomba on Saturdays. I said that there was an open chemist on Ruthven Street that they could try. William then volunteered us to go and get them for her. We did but I was not happy in the slightest. By the time we got back to the church, I had missed my little girl walking up the aisle. After the ceremony, it was lovely to catch up with old friends and relatives that I had not seen for ages. We went back to Mum's house but William refused to allow Tracey and Clayton to stay there, let alone William junior. He procrastinated and mucked about for so long that by the time we pulled up in the car park of the reception hall, William junior was so far past his limit for the day that he was crying his little heart out. He got so worked up that he threw up all over the car. Of course, then William said, 'Go and get Brianna, we need to take William junior home as he is sick.'

I walked into the reception hall and collected Brianna, pulling her away from the wonderful time she was having and along with Mum, we walked back to the car. I told Mum that night I was pregnant again and she said it was a good thing that I had not been involved in the bridal party. She had not worked out that I was pregnant as it was not showing so I failed to see how it could have had any adverse effect on any dress. However, I was seething about other matters. William had orchestrated getting his own way and I had neither seen my little girl perform her duties as a bridesmaid nor had I been allowed to attend the reception. It was a long and very hungry ride back to Brisbane that night.

My brother, Jonathon, and his girlfriend, Debbie, were married less than a month later. This wedding was in Brisbane. It was to be a garden wedding in Debbie's mother's garden. I had made the wedding dress on this occasion. Again, the night before the wedding, William started an argument about not wishing to attend. We did attend and it was quite pleasant. Mum was there and all the talk was about Brianna starting Grade 1 very soon. William stood like a statue out of everyone's way until he thought he could convince me to leave the celebrations early. It was on our way home from the wedding that William was pulled over by the police and he went straight into one of his spiels and I witnessed what I could not believe. He was never asked for his licence and we were on our way home again.

Brianna started year 1 at St Elizabeth's Catholic Primary School at Ekibin in Brisbane. She was so excited and proudly told everyone where she went to school. She was doing reasonably well, in my opinion, given the different twangs that emerged in our house due to different cultural influences. Every afternoon, William would roll up a pamphlet or something similar and practice alphabet sounds with Brianna. If she got it wrong, she got a swat on the head with the pamphlet. I do not believe in fear-based training or child rearing but William was always right. Brianna was blatantly not happy with it and one day she wet herself as she had been too scared to ask William if she could go to the toilet. After this, I did all of Brianna's homework with her.

Just over halfway through that year, I was called to the school to discuss allowing Brianna to just continue at her own pace with no pressure and to let her repeat year 1 again the following year. The problem for Brianna was that William corrected everyone's speech, and I mean everyone. Strangers and friends alike. I was the biggest target of his wrath in this area and to this day, he still does the exact same thing. So poor Brianna hears Mum pronounce words one way, William another, him constantly correcting Mum and her speech and pronunciation of words ends up somewhere in the middle. I was led to believe, by the school, that her other subjects were also falling behind so I agreed to her repeating year 1 and for there to be no further corporal punishment involved with homework. There most certainly had never been anything of the kind with Tracey and Clayton that I had ever witnessed.

I was shocked to discover when I received Brianna's report card that both her Maths and English marks were over 90%. Why then did she need to repeat? I left it be as it was and Brianna very quickly slipped back into school and developed a friendship with a young girl who only lived further up the street from us in Tarragindi. Brianna would visit her house and vice versa. She seemed to be a lovely girl. They developed quite a friendship as the year wore on. One day at school, Brianna's friend had taken money from a teacher's purse that had been left in the classroom during lunch break. Brianna scolded her and took it from her and went in to put it back into the purse. And, naturally, she was caught in her act of kindness and, as her friend lied and refused to change her story, Brianna had to bear the wrath of that lie. I used every trick in the book to determine the validity of Brianna's version and she was telling the truth in my opinion. It was not to matter; the girls were no longer friends and Brianna was being victimised by the nuns. I was devastated by the way my daughter was being treated in a Catholic school. William and I decided to take Brianna out of school early for the year. William went in to see the head nun and "ripped her a new one" for the way she had been treating Brianna. She was incensed as she claimed that no one had ever spoken to her in that manner, to which William 's reply was, 'Well, it is high time they did if this is how you treat young children.'

Once the other parents started to note that Brianna was not at school anymore and began asking questions as to why, I got a phone call from another parent. It transpired that Brianna had not been alone in her victimisation at St Elizabeth's. There were many more children that were in the exact same position and the parents were all banding together and intended to take on the school and go to the authorities. They wanted William and I to join them. I was so relieved to know that Brianna had not been singled out and I thanked them for advising me but I could not get involved with all the other issues that were going on in our lives. Brianna was enrolled in a state school for the following year and we would try our best to repair the damage they had caused her.

It would be many years after Brianna was no longer at St Elizabeth's that William and I would learn the truth about Tracey having private conversations with the head nun at the school and it was she who then reported William and I to children's services. The accusations and claims were false but they proved to have a devastating effect on our lives.

In early June of 1983, I had an ante-natal appointment at the Mater at which my obstetrician had promised me that he would make sure all was in order and I could then be admitted and have my labour induced. The reason for this proposed action was that William was due to leave for a month on a trip to Japan and this was the only way he could get to see his new-born baby. The baby, of course, had very different ideas to mine. The baby's lie was oblique and it would be far too dangerous to induce labour in that situation as the cord could prolapse and cut off the oxygen supply to the baby. The result of this was an emergency Caesarean section. I left the hospital that day extremely dejected. I was going to be alone in having this baby, which was not the way that I believed things should be. William flew off for Japan.

The following week, the baby stopped moving so I was placed into the Mater hospital. The children were in Toowoomba with Mum. I was to be induced on Thursday but the labour ward had become so busy that it was put off until Friday. I was taken to the labour ward and had the Syntocinon Infusion started around lunchtime. It seemed that nothing was going to move this baby as no contractions were occurring. It was not until after 17:00 that they kicked in. My obstetrician had popped in to see how I was going just after this stage and claimed he had ample time to go and perform a Caesarean, especially as my last labour had been 18 hours long. He was to learn that all-time favourite lesson—never second-guess a baby or a multi. Isabelle was born at 20:01. She was a very deep shade of blue with very red hair and no amount of effort seemed to be encouraging her to take her first breath. Even I was up and tapping her feet encouragingly. Eventually, she decided to join us and filled the room with her crying, such a beautiful sound. It was not one that I would hear terribly often though as Isabelle turned out to be a model baby, the one that everyone dreams of having.

William junior was only 15 months old when Isabelle was born and they were as different as chalk and cheese. William junior was a real mummy's boy and still refused to even hold his own bottle. Every time he saw Isabelle at the breast, he insisted that I hold his bottle. Trying to appease him was no mean trick. Isabelle slept through the night from one and a half weeks of age and only had three breastfeeds a day. Even when she woke up, she did not cry. I would find her laying there with her eyes open, staring at nothing. Billy was a true tantrum-thrower. His scream was something to behold. His antics never once seemed to bother Isabelle, she would sleep on.

Isabelle and I went home to an empty house. It was a bit bizarre at first, but in the time we had together, Isabelle and I forged a bond so strong that it would stand the test of time. My brother, Jonathon, went to Toowoomba and collected the other children and we went along our merry way for the first month of Isabelle's life. Isabelle was one month old when I had to get both her and I all dressed up and head to the airport to collect William so that he could meet his new daughter for the first time. I had a double abscess in my groin at the time and was in an enormous amount of pain. Trying to walk in high boots did not help the situation in the slightest. Once back home, Isabelle required feeding, which was totally disrupted because of Dad being home and all the other children being so overexcited by all the activity. Isabelle, for the very first time in her life, did not feed well. By 03:00 the following morning, Isabelle required a feed. As I went to get out of bed to get her for a feed, two things happened. Both of the abscesses burst and I had pus running down my leg and William started moaning and complaining about the fact that he had been told "this child" slept through the night! I settled Isabelle and then had to sit in a salt bath to try and draw out as much of the pus as I could. The following morning, Isabelle woke up with a rash and William's first response was that she needed to be bottle-fed as the poison in my system was affecting her. I thought long and hard and decided that I would allow her to be bottle-fed until I felt better.

The rash worsened and I wanted to return her to breastfeeding but William was against the whole idea. I was beginning to feel a little bit of déjà vu! He had also come up with some wondrous reasons for William junior not to be breastfed as well. Poor Isabelle was to suffer the consequences of this change as she was lactose intolerant and took a long time to settle into formula feeding. She was still a dream baby and a truly wondrous judge of character, as it turned out.

My mother had not seen Isabelle either until she was a month old. I had never, ever actually heard Isabelle scream until my mother took her for a cuddle. Isabelle screamed so much that I jumped and grabbed her, imagining that a nappy pin had come undone and was digging into her! The screaming immediately stopped but I did a myriad of checks to ensure my baby's safety and could find nothing. All present were making jokes about how it was Mum that had caused her to scream. Mum was rather indignant about such remarks and again took Isabelle to prove her doubters wrong. Isabelle screamed again until I took her back. This scenario continued several more times before Mum decided to leave well enough alone.

That would not be the only time that Mum would feel Isabelle's scorn. She was talking very eloquently when Mum was paying another visit to the family. Isabelle seemed to be enjoying proceedings but then turned to Mum and said, 'I think it is time you left now, Grandma, you have been here long enough!'

Mum was flabbergasted by the comment, which I laughed off and tried to make light of but Isabelle had been deadly serious and was not overly impressed that her suggestion had not immediately been instigated.

Mum was not the only person to feel the wrath of Isabelle's tongue. Isabelle always thought she had the mark of her father as well. To name just a couple of occasions when Isabelle 'called it as she saw it' were when William had been eating a hamburger from the corner shop and Isabelle walked up to him and said, 'You eat like a pig, Dad!'

On another occasion, Isabelle became quite cross with her father's actions and turned and said, 'You are getting right up on my nerves, Dad!' Isabelle was such a joy to have around and always managed to make me laugh. She also proved to be the one I could totally and completely rely upon when I needed it the most; more on that to come.

When William left in early August 1984 for an around-the-world trip on a ship, Isabelle could not yet walk or talk and I was pregnant again, although no one yet knew except William and I. It was an extremely difficult four months, financially, in particular. William had decided to take this job on the lowest-paid class of ship as it would be in dry dock in Germany for approximately one month and he would be able to fly to England to visit his parents, whom he had not seen for many years. At the same time, he decided to take a sub of $100 from each pay so that he could treat them whilst he was there. I agreed to this arrangement because it meant so much to him; at least, I believed the money would be used to treat his parents. It meant that William had left me with only $200/week to pay rent, bills, debts from his first marriage and feed six people. I had never been forced, before or after that time, to feed my family and myself such utter shit in order to survive. The truth was something of a different story. More to come on that specific period of time later.

When William arrived home on 27 November, he had almost $6,000, his final payment from this extremely long trip, which he threw up in the air in the lounge room and had it rain down all over the children who collected it all up again. So much had gone so totally wrong during that four plus months but that evening, I dared to believe that maybe we were turning a corner. William had bought himself a lot of things with the sub he had taken—winter coat, leather gloves and boots along with a tool kit from Germany. He had bought a couple of things for the children but mostly for himself. How wrong could I have been?

The following morning, William went and purchased a brand new mower. I had just spent so long dealing with having to take the mower apart every time I mowed to reset it all so that it would work. I had gone so many times to the mower shop for parts to fix it up that it had become a labour of love. William junior did not know that this contraption that cut the grass after Mummy spent a lot of time fixing the issues was actually called a mower. As far as he was concerned, "The Problem" cut the grass and even when replaced with a much newer model, it was still referred to as The Problem by a certain gorgeous little guy I once knew.

William had always been a dreadful money manager but he seemed hell-bent on ploughing through the pay he had received in lickety-split time. Before Christmas, he had also bought a computer for the family, an Amstrad 646. This computer required that the user sit and print in the entire programme for any game, which would take many hours to complete. If, at the end, there had been even one single typo, you would need to go through the entire thing again to establish where the error was to correct it. It was so totally basic but, at the same time, certainly created many hours of fun for the children. They also had the very top of the range gaming machines such as Dick Smith games and Intellivision Video Games Console. The games for this machine were rather expensive at the time, $25-$30 each. Our children did not want for entertainment even back in the early eighties.

By the time Jasmine was born, eight days late and only 13 hours before my own birthday, things were not looking too good again but there were many, many reasons for it this time. Whilst William had been on this extensive sea journey around the world, we had been left with only a minute income to cope for such a long period of time. We ate what could only be described as rubbish food that was the cheapest of the cheap, the phone was disconnected due to William 's reverse charge phone calls from the other side of the planet, we fell behind with the rent as there was just no money to pay it and the debts left by William 's previous marriage were also falling way behind. To add insult to injury, Tracey ensured that this would be one of the most tumultuous periods of my life. She bluntly refused to do a single thing to help around the house but still expected to be driven to and collected from friends by me.

As already stated, William had many other things that he considered to be much more important than contacting Tracey. I asked him to do so many times as I knew it would only lead to much more aggravation for William and I in the long run. The phone had been reconnected and William also received calls from Jane Wilson requesting he make contact with Tracey. As far as William was concerned, Tracey had left the family home and he stated, 'If she wants to see me, she knows where I live!'

What had transpired was that Tracey's plan did not work unless her father kowtowed to her every whim. When he refused to go and see her, on her terms, she had to think of another way to get me out of the picture. If she was ever truly honest with herself, she knew that I held excessively high morals, ethics and standards and if I was to believe a wrongdoing on the part of her father that I could not have tolerated, then she would have been able to break up the marriage.

She went to my brother, Jonathon, and told him that her father had sexually abused her. She told him that he could not tell me, which is exactly what she wanted to happen in truth, so that I would believe badly of her father and leave. Jonathon chose not to tell me anything; he stopped speaking to me without any explanation. He did, however, tell his then wife, Debbie, my sister, Emma, and her husband, Adam, and my mother, of course. Not a single one of them, all of whom claimed to love Brianna, thought it was unacceptable to withhold this information from me!

It was my practice to pack and unpack William's suitcase for all of his trips at sea. When I emptied his suitcase following this trip, I found a Christmas card to him from his brother's ex-wife, which I considered to be way too intimate from a sister-in-law. I confronted William as to whether he had, in fact, had an affair with her whilst he had been in England. To add to this card, there had been the fact that he had actually stayed with her whilst in England and the fact that he had called more than once from her place and hung up without explanation when she re-entered the property before our phone was disconnected. There was also the story about his brother who had threatened to come to the ship when it had finally docked in England to kill him. William claimed that if he tried that, the crew would kill and dispose of him as once on board the ship, he was on Australian territory. I never really understood when he had called to ask my permission for this to proceed? Then there was the time when I could not get through to him at all and was beginning to have some major doubts about what was going on until a huge floral arrangement had been delivered to me. Despite all the evidence to the contrary, William vehemently denied wrongdoing on his part and it would be almost a decade before I found out the truth.

I was to learn many years later—six years two and a half months, in fact—that because Dad had not come running as she had planned, it was necessary to devise another plan to get his attention enough to get me kicked out of his life. She, of course, had gone to Jonathon. She was banking on the fact that he would rush straight over and tell me, I would tell William, he would go running to her to find out what was going on, she would have planted the seed of doubt in my mind and I would no longer be able to trust my husband, and would leave. This would give Tracey everything that she had wanted and had been planning for. But Jonathon refused to speak to me. I have never truly understood what blame I had in what had occurred, depending on the version of the story Tracey told at any given time, before I was even living back in Brisbane, let alone in the same house as them both.

If only Tracey had been .0001% as clever and cunning as she thought she was, she could have very simply had all of her dreams come true if she had actually told me what she was accusing her father of; he would not have seen me or my children for dust. The golden opportunity to get exactly what her heart desired and Tracey totally wasted the opportunity!

But she was not, and I was treated like the proverbial mushroom by all—kept in the dark and fed a load of bullshit!

Fear grows out of the things we think;
it lives in our minds.
Compassion grows out of the things we are,
and lives in our hearts.

-BARBARA GARRISON

CHAPTER 10

MORE JOYOUS EVENTS

Jasmine had made a rather quick entrance to the world once she decided to get moving. I had been completely unable to sleep the night before her birth. I watched television or the huge fish tank of tropical fish we had and went to the toilet extremely frequently all night. By about 07:00, I went in to wake William as I felt a bit funny. I was not in labour. I was certain of that as I had not had a single contraction as yet. That morning, we had a meeting with children's services and that afternoon was my ante-natal appointment so it was to be a busy day. I went about my business of getting the children up, fed and off to school, for those that went.

William was convinced that the baby was about to be born and insisted on calling my girlfriend, Sally, who was the pre-organised babysitter for this birth. I told William that he was wasting Sally's time as nothing was going to happen but over she came and I made her a coffee and we sat at the kitchen table. All the while, William was trying to get me motivated to get into the car and head to the hospital. Eventually, Sally joined in and I gave up and agreed to go and get checked out at least.

We were sitting outside the admissions room at the Mater Mother's, it was approximately 10:30 and it was my friend, Marg, who was on duty. We had completed our midwifery training together at this very hospital. She had gone into the office to sort paperwork after I had told her that I was there under false pretences as I was not in labour. She had said that as I was 8 days late, it was worth a check and I may well be induced anyway, which would save me having to sit in the clinic that afternoon.

As soon as she had said those words, I came over severely nauseated and needed to throw up, the tell-tale sign that I was in transition, a sign I knew all too well. This meant that the baby was about to start its descent down the birth canal as I was fully dilated. We went immediately to the labour ward. I, at least, was finally having contractions. The midwife tried and failed to "rupture the membranes" of the amniotic sac that the baby was in. It transpired that during all my trips to the toilet overnight, I had been releasing amniotic fluid as well as urine and it was such a controlled leak that I had been unable to pick up on the particular odour that amniotic fluid had.

Jasmine was born at 11:09. That was most certainly my shortest labour and could very easily have occurred on the kitchen floor at home if I had not listened to William. Believe me, he would dine out on that one for so many years it was to become very old very quickly!

I had precious little time to bond with my gorgeous new baby girl as the demands of family life got rather out of hand. I had been sent home when Jasmine was less than 48 hours old and was expected by William to get straight back into the cooking, cleaning and many other duties that were seen as mine alone. I was breastfeeding Jasmine but yet again, William was none too happy with that idea. I had witnessed this jealousy in fathers so many times whilst working as a midwife but had never truly expected to have to live it myself. I was determined to ensure that my children had the very best I could provide but William was equally as determined that it would not come from breastfeeding. I used every trick in the book but the pressure was becoming too great, even in those first few days after having given birth.

Mum brought Brianna back just in time to start the new school year. Mum definitely had something on her mind but she was not about to impart it to me. I was ironing after the washing dried, trying to get the baby's clothes ironed as well as school uniforms for the New Year. Tracey was over to beg her father to allow her to move back home and in the middle of all the mayhem, Mum bailed me up in the hallway to announce that she would never stay in our house again whilst William was at home. I questioned and questioned her as to why she had made such a decision but she refused to say. Hindsight is a wondrous thing, as we all know, but I have to ask myself how a mother, who claims to love a grandchild so much that she actually wanted to adopt her, could hold on to information that could possibly imply that the child in question could be in danger? Not to mention Isabelle or baby Jasmine who was just days old. It is incomprehensible for me to come up with any reason why you could allow even the slightest possibility of sexual abuse to be kept locked in the cupboard and to knowingly and willingly put so many children at risk. That, in my eyes, is culpability as accessories for whatever crimes are then committed on and/or against those poor little children.

William allowed Tracey to move back into the house, totally against my better judgment, but then I had so little say when it came down to it. Mum left and the children went back to school. William had spent so much money since returning from overseas that I needed to return to the workforce pronto. Jasmine was two weeks old when I returned to work, desperately padding my breasts to prevent milk leakage whilst I was working. It had been a bitter pill to swallow, having to return to work and leave my new-born baby so soon. But if I wanted to continue to feed my children, what choice did I have?

William had taken a 12-month leave of absence to give him the time he needed to get to know and be with the children again. I was no sooner back at work when William brought Isabelle and Billy to collect me from my early shift in Kangaroo Point. We lived in Tarragindi at that time, almost 10 kilometres apart, and as I did not finish until 15:00 and it was directly in front of the southern side of the Storey Bridge, it was peak hour traffic and not a quick journey home. He had left Brianna, seven years old, in charge of baby Jasmine, two weeks old. I was absolutely furious with him and threatened him with what I would do with life and limb if he ever did that again!

Tracey slept in the front room with Brianna, Isabelle and Jasmine. Somehow, the bassinet managed to get upended and Jasmine ended up on the floor whilst Tracey was watching the girls. Jasmine was fine but the lack of care on Tracey's part caused me huge amounts of stress. She did not believe I had any right to bring these children into her family. What lengths was she prepared to go to in order to achieve her objectives? She had no qualms about becoming incredibly intoxicated, underage, and then vomiting all over the floor of the bedroom she shared with her sisters. I was not impressed as this had been my one no-no if she returned home.

William 's desperate need for me not to be at work again raised its head and it was April when he decided to go back to sea. This was another pattern that I witnessed. I was only permitted to work for three months at a time, then he would use any excuse he could to ensure I gave up again. It was as though he wanted to force me to learn to get on with Tracey whose disdain and disrespect were blatantly obvious to everyone. My friends could not believe what she did and how she acted towards me. She had one persona for Daddy—the sweet little angel—and the other—the devil incarnate—for me when Daddy was at sea!

William had joined the ship in Brisbane but had only made it as far as Frankston in Victoria when he was taken to the Frankston Hospital where he was diagnosed with left lower lobe pneumonia. His temperature was so high that they had to use ice in an attempt to cool him down. I was to finish on Sunday after he had left on his voyage, which was to go to the Persian Gulf where conflicts were occurring between warring nations in the region. I had not been happy about him taking this job even though there was an extra $250,000 insurance per seaman to be paid in the event of death caused by the conflict. I had the call on Saturday night that he was in hospital.

I spent much of the coming week on the phone to the hospital. He did start to improve but they refused to allow him to be discharged or travel home unless I was there with him. As I was a nurse, they were happy to discharge him into my care. I left on Friday morning on a bus bound for Frankston. It was the hardest thing I think I have ever done, left Tracey in charge of Clayton, Brianna, Billy, Isabelle and Jasmine, now four months old. It was the Mother's Day weekend and I did not wish to leave my children but I was torn as to what was the best thing to do. My mother had refused to stay with the children so off I went. The bus went through Toowoomba so Mum came to see me as I went through there.

I called home on our scheduled stops and could only pray that everything would be okay. I arrived in Frankston around 10:00 the following day. The coach driver actually dropped me at the front of the hospital. I immediately went to see William; he was exhausted and still not looking terribly well. I had booked into a motel close to the sea. William was discharged the following day and immediately went to sleep in the motel room. I tried, in vain, all day to contact home but it was constantly giving the engaged signal. I was in such a blind panic with not being able to speak to my children that I did not call Mum to wish her a Happy Mother's Day. It was not exactly at the top of my priorities at that time and I heard about that error for a long, long time to come.

When I finally was able to make contact with home, they claimed they had been trying to win a contest and were on the phone to the radio station all day. I did not believe that story in 1985 and it most certainly sounds even lamer now. Nevertheless, there was absolutely nothing I could do to alter the situation, given that we were at opposite ends of the east coast of Australia.

William and I flew home on Monday. There were two extremely memorable occurrences from that day, which would always stick with me. The first was the cost of the taxi from Frankston to Tullamarine Airport in Melbourne costing $45. It had been paid for by the shipping company but it seemed such an astronomical amount of money to me at the time. The other was the dreadful landing in Sydney en route to Brisbane. I have never had such a rough landing before or since but it would turn out to be 25 years before I would fly again, only to discover that I had developed a habit of panic attacks/air sickness—neither of which I had ever experienced before. I had always relished flying and now that had been taken away from me by one dreadful pilot!

William eventually recovered from the pneumonia and went back to sea. But, for the next two and a half years, he would be on a ship only for a maximum of 10 days before he would again get sick and be diagnosed with left lower lobe pneumonia. His final trip had been coming to an end in Western Australia out from Fremantle where both he and another seaman were taken off the ship sick before the ship continued its journey to the Suez Canal during the conflicts that were occurring in the area. The problem created by leaving the ship that day was that the Customs Officials who had been taken to the ship to clear the seaman to be taken off had not brought the correct stamps for the task in hand. William had been stamped out of the country but had not been stamped back in. This was an issue he should have sorted immediately upon recovery from that illness. He did not, of course, and was an illegal alien for a good few years. The immigration department, once advised of the situation, had been given the passport for correction, and lost it for months. It was eventually sorted but I sometimes now which it had not been.

In those two years, I had another daughter. Bianca was born on 6 February 1986. It was not the easiest of births, to say the least. I had become pregnant again so soon after having Jasmine that I decided not to return to the Mater Mothers but to go to the newest maternity hospital, which was the QEII Hospital. It was much closer to our home and seemed to make perfect sense. Everything about the hospital was just easier and more laidback, which suited me. I was only about two weeks from my due date when I attended the antenatal clinic to find that the baby was in the breech position and they wanted me to be admitted to the hospital for observation. I was in the hospital for one week and I managed to not be home for Jasmine's 1st birthday. I was devastated but I already had everything organised for William; I would never forget her running down the hospital corridor on her toes in her pink and white striped dress. She was gorgeous.

The baby had turned to the correct position and I was allowed to go home. The following morning, I was watching the television when a rocket was launched from Cape Canaveral and the rocket blew up, killing everyone on board.

It was to be a short reprieve for me, however, as at the next antenatal appointment, the baby decided it would be feet first again so I was admitted and booked in for a Caesarean section to be performed on 6 February. I had been in hospital since the previous afternoon, having put myself through agony trying to contact my previous obstetrician for his opinion and getting nowhere.

I had reconciled myself to this action in a manner of speaking. I was being cared for by many of the midwives that I had previously trained with and worked alongside so I was fairly comfortable. I had a dreadful night with the baby doing somersaults the entire time. I was having some contractions but the nurses' view was that I was having a C-section shortly so I shouldn't stress about it. Not one person, friend or not, even bothered to check the position of the baby before I was taken to the theatre.

This was where the nightmare really began. The anaesthetist tried and failed several times to insert an IV. There is a picture of the massive bruise he left on the inside of my left arm. But that was child's play compared to what was about to happen.

It was then time to try to insert an epidural into my spine. After three failed attempts, he was finally satisfied that he had succeeded and that I was ready for the procedure. I was raising my legs to prove what I was shouting, 'It has not worked, I can still feel and move my legs.'

The anaesthetist pinched the lower section of my pregnant belly and asked, 'Can you feel me touching?'

I said in reply, 'The skin is numb but that is about it.'

They considered me ready for the procedure. I was already on a knife's edge for many reasons. I was absolutely certain that I did not need a Caesarean. William refused to be in the theatre with me even though he would not have been able to see anything. Nobody had even checked the position of the baby since I had been admitted. After the failed attempts at inserting an IV and the epidural, I knew this was not going to go well.

They cut the skin; all was well. As they started going through the layers, things were not so well. I was feeling everything, and I mean everything! Instead of immediately putting me under a general anaesthetic, they decided to give me a dose of morphine, which sent my blood pressure underground, and they had to then use epinephrine to get it back. I felt every single movement they made and when they pulled my daughter out, my first question was, 'What came out first? How was she delivered, what position?'

She had come out head-first. She had turned during the previous night and not one single person had bothered to check the baby's position. I had endured a Caesarean section with no anaesthetic unnecessarily due to the incompetence of the staff of the QEII hospital. I was extremely happy to have a healthy baby daughter but I was devastated at the manner of her birth.

They were not done with me though. I finally made it to recovery where I started vomiting, post trauma probably. They gave me Stemetil and again they lost my blood pressure. Again, I was given epinephrine to return to some assemblance of normal.

After being returned to the ward, I was in agony but no one was game to administer pain relief now due to the reactions I had already suffered that day. Eventually, I was given something and all was well. I was done. I would never again want to fulfil my dream of having 12 children. It would need to be as it was; I could never again put myself through this crap.

William rocked up with a card for me. As always, he had written my name and address as if he was going to post it. I failed to notice that the address on the envelope was not our current address. Given everything I had been through to bring OUR child into this world, I considered it to be somewhat rude of him to get the shits with me because I didn't notice what was written on an envelope! We were moving house. Just after this ordeal, I could have cared less but it was a bigger house, which in the long term would be nice.

It seemed that I was to continue to be plagued with issues during and after this birth. I was suffering the most excruciating pain from the tip of my shoulder across my abdomen to my groin. I thought I was having a heart attack at one point. It turned out to be severe wind pain and was finally relieved by an old wives' tale—peppermint water.

The move had already begun when I came home from hospital with my gorgeous new daughter. I had called my mother whilst in hospital to advise her that I finally had a daughter that was the same as me, born with ginger brown hair and looked like her mum. My contribution was minimal, although it did not stop me trying until my dislocating knee decided to stop me in my tracks. It seemed I was extremely weak and was going to take time to get back to my usual self.

I was ready to move forward, new daughter, new home and hopefully better life. As Bianca grew out of things, I sold or gave them away. I was determined that I had finished and would just have to learn to live with my unfulfilled need to have 12 children.

It was not the only disappointment that I was to suffer with this pregnancy. My GP was pushing me to go on and study medicine; he offered me a permanent job within his family practice without question. I would visit Stan on many an occasion for medical problems and we would spend an inordinate amount of time discussing other patients (no names) and he would brainstorm with me and request what my diagnosis would have been and once satisfied that I agreed, he would again give me the hard sell on doing medicine before we would ever get to the reason, I had actually made the appointment for that day.

As I had finished high school after year 11, I would first need to complete a bridging course to give me the required eligibility to enter university to study. I had gone to an information evening at a Coorparoo High School where the courses were completed and was all set to embark on a mammoth journey to undertake my dream of doing medicine.

William, as always, had very different ideas. My responsibility was to him, my children and my home. This course of study would ultimately mean that I would not be there for him or the children and that was not fair to put that burden on him. He was such a control freak that he never once stopped to realise that once I was trained, he would live in the lap of luxury on a doctor's wage and so would all of our children. But I was his possession and I was his to do with as he saw fit. I could not see a way to fulfil my dream and keep the man I had foolishly chosen to marry happy. I had very quickly learned that if he was happy, life could go along fairly smoothly. But if crossed, life would become unbearable and William's demands were many and large. I did not actually realise the full extent of just how large for many years. But I had made the decision to marry him to get away from my mother and I had every intention of trying to make a real go of it. I did love him; I just didn't always like him too much. And there was never, ever going to be a time when I gave my mother the opportunity to say 'I told you so!'

I settled into my new life, in a new home and tried to make the best of it. What else could I do?

Families are messy.
Immortal families are eternally messy.
Sometimes the best we can do is to remind each other
that we're related for better or for worse
And try to keep the maiming and killing to a
minimum.

-RICK RIORDAN

CHAPTER 11

LIFE WAS ABOUT TO GET REAL

William continued to attempt to go back to sea but every time he was thwarted within the 10-day time period. I had gone back to work at Sunnybank Private Hospital doing night duty. It was a great job but, as always, I was never actually allowed to get the amount of sleep that my body required to function as I had responsibilities to William and the children! William was, naturally, exempt from the same rules. He never, ever did a night feed or tended to any of our children at night unless I was actually in hospital having another child. Since day one of our marriage, William's sleep and William's needs were sacrosanct and definitely came before that of any of the children and most assuredly before mine.

I had come home from work one Thursday morning after having completed my four nights for that week and ready to fall asleep immediately. William wanted to have fun, I did not. William wanted to have another baby, I did not. He went on and on and on and on, as he always did when he wanted what he wanted and it made absolutely no difference what my thoughts or feelings on the matter were as he would do what he wanted, one way or the other! If I did not comply with his wishes, he would take it out on the children and me later. It was just easier to give in and shut up.

And, of course, I fell pregnant again, bloody rabbit! It was the most diabolically difficult pregnancy that I have had. From the moment of conception, everything was so totally alien to that which I had ever experienced in any other pregnancy. I continued to work for as long as I could but it was nigh on impossible for me to do everything I needed to do at home, work and feel as awful as I did. My last day of work was to be 10 November 1986. William's last day of work was 11 November 1986. The difference between us was that William would never, ever work again. This left us to try to survive on government handouts and any work that I could do. But, as William made so very clear, he was a "sick man" and the care of him, the children and the house was my responsibility!

I battled on through this excruciating pregnancy as best I could. I had root canal, excision of a groin abscess, urinary tract infections, etc. Whatever could go wrong, went wrong. I spent the entire pregnancy feeling totally uncomfortable, mostly having to sleep in the lounge on a camp bed or the couch so that William's precious sleep was not interrupted. I was so determined to have a trial of labour with this pregnancy, never again to have another C-section. I had made the unilateral decision that I was returning to nursing full time and would take over the mantel of breadwinner for the family as William had no further interest in providing for his family, despite the fact that there were many areas in which he could have gained employment that did not involve air-conditioning or dust—the only things that he had to avoid.

I made no bones about the fact that I was taking over and things would return to some sort of normal. William was perfectly capable of looking after the children, even the baby when it was born. I was so determined to return to the workforce as soon as possible that I—who was the world's greatest advocate for breastfeeding—made the decision that this baby would be bottle-fed from the off. There were no arguments on that from William, naturally; he totally disagreed with me breastfeeding for extremely selfish reasons.

As the pregnancy progressed, my workload failed to decrease and I was becoming more and more exhausted and uncomfortable. My determination to have a normal delivery and get back to work was beginning to waver; the pain and discomfort were almost unbearable. The lack of sleep due to these things made my body scream for relief. The only way I could see that happening was to give in and get the baby delivered. My obstetrician had been in agreeance with me trialling labour but I was done and the C-section was booked for 38 weeks. It was all I could do to make it that far. We had another daughter, Rosemary. She was born on 2 June 1987. I was so exhausted but yet to fully realise that the fun was only just beginning. If I thought that being pregnant with Rosemary was incredulously difficult, I was most certainly about to learn that life with her was going to be a roller coaster ride direct from hell.

She refused to feed and spent the greater percentage of her time screaming. Nothing anybody did for Rosemary was good enough. I was a brilliant midwife but Rosemary got the better of me. She hated the capsule with a passion, she hated going out even more, she hated to sleep, to eat, to be cuddled…in fact, there was nothing I could find that would actually soothe this tiny baby until I discovered the white noise on television.

William's sleep was being too disturbed by the baby so we were relegated to the lounge. I sat on the couch and watched Pat Cash win Wimbledon and Wayne Gardiner win the 500cc Grand Prix. I had to constantly rock the bassinet or the screaming rained down and so did the wrath from William. The white noise was great but I still had to rock her and consequently, I was only able to catch snippets of sleep here and there. There was no reprieve from the rest of my daily duties of getting children up, lunches to make, take them to school, wash, iron, housework and on and on and on.

The opportunity to return to the workforce was becoming a distant memory as Rosemary ruled the entire household with her screaming. No doctor could find any sort of reason for it and I used every trick I knew but nothing worked. She was only a few weeks old when we took all of the children to Alma Park Zoo. Rosemary screamed the whole way there, the entire time we were there, all the way home and for three hours afterwards, seemingly as punishment for us all daring to have removed her from her comfort zone, not that she didn't constantly scream there too. Every time she was taken anywhere, to doctors or to the shops, she would scream for the entire journey and always for three hours afterwards. It just became part of life and took a full year before I started to be able to get any sort of decent sleep.

Whenever I brought up the subject of going back to work, William was determined that he was "too ill" to look after Rosemary, let alone the rest of them, so again it went on the backburner. I was, however, determined not to lose my years of registration that, despite William 's best efforts to thwart me, I had worked hard to achieve. I was on the 6th year and I had no intention of going back to first-year wages. I had three years from the day I had last worked to complete some documented work in order to retain my years of registration. It could have been as little as one hour but as long as it was documented, I would be fine. That too would be taken away from me.

There was nothing for me to do but obey "the master and chief" and do as was expected of the dutiful wife to the very best of my ability. We grew to accept that life would never again be our consensus of "normal" with Rosemary as part of the family. As she grew, she was no less troublesome but was developing into a very clever little girl. Her hyperactivity was draining on the entire family but mostly on me. I had to have eyes everywhere to keep up with her and her mood swings. Rosemary's reputation preceded her wherever we went, our GP wanted to have some blood studies done on her but stated adamantly that she could not have that blood taken at the surgery as there were just not enough people on staff to cope with Rosemary! I, alone, took her to a much larger collection agency once I had forewarned them of what the outcome of drawing blood would mean for them. It took six of us, including me, to hold Rosemary still enough for one nurse to be able to draw the required amount of blood. Rosemary, as always, screamed for every single second of that time and for a long, long time afterwards. Had a police officer heard the shrill, he would probably have called SWAT! The children's school decided to offer family portraits at a greatly reduced price and it was an opportunity for us to have one done. Rosemary had other ideas, as usual. The picture looked as if we all had a knife stuck in our backs and were being forced to partake against our wills. Every family picture attempted at home ended the same. It was a futile exercise...

I fell pregnant again in 1988 but still held on to the hope that I could resurrect my nursing career. For this entire pregnancy, I felt that something was not right. Of course, I did not for one second suspect that there was anything wrong with the baby, instead believing that it was me. I was 31 and would be 32 when I would have had this baby. William 's first wife had been 32 when she died and she had been pregnant when diagnosed with a terminal illness. I was beside myself with stress for the greater part of the pregnancy and, of course, as was my nature, said no one of my morbid fears. It was just another box for my compartmentalisation. Billy had told me when I was pregnant with Rosemary that if I had another girl, he was leaving home. Indeed, when he was brought up to visit me in the hospital after her birth, he had packed his preschool bag with what he considered he needed and informed me he was leaving. I considered it best to at least attempt to determine the sex of this baby before I announced the pregnancy to the other children. I went to a doctor on the Terrace in Brisbane who reputedly had the best ultrasound machine in Brisbane at the time. I explained my need to know the sex of the baby and try as he might, he could not get the baby to uncross his legs and move them just far enough to be able to determine his gender. I went home extremely deflated as I had so wanted to be able to finally tell Billy that he would have a baby brother at last.

I, again, for whatever crazy reason, was determined not to have another Caesarean section. It was a hopeless dream as I had already had two Caesareans but that did not stop my pregnant brain going to some weird places. I was just so determined to return to work that if I was able to deliver normally, I would have a very much shorter recovery time and would be able to try to talk William into letting me save my registration. As the pregnancy progressed, I became more and more stressed about what was wrong. My mother did not know about this pregnancy, the only one that I had not told her about. My aunt and godmother, Mum's sister, had died and in January 1989, my sister, Emma, had to have a hysterectomy. That was it, the empath that I was could never rub salt in that wound by telling Mum now. Once I accepted that I would have to have a Caesarean again, I begged my public/private obstetrician to deliver the baby on 18 April as then at least it would mean something to Mum—her wedding anniversary. He was unable to get a theatre slot for that day so I was booked for 20 April.

I awoke from the anaesthetic in recovery with a nebuliser mask on, I was very displeased and tried to take it off. I had, apparently, suffered an asthma attack whilst under the anaesthetic. There had also been a considerable amount of bleeding due to the fact that I had suffered from a Grade 4 placenta previa—the placenta was fully covering the birth canal and the baby could not be delivered normally through the vagina. But that was the easy bit; my beautiful baby son, Mitchell, was born with an imperforate anus and a hypospadias—he was born without an anus and with a deformity to his penis. I was devastated that whatever power was at play was making an innocent gorgeous little baby do the suffering instead of me. I would have swapped places with Mitchell in a nanosecond, no baby deserved to look down the barrel of a lifetime of issues and pain.

William finally had a little brother, seven years his junior.

Mitchell was barely 24 hours old when he required his first surgery to perform a colostomy. It was established that his imperforate anus was of the worst possible type. He had only an ascending colon and transverse colon, there was almost no descending colon and there was also no circular anorectal muscle structure and, of course, no anus. The hypospadias was also of the worst possible grade, it was a basal hypospadias, which meant that the urethral opening was at the junction of the scrotum and the base of the penis. Mitchell would require many corrective surgical procedures to bring him to some assemblance of a normal anatomy and function.

I was still in a state of bewildered devastation whilst my new baby son was transported to the Mater Children's for the colostomy surgery to be performed. My husband was so concerned for both my welfare and that of his brand-new son that he sent his two eldest children, Tracey and Clayton, to sit with me whilst awaiting news of how the surgery had progressed and when he would be returned to the Mater

Mothers. We had wonderful neighbours who had already cared for Rosemary on many occasions to give us a break so William using the excuse that he could not leave Rosemary or the other children with Tracey and Clayton and/or the neighbours fell rather short. What it really meant, as usual, was that I do not have to do anything that I do not want to do and no one can make me—William's go-to argument on all matters. So I sat in a state of despair on the balcony of the old Mater Mothers, having to endure Tracey and Clayton's endless arguing, mostly about Tracey's upcoming nuptials. It was the longest and most upsetting evening I had endured for a long, long time. I was often asked why my husband was no longer in the picture and how I would cope alone. My go-to phrase had become, 'I am a married/single woman!' Even at school, some of my children were asked what had happened to their father and how their mum coped so well on her own as they only ever saw Mum at school events or when they ran into us at the shops, etc.

Mitchell's first six months of life were very difficult for him as it transpired that he also had an extremely severe lactose/sucrose/fructose intolerance. He had three more major surgical procedures by the time he was six months old. The first was to create an anus and a muscular trigger system of muscles in place of the normal rectum. My mother had come down to be with me for this surgery but left as soon as she possibly could. I never could work out why she even bothered, other than to big note herself. Following this surgery was a lot of home nursing care, all of it by me as William would not go near it; that was one of very few times he ever acknowledged that I had any abilities as a nurse and used them to his advantage, as was his way. The second operation was to create a urethra for Mitchell. For this procedure, they had to use his foreskin. The procedure was normally performed in two different surgeries but due to the complexity of Mitchell's issues, the surgeon decided to attempt to perfect a new urethra in one surgery. Mitchell had a circular suture line around his penis and had a catheter in situ. Unfortunately, the catheter kept blocking up and it involved many return visits to the Mater Children's. William even managed to come with us on one of these occasions, in the evening, having left the neighbours in charge of the rest of the children. Funnily, I did not actually need him to accompany me on this occasion. As always, when I truly needed him, he refused to be there and when I did not need him, I could not get him out of my hair. The truth was that he only ever saw fit to go with me to have a go at someone or to try to prove that I had done something wrong to cause the current situation.

Mitchell's final restorative surgery was to close the colostomy, create an anastomosis of his bowel to finally connect what large colon Mitchell had to the newly created rectal trigger and anus. This was a particularly difficult surgery as Mitchell's ascending and transverse colon had continued to grow normally in the first six months of his life. However, what little descending colon there was, now attached to the rectum/anus, had not so it was a very difficult job to join differing sizes of bowel together. Of course, the most difficulty was to be for Mitchell as he tried to pass motions to a point that then would take, on occasions, up to 18 hours to pass through the very much smaller second stage of his bowel past the anastomosis. He would scream in agonising pain and the only relief he seemed to get was lying on the warm waterbed that I had at that time. Life was just a series of degrees of pain for my Mitchell, the bravest little soldier I had ever known. But for all of the agony, Mitchell nearly always had a smile on his face and could light up the room with his laugh.

Apart from trying to care for my beautiful new baby boy and all the extra care that entailed—washing and drying at least two dozen nappies twice a day—I was to make the flower girl dresses that Brianna and Isabelle would wear to Tracey's wedding, which was fast approaching. Fortunately for me, my wonderful neighbour, Dotty, who was a brilliant seamstress, was making new outfits for Billy, Jasmine, Bianca and Rosemary to wear. This lessened the load on me dramatically. William had decided that he wanted to wear a particular outfit, white suit jacket, black trousers, etc., so I hired everything that he wanted. There was, however, no money left for me to get an outfit. I was offered an old dress of Tracey's that I was to wear with a black jacket. 10 days before the big event, Tracey and I were in David Jones at Garden City, buying last-minute requirements when my foot went out from under me on their super slippery floors. I dislocated my knee again. I managed to get it back into place and Tracey got me home. It had never been this swollen before and I was in agony. I rested as long as I could but it seemed there was not going to be any guardian angel to pop in and help me so I had to soldier on.

The night before the wedding, I had to do what felt like hundreds of braids in Brianna and Isabelle's hair so that they would be all frizzy the next day. In the morning, Tracey and her bridesmaids were getting ready next door at Dotty's. Not once did anyone check if I needed any assistance. I was in agony and struggling to get, not only Brianna and Isabelle ready for the cars to the church, but also Billy, Jasmine, Bianca, Rosemary and Mitchell, who of course required a lot of attention. I had not been included in any hairdos or make-up and whilst everyone else was ready for the off, I was struggling to get myself dressed and made up with my extremely swollen, bandaged and agonisingly painful knee. There was a point when I thought it would be best if they all just went and left Mitchell and I at home but that would have just given Tracey even more to bitch about.

At no point during either the wedding or reception were we ever introduced to Carl's parents so it became extremely obvious to me that Tracey had been very busy telling tales about her wicked stepmother. It was all I could do just to be there so I was not about to create a scene by hobbling over and starting a conversation. We left the reception as early as possible due to my level of pain and Mitchell's need to be in his own environment.

We learned later that after we had left, they had brought out the wishing well to get money from their guests. They had also, at a slightly later date, had a chicken and champagne breakfast, to which we were not invited.

My priority was trying to remain well enough to care for my children, especially Mitchell. I was referred to an orthopaedic surgeon, Dr John Morris. He had the worst bedside manner and was an arrogant beggar but he was a brilliant orthopaedic surgeon. He told me that I had total muscle wastage on my left outer thigh and required surgery to try to improve my knee. I asked if he could guarantee that it would be cured, which, of course, he could not. It made very little difference; I had a husband who would not look after our children so that I could have surgery and recovery time so I had to decline the surgery. Over the ensuing months, as Mitchell had operation after operation, I just had to keep putting one foot in front of the other, sometimes very painfully. But my knee did start to strengthen a little with the help of a knee guard, which I had to wear all the time for support.

Time moved on and I was consumed with caring for my children. Mealtimes were often more fun than one could ever imagine. I would have to prepare special meals for Mitchell due to his bowel requirements, a special meal for Rosemary who was hyperactive and many foods made her worse and a different meal for the rest of us.

If, however, we were having Chinese food for dinner, then I would also have to prepare something different for Billy who bluntly refused to eat Chinese, which the rest of us loved. There was never a dull moment.

Mitchell's first Christmas and birthday were causes for great celebration, even more than normal, given all that he had been through. He was spoilt rotten naturally due to all the pain he had to deal with through his short life. Mitchell was such a jovial little soul, despite his difficult start to life.

The bond between mother and son was an extremely strong one that would never be broken despite the best efforts of many who would try in Mitchell's future.

A house divided cannot stand.

-MATTHEW 12:25

CHAPTER 12

LIFE AFTER A CAREER

Mitchell continued to flourish but would, forevermore, have a problematic life. The universe had compensated; Mitchell would have a special intellect that, in the future, he would choose to use wisely. I had accepted my fate to become the mother/housewife/slave to the family and absolutely relished the time I spent with my children and in my garden.

I did wonder if Mitchell would become too spoilt if he was to be the last child I had and I did still have my dream of having a family of 12 children. The discussions that William and I had had been before that fateful night in December of 1990 so we had been actively making an attempt to conceive another child. I had nothing outside of my family to look forward to in life and I was always fully responsible for the care of all the children so any and all burden was on me and me alone.

The day after that fateful December night had been one of great significance, I was just not going to realise that significance, and what it actually meant, for another quarter of a century! I had woken up as normal believing that the events of the previous evening were over and done with and that life would now be able to move forward minus the burden of Tracey's false claims.

What actually occurred was the complete opposite of that initial hope. William, once awake, had morphed into some sort of being that I no longer recognised. His entire demeanour and character were not that of the William that I had known up until this point. He found fault with every single thing that I said or did and was continually combative. It was not long before he had me in tears and that was going to be something that was to become what passed as normal life for me.

At first, I thought that his bizarre behaviour was as a consequence of learning what Tracey had accused him of and that he was truly having difficulties with the reality of it. But as days wore on and I realised that it was not only me but also the children that were bearing the brunt of his wrath, I began to do everything in my power to help William deal with what I believed to be stress and/or depression over the false accusation against him.

I wanted to take Tracey to court and clear my husband's name officially. I was convinced that this would help him. William would not allow me. He all but blamed me for putting our other children in peril if I did such a thing. My argument was that they were in more peril if I did not clear his name. I believed it to be my right as his wife to do so. It did not happen.

As previously mentioned, the night I was called to Toowoomba was a mere six weeks later. I was not to learn of that night until the late 90s. It was obvious then that the accusation really had not been the cause of his total metamorphosis, which then put doubt in my mind as to the validity of Tracey's claim but still not a single step closer to understanding who the person was that William had become or, more importantly, why.

I was pregnant and, again, between seven and eight weeks, I started to bleed. At first, I thought it was just from the stress caused by this new vindictive William that had suddenly turned up in my life. I was convinced though that I would again miscarry and the prospect devastated me, not that there was any true concern or support from my husband. This lack of empathy was not new where William was concerned but it was definitely very much more pronounced now.

Following an ultrasound, it transpired that I had, again, been pregnant with twins as there were two amniotic sacs in my uterus. One had miscarried, the other was very much still a viable foetus. I was both sad and ecstatic. The bleeding stopped as predicted and the 2nd sac would reabsorb into my system as time went on. I could breathe again…well, as far as the pregnancy was concerned.

My life, however, would never be the same again. It was during this pregnancy that William would show his true colours for the first time. Apart from verbal, psychological and sexual abuse, William descended into physical violence. We had been at the kitchen table and he had started an argument with me over nothing, as was now the norm, and when I did not respond in the exact way that he had demanded, he grabbed a handful of my hair and dragged me from the kitchen down the hallway to our bedroom and threw me onto the bed. I was shell-shocked, what had just happened? This was a whole new low for William. I had long known that his brother, Stanley, was a wife-beater but William used to abhor his actions and I had never seen this coming! What was I to do now? I had had six children with him at this point and I was pregnant with number seven.

His grandfather, also William, had walked out on his grandmother just after giving birth to their 7th child and run off with a musician and started a whole new family. I was never, ever going to allow my children to be part of a broken home as their grandfather had been. I also would never give my mother the satisfaction of saying, 'I told you this would happen'. Being treated as the proverbial mushroom by everyone in my life meant that I truly believed that it was only me that was being mistreated/abused as I protected my children in every way that I could; as I would do anything and put up with anything for the sake of my children, the decision had already been made.

William had gone again to the department of housing to request a larger house due the impending new arrival. They had said to let them know once the baby was actually born. I hated the fact that we lived in public housing and never told a single soul this fact unless they already knew or also lived in the same situation. My mother had brought me up to be a snob, well and truly, and as much as I tried to get rid of that part of me, it always stigmatised me to the point I would always look over my shoulder if I ever entered a second-hand store or op shop. I really have not changed that much. My circumstances have certainly changed and I have other ways of getting what I need, or perhaps they are just smarter ways.

The pregnancy progressed without a hitch. In fact, it was, apart from a lousy husband, one of the better pregnancies that I had. The OT was booked for an elective Caesarean section at 38 weeks. I had to go into hospital the afternoon before as was the norm in those days. It was gut-wrenching having to leave Mitchell with his father, whom I now trusted about as far as I could spit. I just could not stop loving this creep no matter what he did to me.

The following morning, 19 September 1991, I was taken to the OT and had a fantastic doctor put in an epidural, which actually worked. They were a fantastic crew in theatre that day, more so because I was alone as always, so they were trying to compensate for my absent husband, whose needs always came before mine.

My gorgeous son, Zach, was born and I was amazed to see a crop of red hair; I already had two daughters with red hair but to have a son was new to me. After the surgery was complete, I was taken to see my new baby boy. He was absolutely gorgeous and was frowning. I had finally managed to produce a son that was the spitting image of his father, frown included. All he needed was a mini pair of glasses and the only difference then would be the fair skin and red hair as opposed to his father's olive skin and black hair.

It turned out that the anaesthetist had injected morphine into the epidural for pain relief. It worked a real treat as far as pain relief went but I started scratching myself to death, developed a severe rash and was very agitated and uncomfortable. My girlfriend, Pattie, was the midwife in charge and she very quickly organised a Phenergan injection to help calm the effects. She asked if I had been given morphine before and I told her about Bianca's birth. She then told me that I was allergic to morphine and to never allow it to be administered to me again. It would take more Phenergan injections to help relieve the symptomology and I would never again forget the effect it had produced in my body.

Zach was a beautiful little fellow. The first night after his birth, he had been brought to me for breastfeeding, which he did extremely well. I had finished feeding him and he was asleep in my arms and I was just savouring our alone time. It was in the early hours of the morning and watching him sleep so peacefully in my arms that was a truly beautiful time. Due to the time of day and the added effect of the Phenergan, I must have dozed off whilst holding him. I was jarred awake with a huge fright to the sound of the largest fart I have ever heard a brand-new baby muster. Zach was so lucky that my instincts prevented me from flinging him across the room with fright. I very promptly got him back safely into his bed.

No one would believe me about Zach's gaseous abilities until my girlfriend, Kitty, just happened to be coming through the door on a visit as Zach let one rip. She was completely astonished that this tiny little bundle had produced so much gas. God help the ozone layer with Zach on the planet.

We went home rather more quickly than usual as I felt so much better than I ever had after a Caesarean due to the competence of the anaesthetist, the only slip having been my allergy to morphine. Mitchell was very pleased to see his mum but I was even more excited to see him. He didn't seem to really mind there being another baby but he was having none of me breastfeeding Zach. I was his mum and this was a step too far. I continued to try for as long as I could but Mitchell was just so upset that I had to let it go again, much to the delight of my husband.

I was barely back into the swing of things when we were notified that the housing department had a house for us in Sunnybank Hills. It was our house, it had five bedrooms and unlike with other transfers, we were not being given the choice of three properties. It was this one or we stayed where we were. William went into the city to get the keys and we went to view the property. Compared to the houses we had lived in since our marriage, this was a mansion. It was a low-set brick home with a double lock-up garage, storeroom with toilet and basin and a laundry. There were indeed five bedrooms and a bathroom with separate toilet inside. The kitchen was not huge but had heaps of built-in cupboards and a range hood. It even had space for a dishwasher. The lounge/dining were open concept and, although somewhat narrow, certainly workable. It was a long narrow house and was very deceiving from the front as to its actual size. The houses on either side were double-storey so this house was rather dwarfed by them. On the bedroom/bathroom side of the house, the neighbour had full access right up to the house. He even had pot plants against the house. Either end was fenced off, an agreement made between the neighbour and the previous owner of the property. I was unsure about this arrangement but apart from that, I was sold.

So the documents were signed and exactly one month after having had my 4th Caesarean section, I started to move that which I had been packing for months in preparation for this move. From Tuesday, I was doing a 05:00 run—empty the wagon at the new property, back to get the children up, fed, dressed and taken to school, wait for William to pack the next load into the wagon and my girlfriend's sedan, do the next run, get it all into the house, back home and eat and see my new baby for a short while, do the next run, back in time to collect the children from school, do homework whilst William packed the wagon, do the next run, then home to do baths, dinner, school lunches whilst William packed the wagon for the 05:00 run the next morning. I did this for the rest of the week. Saturday was when my brother helped William get the big things to the new house with his trailer. William and I had taken the fridge in the back of the wagon on Friday and that had ultimately killed the car, although she did still keep moving for another couple of months almost. On Sunday, I was at the house lifting the carpet and trying to get all the wood edging up. My body was done and I had to go back to Sunnybank Hills and admit defeat. Jonathon and William went back to finish off and I knew full well that it was not left in the manner that I would have considered acceptable but I had, as always, been used and abused to the point of complete exhaustion and had, as always, had to learn to live with second best. It was, of course, I who had to return the keys for the old property to Belmont on Monday. It was I who was responsible for getting the new house into some assemblance of order, not forgetting just how "sick" William was. I worked as furiously as I could to get the main living areas acceptable.

It was on Tuesday that Mum and Emma came to visit. The visit was for the purpose of meeting Zach and had been arranged before we even knew we were to move but now had a dual purpose. I had told Mum not to hold any expectations of tidiness as I had so little time and energy and we had only officially finished moving items in on Sunday evening. She was flabbergasted as she walked in, claiming it was immaculate and that no one could possibly have known that we had only just moved in unless they were told. These extremely rare praises from my mother did give me pride but they were always very short-lived and would be shortly followed by a nasty barb, or 10.

The next challenge was to get all the primary school children into their new school. Brianna was to stay at her current high school as she was in her first year there. It was to be a trial of how well she did—having to leave on a 07:00 bus and not getting back home until 16:45 at the earliest. This lasted until the June holidays of 1992, when she became exhausted from the travel and her grades began to suffer, or at least that was what I had thought was the reason for the decline. We moved her to Sunnybank High School but there were a couple of subjects that she had excelled in that were unavailable to her at this school so it would be a "wait and see" as to how well she would do here.

Living in Sunnybank Hills was somewhat of a trial for us, or at least for me. There was absolutely no privacy with this property, I felt like we were living in a goldfish bowl. This was helped very little by the fact that the department of housing had bought this house as emergency housing for those in need and the first residents had run amok, actually had set fire to the kitchen, the children had climbed all over the roof and played with hoses and ended up doing a midnight flit without informing housing. The die had been cast and we were labelled from the off as exactly the same ilk as the previous tenants. This made me feel truly sick to my stomach, knowing that I had been brought up middle-class and to be a snob and the fact that the only reason that I could not afford my own home was the fact that my husband was a controlling narcissist who had lost me my career. But none of that was anyone else's business and whilst it got airtime in my mind, it certainly never made it out of its box fully. Also, the fact that the housing department had removed an outdoor room, which had been at the back of the property and had afforded so much privacy, left us completely exposed to not only the neighbours but also to the elements.

The master bedroom was on this side of the property, unlike the other four, and was fully exposed to the neighbours. On Ekka Day, 1992, we had a rather large awning installed on this bedroom window and at last, I felt a modicum of privacy but there was still nowhere to sit at the back of the house without the sun melting you in the effort. We had a 5m x 2.5m cover installed so that we had, at least, a small space to take refuge from the elements and where we could have a BBQ when desired. We worked hard to create a garden, my great love and life began to make some sense but I always believed that moving to this house had been the biggest mistake that we, or I, had ever made. Within the first 12 months, the neighbour on the bedroom side had made his feelings about us perfectly clear and there was a fence erected as a proper boundary between the two properties. It would be more than a decade before we spoke to each other again. William and I had sought assistance and had organised a mediation meeting between us but that neighbour had refused to attend. Isabelle was extremely pleased, for one, that there was now a clear boundary as she had often accused the neighbour of looking in whilst she was getting dressed. I was so livid, but what I realised at that time was that I needed to have an eagle eye much, much closer to home.

Whilst life in Sunnybank Hills was far from expectations, Zach continued to thrive and was the dream baby and little boy. He could always bring a smile to my face and calm me when I was down. Indeed, that would turn out to be the trait that would continue into adulthood with him. Once he put his arms around me, all was right with the world, even if only for the length of that embrace but it gave me the strength I needed to move forwards, and always will.

Children without families are the most vulnerable people in the world.

-Brooke Randolph

CHAPTER 13

JACK

Jack's arrival into this world had been nothing short of amazing. His dad, William, had had a vasectomy performed in England after Clayton had been born as the cost of living was such that they could not afford more than two children, which they now had. After moving to New Zealand, William and Angela had fostered two children, increasing the children to four. That had sadly ended when they had moved to Australia and that was where William had his vasectomy reversed, at the Princess Alexandra Hospital in Brisbane.

I now know and fully understand the full cost to Angela of William having gone through that reversal procedure and allowing her to become pregnant; it had been a cost not to be taken lightly. This I know from bitter personal experience since, meaning that neither Angela nor I took the decision to have children lightly because of the consequences to us. I knew just how much Jack meant to Angela because I knew her at the time, also because I knew the costs to myself, but I also know just how much each and every one of my children mean to me. It was a cost that I personally know I would repeat over and over just to fall in love all over again with my beautiful children, and Angela had felt exactly the same about Jack.

Much of Jack's pregnancy and birth I have previously covered but it is from with my own pregnancy with my eldest son, Billy, that I need to start this story. All Jack had ever needed, like all children, had been love and understanding. Jack was unique; he had been in the uterus whilst his mum had acute myeloid leukaemia and no one knew what the result of that occurrence could or would mean in the long term. So, every milestone missed was a major issue and became cause for great concern where Jack was concerned, in some cases unnecessarily, but no one knew what to expect, the medical profession included. I had always had a soft spot for Jack since I had first listened to his heartbeat whilst still in utero. I had become his full-time carer/stepmum when he had been just under 14 months old. I fell in love with him all over again. He also got a new big sister who absolutely adored and doted on him. I cannot, in all honesty, say that Tracey and Clayton ever felt the same way about Brianna. What sort of a threat could a two-year-old really pose? Jack witnessed all of their animosity towards both Brianna and myself.

Jack could see no good reason to talk, walk or eat particularly much. He was his little personality entirely and had no intention of fulfilling expectations placed on him by other people, be they family or the medical profession. It was whilst I was attending an antenatal appointment with Brianna and Jack that a dear friend and previous colleague happened to be in the clinic. She stopped for a chat. After observing Jack for a short while, she had asked what was wrong with him, what had been going on with him, etc. I explained my concerns and she immediately stated that she would get an appointment for him to see a paediatrician at the Mater as soon as possible.

We visited Dr Thearle and he did have some major concerns that Jack was so far behind meeting milestones and, with his history, made the decision to run a battery of tests to attempt to get to the bottom of it. By far the greatest concern for everyone was that Jack was not even attempting to walk. One of those tests involved us travelling to the Royal Brisbane Hospital for endoscopy examinations. I had Tracey, Clayton and Brianna in tow as well due to the school holidays and I was heavily pregnant with William junior. William was at sea at the time so the entire weight of this full day fell on me.

Tracey and Clayton would not stop complaining about being bored and driving me insane. Jack, naturally, was whingy as he had to fast and did not understand what was happening to him, the poor little guy. He was given an oral pre-med and became rather sleepy. When the time came for the procedure, I had to leave Tracey and Clayton to look after Brianna whilst I carried Jack and got onto the patient transfer bus to go to the building in which the procedures were to be performed. I waited whilst it was performed then had to again carry Jack onto the bus and back to the ward. He was extremely disoriented and it was rather distressing to watch. Once the staff cleared him for release, we trudged to the car and headed home. That was when the real fun began. In order that Jack not hurt himself, I had set up the playpen in the lounge with tons of cushions, toys and rugs as he was falling all over the place as he continued to recover from the effects of the anaesthetic. I was so exhausted from the day and the fact that Tracey refused to assist and my ankles had swollen to be the size of footballs, the best I could do was sit on the couch in front of the playpen and console Jack as best I could. By the time he finally went to sleep for the night and I had sorted Brianna, I fell into bed and crashed.

All the test results revealed no real medical reason for the fact that Jack was so far behind what would be classed as within normal limits by those who mandated such limitations. Of course, their other avenue of investigation was family history. This was very difficult for me to ascertain but I continued to ask my new mother-in-law, Daisy, for any information that she could provide to assist her grandson. She consistently repeated that there was nothing noteworthy with either of the boys she had given birth to or within the greater family. They were of the generation where you did not speak of imperfections ever. Angela's parents were adamant that there was no family history to suggest that Jack's perceived issues came from their side of the family.

The only thing we knew for sure was that William had an aunt who had fallen into a fire at 18 months of age. The family claimed that she had gone mad after that and had spent her short life in a mental institution in England until her seemingly early death. The decision was made that Jack would go into the Mater Children's Hospital for the purpose of being observed and to give me a break for the three weeks I had left before Billy was due to be born.

We visited Jack as much as we could but I was reminded that this time was meant to be for me to rest as Jack was very high maintenance. He could not understand why he had to stay there and it broke my heart every time I had to leave him. Nevertheless, I spent as much time with him as I possibly could.

As previously stated, Billy decided to arrive almost a week early and caused quite a degree of trauma to me. He was born Tuesday at lunchtime but I was not released from hospital until Saturday. He was going to prove to be a difficult baby and his father would prove to be even more difficult. More on that soon.

Once Billy and I were settled back in, Jack began making home visits on a Saturday. It was wonderful to have him back home but he was less than impressed with his new baby brother. On his first visit home, I had sat Billy on top of the bouncinette so that I could spend time with Jack but easily be able to pick up the baby. What I had not expected was that Jack would stand in front of the bouncinette, raise his foot and bring it down as hard as he could on the front bar of the bouncinette, causing Billy to fly up in the air. Thankfully, I was able to catch him without any harm having been caused. This was only one incident. On another occasion, Jack tried to strangle Billy. I understood why he felt animosity towards this baby who got to stay in his house and he had to go back to the hospital.

Jack was diagnosed as psychotic at age two. This really was a sign of the times as any true medical professional knows it is impossible to label a child in this way when he can barely walk or talk and was quite withdrawn. That was the label they gave him and between that and Tracey's lies to children's services' worker Jane Wilson, Jack's three weeks in hospital were blowing out into months.

Having needed to return to work when Billy was three months old, my time became even more limited for hospital visits to see Jack. We were, however, at the Mater Children's every weekend, whether Jack had made a home visit or not. The staff was fully aware of the family dynamics and needs and the fact that I was a registered nurse and working. This did not stop the totally unrealistic expectations that we would be at the hospital every day to see Jack. They were also unaware of the unrealistic expectations placed on me by my husband during this time in my life. We were unaware of the fact that Tracey was busy telling tales to all who would listen. I was, after all, only the "stepmother" (a label I abhor, especially where Jack is concerned) and I had a beautiful baby boy who was not receiving the attention that he deserved due to the expectations placed on my time. There was no sound reason as to why William could not have taken himself, Tracey and Clayton to visit Jack every evening if he had so chosen to do so. William always had better things to do with his evening. More on that in the next chapter.

I was becoming more and more exhausted as time went on, I could not work out why. I had to keep going to work, caring for the family and going to see Jack. It was becoming increasingly obvious that Jack was not coming home from hospital but I could not, at the time, work out why. I had worked my final night duty shift for the week when I got a message that the Mater Children's required me to attend a meeting that very Friday morning. They knew that William was at work so why did they want to see just me? I did not normally have the babysitter come to care for the children on a Friday but had to call in to ask if she would mind. I got her home and ensured all was well, then set off for the Mater. I was absolutely shattered, in incredible pain but had to endure several hours being berated as to why we were not at the hospital to be with Jack on a daily basis. I reminded them of the situation. I was sitting there in my PAH work uniform. I was bewildered and then I was informed that the decision had been made to place Jack into temporary foster care. Why would they want to do that? Why could he not just come home to his family? This just didn't make any sense to me at all, there was no logic to their arguments but every time I tried to make a sound argument, they shot me down with what seemed like utter rubbish of equal standing to a diagnosis of psychosis for a two-year-old. Something else was at play here but I could not figure it out. A room full of supposed professionals against one "stepmother", seemingly orchestrated to ensure William was not there and all the blame was being laid squarely at my feet. I refused to give them the satisfaction of witnessing me cry.

After the barrage, I went straight down to Jack, held him tight and cried my heart out. I spent a long time with him then, trying to work out my next move. I eventually left and called in to see my sister-in-law to let her know what was going on. I then went home and took the babysitter home and did only what I had to do for the rest of the afternoon—wait for the time I had to drive to Fisherman's Island to collect William from work. As we drove, I relayed all of the day's events and all the intricacies of the meeting/crucifixion of me at the Mater. We were driving straight to the Mater and upon arrival at Jack's ward, William announced that we were there to take our son home. Of course, they delayed and delayed (as was the normal procedure) in order to get the doctors and security to the ward.

Once there, the doctor stated that if we attempted to take Jack out of the hospital with us, they would send the police to our home and they would forcibly remove not just Jack, but all of our children. One would have thought that they would need to have some grounds for this type of action but we were living under the **Joe Bjelke Peterson** government and the exact same fate had been enacted on another Brisbane family only weeks earlier. That was the toughest night of my life. I could only imagine what it had been like for William. We had to leave without Jack.

I was devastated by this development and as a nurse, had the feeling that something was not quite right with this whole situation. Children did not get taken from their families without just cause, whether it was found to be the truth or not. There was more to this story and at that time, I felt that we were being kept in the dark as to the real reasons for this action. No one was actually stating any of those reasons, but I sure as heck had a very good idea about them. The categorisations, generalisations and accusations were most definitely pointed squarely in my direction, which only served to fuel the fire already burning in my mind. As previously stated, I became so stressed over Jack being taken into care and having to live our lives in a goldfish bowl, constantly being monitored and judged by other people's perceptions of the situation, that I was forced, due to illness, to give up my job.

Jack moved to a foster family who lived on the far north side of Brisbane. We had been told that we could visit him, preferably weekly, but the foster family were obligated to bring Jack to us only four times a year. Once he was settled into his new home, Brianna, Billy and I would make the minimum one-hour journey, each way, to visit Jack every Wednesday. Jack seemed to be happy enough and he was always so happy to see us all. He loved Brianna and Billy as he became more interactive.

I made this trek every Wednesday without fail. There were occasions when William was home and he did not want to go every time. I never once neglected my duties to Jack, even though I had become pregnant again and, as the pregnancy progressed, it became an even greater effort as we now had to travel to Caboolture. On one of my visits, the foster mother mentioned that Jack had said, 'My dad hit my mum and she went flying across the kitchen floor.' They wondered how this was possible as he had been only a few months old when Angela had died. Then they wondered if it had been me. I said that it had not but I knew the incident to which he was referring. I had been told, by William, that the live-in babysitter/housekeeper had been feeding Jack in his high chair in the kitchen whilst William was in the lounge. Jack had let out an earth-shattering scream and William had leapt up and run to the kitchen. He had not asked what was wrong or even checked Jack, his reaction had been to push Sandy, a very large lady, chair and all across the kitchen and into the back door.

It was after this that Jane Wilson decided it would be a good idea to create a scrapbook of Jack's life for Jack to learn and understand where he came from. I, of course, went to great lengths to create this memory book for Jack. I took great pride in doing it for him. It had every single piece of information in it that Jack would ever need to know about his family, pictures included. It would always be an ongoing project as he grew older, adding new photos, etc.

I could not understand why Jack continued to remain in care when he had a perfectly good home with his family. I also could not understand William 's reluctance to fight for his son. It just didn't make any sense to me. Of course, no one could seemingly provide the answers that I was seeking or, more likely, were not prepared to say.

It had always been William 's intent to adopt Brianna and I would adopt Jack. The choice as to whether Tracey and Clayton were to be included was to be entirely their decision as far as I was concerned. Nothing would have made me happier than to cement our new family but I made it very, very clear to Tracey and Clayton that Angela was and always would be their mother, as well as Jack's, but it would be an honour for me to create this new family moving forward. The law stated that we had to live together for two years before any application for adoption could be made.

On one of the many home visits that Jane Wilson made to our home, we asked her about starting the adoption application process as it had been over two years since we had married. She told us, in no uncertain terms and not altogether politely, that there was no point in even trying as it would never be approved whilst Jack was in care. We were extremely saddened but believed that she knew what the law was and was not just being vindictive.

The time came when William was required to attend family court to sign temporary guardianship of Jack over to his foster parents. I was not required to attend by William so I can only assume that what I was being told was actually the truth. Things were looking even more suspicious in my eyes but I kept my concerns boxed away for the time being.

We had occasion to visit children's services at Stones Corner and were being seen by a different person, a true breath of fresh air. We again broached the subject of adoption. It was then that we found out that Jane Wilson had been vindictive and had lied to us. This lady could not understand why she would ever have made such a statement, especially as she knew it to be untrue. I was absolutely certain now that I knew exactly what was going on but it would still be a long time before I could prove it.

Jack moved to Ipswich for a short time but then the foster family moved further up the Queensland coast, way too far for us to travel with our increasing family. Luckily, we had been able to coordinate one of Jack's visits to coincide with a company coming to our home to have a family portrait taken. That was when Bianca had been a baby. That would be the only glimpse of a true family that we were to get. We asked how often they would bring him down to see us. They stated that they were not obligated to make any such trips and could not see that they would be. We…well, I was absolutely devastated by this. We wrote often and exchanged photos but William had been forced to give up going to sea by this stage and life had become a real financial struggle.

As Jack grew a bit older, the letters were not as frequent but occasionally, we would get some with updated photos. But instead of us being reunited as the family that we should have always been, we would very rarely see Jack again. It was always me who wrote the letters, never William. Tracey and Clayton were both extremely lacking in this department as well. Brianna and Billy and the other younger children would send letters and pictures to Jack, their big brother, but things now seemed to be set in concrete, as with many other areas of my life, and I had absolutely no control over them any more than I ever had.

When truth is buried it grows
It chokes, it gathers such an explosive force
That on the day it bursts out
It blows up everything with it.

-MIA ZOLA

CHAPTER 14

JACK: THE SACRIFICIAL LAMB

I grieved the loss of Jack as surely as if I had given birth to him and there always felt like a permanent hole in my heart where he should be. Not knowing how he was or being able to support and care for him when needed was incredulously difficult. Life went on, of course, as it does, but there was always a part of our family that was missing so nothing was ever quite right again.

My suspicions regarding the reasons for this turmoil in our family were that Tracey had been telling her lies to Jane Wilson. The thought of Tracey having caused Jack to be taken from his family was bizarre but knowing just exactly how desperately she wanted to be rid of me, it was a very strong possibility. As time wore on and more and more evidence showed of Tracey's lies, the more I was convinced of the validity of my thought processes.

I have already spoken of the letter full of lies written by Tracey to her grandparents in England. After our move to Sunnybank Hills, we no longer had contact with Tracey. Well, I will clarify that now. I no longer had any contact with Tracey and I prevented <u>my</u> children from having any contact. She was also not allowed to come to our home, at least whilst I was at home. As to what William did, I will never ever know the truth. I do know that Clayton was in constant contact with her, however; always the dutiful little puppy doing all it could to please his master, with the tail constantly wagging.

The 1990s were turning out to be rather illuminating from my point of view and, most certainly, not for the betterment of myself or our family unit. I was out shopping on one occasion, not my usual haunt, but there had been something in particular that I could only get from Sunny Park Shops. I had decided that I would just use the chemist that was there rather than having to stop on my way home in order to attend our regular pharmacy. I will always be extremely sorry that I had made that decision that day.

I stood at the counter, handed over the prescription that I required and was about to say that I would return for the script after I had been into the shop, when the assistant said, 'Mrs Breen, you would not be related to Tracey, would you?'

I said, 'Yes, she is my stepdaughter.'

What followed was first her deepest sympathy for me, then a barrage of stories about what a truly evil person Tracey was. She went on to elaborate with stories of how she had lied so profoundly to every friend that she had made, and all of them would leave her in the end. And she walked away after deeply hurting them and acting as if it had all been their fault. All I was hoping was that the ground would open up and swallow me right there and then. That encounter had such an impact on me that whenever I think of it, I get a shiver down my spine.

The laws regarding Freedom of Information had changed and I had an opportunity to put a few ghosts to rest. I personally had absolutely no intention of contacting Tracey for her permission to get information from the department of children's services regarding the conversations between them and Tracey. I, of course, had to do all the legwork; i.e., phone calls and requests for information. The result of this request was that we received documents in June of 1993.

Although these documents were extremely heavily redacted, there was ample information for me to know who the Judas was in our family...well, one of them at least.

Tracey Breen is a pleasant, slightly overweight, 16-year-old girl. She has spent too much of her life from too young an age looking after babies and younger children and she is very aware of this. Following their marriage, there was a period when William and Ellie both worked and kept Tracey home from school to care for Jack—J.A.B. were notified and visited the family at this time. In May 1984, this department received a complaint from the head teacher of Brianna's school who stated that Tracey had left school and was at home caring for the younger children—William and Isabelle. As a result of this complaint, a home visit was made. Tracey was at home alone with William and Isabelle and stated that Ellie was working as a Blue Nurse, William was at sea. Over a period of approximately two hours, Tracey very eloquently described her situation.

Tracey was born in 1968 in England. In 1970, she became a big sister to Clayton. In 1974, the family immigrated to New Zealand where they had lived for four years. I had never once heard Angela or William state that Tracey had spent 'too much of her life from too young an age looking after babies and younger children.' There had been no babies. Tracey had only been a toddler when Clayton was born and he was so large that his nickname had been Cassius Clay in the maternity ward. I very much doubt Tracey did terribly much in the way of babysitting Clayton as Angela was a stay-at-home mum. The foster children that Angela and William had in New Zealand were of similar ages to Tracey and Clayton so no babysitting there either.

In 1978, the family had then moved to Australia. It had again been just Tracey and Clayton with Angela as a stay-at-home mum. It was within the next year that William had had his vasectomy reversal and Angela had become pregnant. William had also sponsored Angela's parents so that they could come to live in Australia and for a time, they had lived with William and Angela. This had caused a large amount of stress as they loathed William and the feeling had been quite mutual from William's point of view. Still no babies to care for.

By the time Jack had been born in 1979, Tracey was 11 and Clayton was 8. Having been born a diabetic baby, Jack had to stay in the neonatal intensive care unit in a Humidicrib followed by a stay in a normal cot until he was ready to go home. Angela was in the Mater Adults and as previously stated, we midwives would take Jack to visit his mum as often as we could. When Jack was taken home by the family, there was first his father who was more than capable of caring for a baby. There were his grandparents on Angela's side and there was also the team of midwives that called in to bathe and feed Jack, cook, clean and whatever else would make the life of this family easier. If Tracey had been called upon to spend too much of her life from too young an age looking after babies and younger children, I most certainly have never been made aware of it. That would be outside my remit as we were not married then and Angela would most certainly have had something to say if William was using Tracey to get out of what he, himself, should have undertaken. Angela also had day visits to her home and I am certain she would have been told by Tracey if things were not right. After Angela's death, William again had a lot of outside assistance. One of the midwives, Sue, had often taken Jack to give William a break. William had taken the opportunity, when offered, to place Tracey and Clayton in temporary foster care to give him time to grieve for his wife.

As is generally the case with lies, the story changes and when held up to tight scrutiny, the holes very quickly begin to appear. As the African proverb states:

A lie has many variations, the Truth none.

According to the National Archives in Canberra, William first went back to sea after Angela's death in July 1980. In order for him to be able to do this, he had a friend of Angela's from New Zealand, Sally, move into the family home in the capacity of babysitter/housekeeper. At the time that William and I were married, 10 December 1980, we were both at home to care for all of our children. I had returned to the workforce at the Mater Mothers in South Brisbane and worked over the Christmas period. I had prepared Christmas Day lunch, with a whole lot of 'my mum did not do this, my mum did not do that, my mum used this, my mum used that, etc.', eaten as a family, then I had gone off to work a late shift. William had been home as well as Sally to care for the children. William had gone out to sea on the W. M. Leonard between 13 January to 18 January 1981. It was during this period of time, one week, I had started to bleed in my pregnancy, had been prescribed a muscle relaxant and had to immediately cease work. Sally had been a godsend to me in that week. The medication had knocked me out and she had been invaluable in taking up the slack for me. I have always been a perfectionist to the point of OCD and have always found that it is far better to complete the work myself rather than delegating as, most times, even I cannot meet my own exacting standards so there is no point in getting someone else to muck up a job that I will only need to redo anyway. This was the result of having been traumatised and abused by my adoptive mother and having been made the slave of the family and on whose shoulders the entire weight of the household sat. This was why I failed to see a time when the laziest, most unhygienic young lady it had ever been my misfortune to come across could make such completely and blatantly false claims. I still cannot see where Tracey could make the claim:

Following their marriage, there was a period when William and Ellie had both worked and kept Tracey home from school to care for Jack.

Of note here was that there was no mention of Brianna, who did not turn three until 15 January. Who had been caring for her? Had Sally perhaps been looking after Brianna but Tracey specifically placed in charge of Jack? Of course, this had not occurred except in the mind of the psuedologue.

Tracey had commenced high school at Holland Park State High on Bapaume Road in Holland Park when the school year began in 1981. It had been a difficult adjustment for Tracey from primary school to high school. She had not been the brightest student and I had tried as best I could to understand the curriculum that had been so different to that which I had studied so few years earlier. Tracey had also struggled to accept my help. I had studied Maths A and Maths B at senior level and had tried to make things easy for her to understand but she was not going to accept my help and I just had to understand that this child was still desperately grieving the loss of her mother. I had tried to focus my efforts on this area as she had not received any help from her father. Many times, I suggested that she and Clayton may need professional guidance in the grieving process but William would not have any of it.

Tracey's school work suffered as the year progressed but I felt that my hands were tied behind my back in terms of offering any valuable assistance to her. As time went on that year, there were an ever-increasing number of stories of sexual harassment by Tracey against male students at her school. I had tried desperately to establish exactly what these boys were doing to her and as she forbade me to contact the school, I had my brother try to speak to some of the boys and/or their parents to try and ensure that they were aware of how their actions were making Tracey feel and that it was unacceptable. I had to call upon my brother as these allegations were only ever made whilst William was at sea. Jonathon would always return scratching his head and stating that he did not understand what was going on. The lads would always be totally shocked at any such allegation, claiming that they knew nothing about it and hardly spoke to Tracey, and as Jonathon put it, they were half her size and she could have blown them over. Nevertheless, these allegations continued throughout the year until it got to the point where Tracey claimed to be so traumatised by them that she finished the school year early, with William's permission, and refused to go back to school ever.

William finished serving on the Queensland Cement Co, a dredge in the Brisbane River, on 31 December 1981. He was then home full time until May of that year. I tried to establish whether Tracey would be returning to Holland Park High School, which she bluntly refused to do. I spoke with William constantly about the fact that maybe we should be getting her into a new school where she could feel more comfortable. He said that he would deal with it. I had been very heavily pregnant with Billy, William had been trying to rent us a place to live in Laidley and had succeeded and had, in fact, started to move some of our belongings out there until I found out how frequently brown snakes were seen there and I bluntly refused to move.

During this period of time, there had also been another quite large issue that developed. When William had finished on the Cement Co, he had decided that he no longer wanted to drink coffee. That would probably have been acceptable for an occasional coffee drinker but William constantly had a cup of coffee on the go, which consisted of two heaped teaspoons of coffee, two teaspoons of sugar and a dash of milk. He replaced his favoured beverage with tea, which only had half the caffeine of coffee. At first this was not an issue but slowly as the migraines set in, he became extremely difficult to live with, his temper flared regularly and every time I mentioned Tracey and school, I wished that I had not.

The symptoms increased—tremors, chest pains, insomnia, to name just a few. The problem was that by the time all of these symptoms had arrived, it was too far removed from the cessation of the coffee to make any sort of correlation between the two things. William appeared to be okay as long as he did not go to sleep so the result of this was that he would be watching television half the night, finally fall into bed and wake up very late, with an incredulously painful migraine. He even managed to punch a hole in the bedroom wall between his pain and his rage at the pain.

Our GP was running all manner of tests with all the results coming back as perfectly normal. Everyone was left scratching their heads. Even the day Billy was born, he had driven me to the hospital in the small hours of the morning and gone home to bed around

04:00. He had almost missed his birth due to the symptomology he was suffering from.

Due to his incessant television watching, William eventually discovered the reason for all of his symptoms himself whilst watching the Don Lane Show. One of their guests had suffered caffeine withdrawal as a result of having given up coffee, just like William. So, the following morning, I made him a very strong cup of tea, followed rather quickly by more. After some experimentation, we arrived at the correct amount of caffeine to keep his symptoms at bay. Our GP was amazed but agreed that caffeine withdrawal was equally as potent as heroin withdrawal. The difference was that it was harder to diagnose and tended to last a bit longer. For all of William's future, he would be plagued with incessant migraines whenever he did not get enough caffeine into his system.

All of the time that William had been going through the withdrawal, Tracey was still not at school. I had dared not mention it for fear of the repercussions. I could not fathom why Tracey did not want to be at school; she must have craved peer contact. There was absolutely nothing for her to do at home and she rarely, if ever, actually offered to do anything. William's response was that he would sort it out.

William returned to sea on 08 May 1982 on the ship, BP Enterprise. It was a short-term engagement, until 11 May 1982. It was during this period of time that J.A.B. officers came to the house to find out why Tracey was not at school. Sandy had been with me when they came. I explained the whole situation truthfully but of course, by law, she had to be in school and it now fell to me to organise it. I explained to Tracey and set up an appointment with Yeronga State High School's Headmistress and Tracey was enrolled and started year 9. She was very much less than impressed at having been forced to return to school, any school, but now had no choice in the matter. When William had returned home, he had just been pleased that it was no longer his problem to deal with.

As the school year progressed, the same old allegations of sexual harassment were made by Tracey of students from her new school. This time, there were also allegations of bullying made against other female students. On one occasion, Tracey had arrived home on the bus, crying and distraught after one particular female student had bullied her relentlessly all the way home on the bus. I got the full story from Tracey, calmed her down, then proceeded to head straight to the home of the accused. Sandy was still living with us so I had no problem leaving the children in her care. I knocked on the front door and the student herself answered. I went straight into a tirade about her bullying Tracey. She had no idea what I was talking about. She hardly knew Tracey but she thought she had seemed all right. It was I, this time, who walked away scratching my head. On that drive home, I recalled all the wondrous stories Tracey had told the midwives at the Mater when Angela was a patient for quite a period of time. None of them were true and it was then that I had to consider if she had been doing the same with the nurses at the Mater Children's whilst Jack had been an inpatient there. Not everyone could see through the stories; that was not the fault of the nurses. They were responsible for many patients but they were also legally and morally responsible for reporting anything they thought was untoward, in those days, first in handwritten shift notes and second to the professionals in charge of each patient at handovers and weekly meetings regarding the ongoing patient care. It was beginning to look to me as if Tracey had decided to sacrifice Jack in order to get me out of her family.

By the end of that school year, 1982, Tracey had decided that no law could stop her from finishing school then as she would be 15 before the next school year commenced. I tried with everything in my arsenal to encourage her to at least complete year 10 before throwing her education away as it would, at the very least, give her slightly more options. After my personal experience, I advocated that every student, no matter how much they hated school, should complete year 12 purely to give them every single opportunity in the future if they decided that university was required to fulfil their goals and dreams. William 's opinion was that if she didn't want to go, then why force her. I had learned by this stage in my marriage that it was best not to cross William, not if I wanted a peaceful life.

I suggested studying year 10 via correspondence and Tracey agreed to consider it. In the new year, we did organise correspondence for Tracey but I caught her cheating on her assessments many times, which totally destroyed the whole point of the exercise. Tracey stole money from us and also cigarettes. I suggested that she needed to get a job to help fill the time when she was not doing her studies. And the problem was that it would have seemed reasonable that if she was not attending a formal educational establishment, she should start to contribute to her own wellbeing.

May 1984, this department received a complaint from the Head Teacher of Brianna's school who stated that Tracey had left school and was at home caring for the younger children—William and Isabelle. As a result of this complaint, a home visit was made. Tracey was at home alone with William and Isabelle and stated that Ellie was working as a Blue Nurse, William was at sea. Over a period of approximately two hours, Tracey very eloquently described her situation.

I am afraid the entire above paragraph calls into question not only Tracey's storytelling ability but also that of Jane Wilson's. I had, indeed, worked for the Blue Nurses and the paperwork in front of me showed that I worked from 9 January 1984 to 13 April 1984. This letter was signed by the then nursing superintendent of the Blue Nursing Service, Edward Lemin. William 's work commitments for that period of time were 6 January 1984 to 8 February 1984 on the Echeneis (where Billy had been named as Deck Boy by the crew), 13-17 February 1984 on the Cement Co dredge. Both of the above vessels were Brisbane-bound, which meant that William completed a daily shift, then returned home after work. 18 February-6 March 1984 on the vessel, Bass Trader, then 24 March-5 April 1984 on the TNT Carpentaria. William was actually present for quite a lot of the time early this year, especially whilst serving on the Brisbane vessels. I had to be at my first patient by 07:00 to give an insulin injection and my day finished at 15:00. I would only just miss doing the afternoon school run. During this period of time, when I had worked for the Blue Nurses, it had been discussed that as Tracey was not employed and I could earn more money than she could, I would return to work if she would be happy to look after Billy and Isabelle and take Brianna to and from school. Tracey did all but nothing the entire time that I was at work. I would arrive home in time to have a coffee before I did all the washing up and drying that had accumulated since the night before, start any washing that was required, bathe and sort Billy's red raw buttocks because he had not been changed all day, bathe and feed Isabelle whose bottom fared slightly better, vacuum where needed, help Brianna and Clayton with their homework, prepare the evening meal for us all and beg Tracey and Clayton to do the washing up and drying. If this was ever done, it was most certainly not even attempted for at least 3-4 hours. I would have gotten Brianna showered, sorted the school lunches for Clayton and Brianna for the next day and have had a shower myself. I would eventually conk out on the couch and it was during this time that Tracey would come and steal my cigarettes and line them up along the kitchen sink for her personal use.

We were fully aware that a complaint had been made and we were fully aware that Tracey had again been telling lies. However, the department of children's services had a legal document casting aspersions against the good names of both William and I and further, it was full of inaccuracies and downright lies. Not one single claimed event or story had ever been corroborated by Jane Wilson, which could so easily have been done with simple phone calls or conversations. I did not work in May 1984 and I had the proof, she did not enter my house during or after May 1984 and find Tracey home alone with anyone. I did not return to the workforce until February 1985 when my youngest child at that time, Jasmine, had been two weeks old.

A lie can travel halfway around the world while the truth is putting its shoes on.

-CHARLES SPURGEON

CHAPTER 15

THE RELENTLESS CHARADE

Following the previous false statement in the Freedom of Information document was an extremely large redacted passage:

> *When a visit was made on William's return later in the week, Tracey was absent—William and Ellie were extremely hostile and defensive and Ellie had finished work. They stated that Tracey had badly wanted to leave school, that she was happy, that there was nothing wrong with her caring for the children and it certainly wasn't anyone else's business.*

There was no indication of when this was alleged to have occurred but I happen to know that this particular occasion occurred after William had returned from the TNT Carpentaria on 5 April 1984. I did not finish with the Blue Nurses until 13 April 1984. As it was the Easter holidays, Tracey had accompanied Brianna to Toowoomba for a holiday with my mother.

I recall that particular meeting rather well as I had spent all morning having a severe attack of hay fever. I had prescribed medications for this, Polaramine. I had to use these until I got to the point where I no longer had hay fever. The problem was that they always made me drowsy. After explaining all of this to Jane Wilson, I had then sat in the corner of the lounge and left William to do all the talking. Extremely tired and drained was the best way to describe how I had been feeling during that meeting, most certainly not extremely hostile and defensive. William had often been called "brash", "rude", "calls a spade a spade", but I had never heard him called extremely hostile and defensive in those early days either. Confused as to why this was even an issue with children's services as Tracey was over 15, legally able to leave school and paying her way in the household by helping to care for her siblings. As indeed was I!

In August 1984, Tracey left home while her father was at sea for three months; she went immediately to her natural mother's family and asked them to telephone me. She remained with her Uncle Maurice and his wife and they state they are willing to have her as long as she wants to stay. Her grandparents live next door. This branch of the family has been estranged from William and there has been no contact since shortly after Angela's death.

William left Brisbane to join the Australian Venture on 4 August 1984 and was away for 16 weeks on an around-the-world trip, during which the ship was to spend one month in dry dock in Germany. As previously stated, this was a particularly harrowing period of time for those of us left at home. Tracey ensured that these 16 weeks were made even worse for me once she discovered that I was pregnant with baby number three with her father. It was Tracey who became extremely hostile and defensive towards me from then on. As the weeks progressed, her behaviour became more and more unacceptable but there was nothing I could do, as Tracey well knew. The whole family suffered from a severe bout of diarrhoea and vomiting during these 16 weeks and although I had cared for each and every one of the family whilst they were ill, including Tracey, when it came for my turn to be sick, she bluntly refused to lift a finger to assist me in any way, shape or form. It had been my mother's 60th birthday on 25 September 1984 and we all—Tracey, Clayton, Brianna, Billy and Isabelle—had gone in our car with my brother, Jonathon, his wife, Debbie, and their daughter, Rebecca, travelling behind us. Tracey did her best to upset this celebration, as she always had and always would when she was not the centre of attention.

William had spent his birthday, 11 October, overseas. It was later that month, as already stated, that Tracey left the family home at 05:00 on a Sunday morning. After having called my uncle, an inspector of police, for advice and having made a few other calls, I went to the home of Angela's parents, Fred and Phyllis Leeke, on Cracknell Road in Annerley, Brisbane. Tracey was there with her grandparents. I apologised and asked if she would come home. Tracey stated that she was there to stay until her father was back in Australia. I was actually relieved to be able to breathe but I knew then that she thought that she had found a way to get me out of her life for good. Of course, when I rang William after having seen her that day, he had very little interest in making any effort to see her after all the trouble she had been causing the family. He did indeed claim that if she wanted to see him, she knew where he lived. It had been her who had chosen to leave in the first place.

This branch of the family is estranged from William and there has been no contact since shortly after Angela's death. This sentence is from the Freedom Of Information document that I am quoting!

This statement was an absolute lie. William took the children to see them frequently. We all visited James and his wife, Gillian, in Redcliffe. Maurice's first wife was in England. His pregnant girlfriend had been Billy's babysitter when I had worked at PAH. Maurice had gone on to try his hand at acting here in Australia. I also used to visit Fred and Phyllis whilst they had been living in a flat opposite Chardons Corner, Annerley, and after Tracey had been at her with her neverending lies, Phyllis accused me of causing Jack to be taken from the family. I had loved Jack so much that this accusation had nearly broken me but it made perfect sense as Tracey knew exactly how I felt about Jack.

Another small, redacted paragraph followed:

On visits to the Breen home over the past two years, it has been very apparent that Tracey is used as a workhorse—always 'Tracey, get some coffee', 'Tracey, see to Billy', etc.

I have never spoken to a single human being in this manner in my life thus far and believe me, I have had more than enough reason to. I was brought up to act appropriately when guests arrived. I would have been up from the crack of dawn, cooking and preparing and would have the traymobile filled and ready to wheel into the lounge. The tea would be in the teapot and the coffee in the coffeepot, all that had been required was for the hot water to be added and it to be wheeled through. As Tracey's father had already been through caffeine withdrawal and now drank only tea, I would have asked if she could fill the tea and coffeepots and wheel it through. William, like his daughter, needed to be the centre of his own universe and had I said, 'Tracey, get some coffee', his immediate and forceful response would have been, 'I don't drink coffee, get the tea', but I did not see that written on this legal document. I am uncertain of any issue with Tracey checking up on her baby brother. I have never ordered anyone, let alone Tracey, to do anything, even when I was nursing so I find this paragraph both totally inaccurate and completely offensive.

A great deal of tension built up about her father's return, but when he arrived, he made no attempt to contact her. Several days later, when I spoke to him about it, his attitude was— 'she left home, she can come and talk to me if she wishes, but I am not going to contact her.' Tracey eventually did visit but remains adamant about not returning home.

Of course, there was a great deal of tension, on Tracey's part, about William 's return to Australia on 24 November 1984. She was absolutely certain that she had me cornered in a situation of her making and that her dad would end the marriage now and they would go back to normal. When he refused to make contact, even after the intervention of Jane Wilson, Tracey went to Jonathon and told him that she had been sexually abused by her father. She asked him not to tell anyone but hoped that he would, so guaranteeing that I would leave the marital home due to suspicions over her father's conduct. Jonathon did not come to his sister who already had two daughters of her own and daughters three, four and five were born long before he ever made contact again.

As Tracey's grand plan had not produced the results that she had wanted, she did come to see her father and she begged him to take her back to which he agreed just after Jasmine was born on 24 January 1985. Again, this paragraph from the Freedom of Information was full of misinformation.

I would learn after reuniting with Jonathon, through Debbie, that the story that Tracey talked about the day she left home was that when she had arrived at her grandparents' house, they had had a young gentleman living with them. Apparently, when Tracey had gone for a shower later that day, he had raped her in the shower. She then stated that she had told her father and that he and Clayton had come around and had beaten up the gentleman in question. Debbie also advised me that she had heard many versions of Tracey's stories, it just depended on the day as to the version you got.

Obviously, William had been on the other side of the world and Clayton had either been with me or at school. Clayton may be tall now but he took a very long time to achieve that growth and was, until later in his teens, rather small in stature.

What really bothered me in all of these lies was the real truth— Tracey and Clayton had never been allowed to grieve or assisted to grieve by their father, over their mother's death. He had a parade of at least six women in and out of his bed between Angela's death and when we got married eight months after Angela had died. He had the kids sent away for periods of time for his own benefit; how could they not see this as betrayal by their father? Tracey was desperately trying to keep her mother's memory alive as she knew no other way to feel or act. Clayton just copied Tracey, whatever she said, Clayton did. They had both had a mother, she had become pregnant and because of that, their mother had died and all they had been left with was their grief and a baby brother.

As a trained nurse whose favourite specialty was psychiatry and psychology studies, I can so easily see now, as I could when I was first married, the absolute pain that both Tracey and Clayton were in. To them, I was just another in the line of their father's conquests and, having lived through it, I know that Tracey had done her very best to see off all the other "bed buddies" of her father's. At first, the idea of the wedding and having new clothes bought for it had been exciting but the reality had hit Tracey extremely hard. Even today, she is still that little girl grieving for her mother, as is Clayton that nine-year-old boy.

The biggest casualty in this whole web of deceit had been Jack. Whether Tracey considered him the reason for their mother's death or just a means to get me out of her life will never be known for certain but either way, it was Jack who truly suffered. He has grown up with a family who was not his, he has little to no knowledge of his mum, Angela, because his scrapbook mysteriously disappeared after they moved to Gympie. He has no recollection of ever having seen such a thing. He very clearly remembers being told by his foster parents that we, William and I, did not want him. Somehow, they even managed to have Jack's surname legally changed from May to Blaine. His birth certificate states that he is a Blaine. Fortunately, William has always had a copy of Jack's birth certificate, his real one. How was it possible that a children's services worker and a pub owner managed to break the law and have Jack's name changed? Even if said pub owner was the cousin of a legendary Broncos/Queensland 5/8th…

Jack came to visit us one night at midnight with a friend. They were on their way to a bike meet. It had been his lovely friend that had forced him in the door and they had stayed for just over two hours. Jack had been 18 then. We had tried to explain as succinctly as we could what we believed had occurred and the reasons why his life had turned out as it had. I had advised Jack about our receipt of the Freedom of Information document when we received it and he had responded but I have no doubt that he had been totally confused by the whole thing. He had been lied to for just too long. To have been told for so long that we did not want him and to be sitting around our dining table with these same people who were ecstatically happy to see him must have totally blown his ideas of reality apart. We did not see him again, although we enforced that our door was his door and he could come whenever he wished and would be welcomed with open arms.

It was in early 2010, our 30th wedding anniversary on 10 December 2010, when I decided to secretly try to find Jack again. I knew he had been in Toowoomba the last time he had come to visit. I first enlisted the help of my daughter, Bianca, as her partner, Debbie, was incredibly astute with computers and social media and I was certain that they would succeed much more efficiently than I ever would. After several months, Bianca had not even tried to find him so I then asked my son, Mitchell, who has an IT degree and is blessed with knowledge in all things IT. He located Jack rather quickly and indeed visited him at his home in Gympie but Jack was not going to be able to attend our 30th wedding anniversary party as he would be at sea on the fishing trawler he worked on. He was due back into port at Maroochydore just before Christmas that year and Mitchell and he would try to organise for Jack to make a visit to our holiday apartment in Caloundra. Only Mitchell, Bianca and I knew that we had located Jack. Actually, Bianca had gotten rather upset with Mitchell that he had managed to find Jack before she could. I am certain that had she actually tried, she too would have succeeded.

It was Christmas Eve and Mitchell, William and I were sitting on the balcony in Caloundra when I told him what I had tried to achieve but that I had failed as Jack would not be able to come and visit. I was again devastated but, to be perfectly honest, I did not consider that William seemed perturbed about it at all.

Another two years would go by before we actually got to see Jack in the flesh again. I had become a Facebook user by then and had sent a friend request to Jack, which he had accepted. He never actually spoke to me but at least I could show William pictures of him and so on. By early 2013, our marriage was all but over but I had been asked to hang on until after Billy got married in early April. Jack and his girlfriend, Heidi, had a beautiful baby boy, Tomas, on 7 January 2013, which ironically is also Tracey's birthday. I was sending messages of congratulations with no replies, then the next morning, after a dreadful night with very little sleep, I saw on Facebook that Tomas had been transferred to Nambour Hospital due to medical issues. I was so upset and sent through more messages. Finally, Jack broke his silence and said that if we wanted to prove we were grandparents, we needed to get up there today. I knew that I could not make the drive there and back so I called Clayton and asked if he would drive Dad and I up there in my car. We prepared ourselves but when Clayton arrived, he had his girlfriend, Agnes, in tow. He stated that we would be taking their car. Clayton also took $50 from me for the fuel to put in his car!

It was absolutely wonderful to see Jack and to hold him in my embrace. Heidi was so lovely and Tomas was adorable. We talked and took photos and generally had a great time. I bought a teddy bear for Tomas. Eventually, William became displeased that he was not the focus of attention and suddenly became ill, which absolutely frightened the shit out of Jack. He was taken to the emergency department and I went to start making the necessary calls to the children, especially as my youngest son, Ben, had no idea of where we were or what we were doing. The doctors wanted to keep William in hospital overnight, which he was having none of as he could turn it on and off like a tap but he had bitten off more than he could chew this time with his need for attention.

Jack had agreed to come to Brisbane to stay with us for the Australia Day long weekend, by which time Tomas would be fighting fit. True to his word, Jack, Heidi and Tomas came and stayed with us. We had a huge BBQ feast with most of the family present. There were those that were not as well. William and Janet had been travelling and were unable to get back due to the floods of that year. Bianca and Debbie had been evacuated from their unit as the flood waters had completely flooded out the carpark level. They could, however, have made it but chose not to.

The time whilst Jack, Heidi and Tomas were with us, extended by the road closures preventing them returning to Gympie, were the happiest I had felt in many, many years. Clayton was constantly there, not giving anyone a chance to breathe. For the first few nights they were with us, Jack would come and kiss me goodnight and give me a hug. It felt as if time had melted away and everything was as it should be again. Clayton had other ideas. I came and sat at the dining table one evening with Isabelle and William. Clayton and Jack were sitting just outside on the front patio and Clayton was telling Jack all manner of lies about me from when he had been young. William just sat there, saying nothing, Isabelle looked at me, astounded. Could Clayton truly believe the rubbish he was sprouting or had his mind been so filled with Tracey's propaganda over the years that this is what he actually believed? I could not and would not say anything, the damage had been done. I was so depressed at that stage in my life that I could not have changed the outcome even if I had the ability. I got no more hugs or kisses. I seemed to be tolerated. When they were finally able to leave, I knew that would be the very last time that I would ever see or speak to my gorgeous little boy, Jack.

Let no one enter your inner kingdom
unless they come with love.

-AJAME.

Warning: this chapter contains coarse language.

CHAPTER 16

THE NARCISSIST AND THE EMPATH

It was not as if I did not have more than enough information and knowledge of William 's behaviour to know that this was the last man on earth I should ever have become involved with, let alone marry and commit myself to for life. But that was exactly what I did, for two reasons.

Firstly, I truly believed that I loved him and even now, on my part at least, that love was true, real and very deep. I truly gave this man every part of me. I laid myself bare to him. Secondly, this seemed to me to be the only way to get away from my mother for good. It truly was that simple. But hindsight is a wonderful thing and I know now categorically, William never loved me and was incapable of loving any single human being other than himself. He had never loved Angela either. She had taken him in off the streets of England and he had been comfortable enough to live his life with her and create his backstory for the sordid activities that William needed for sexual gratification. Angela's brothers often claimed that they had caught him out with other women and I now have absolutely no doubt that he was cheating on both Angela and I for our entire marriages, 13 years and 32.5 years, respectively.

William was a traumatised child who, instead of trying to improve his disposition, took life for everything he could get and everybody he met along the way as well. William has always truly believed that the world owed him everything. He is a true narcissist/psychopath, voyeur and psuedologue. How had William managed to go through so many years of life without being diagnosed with psychiatric illness and being treated for the same? How had William avoided being charged with all of the crimes he committed against women? These were the two questions I have been asked the most since I left my husband over four years ago by the police, lawyers, psychiatrists, psychologists, counsellors and everyone who now knows the truth of my life. The other question, of course, is why did I not leave him much sooner than I did? I will attempt to answer these questions with complete honesty, which is all I am capable of doing. The truth is sacrosanct to me and always has been. It is the one truth that has kept me from tipping over the edge when life no longer seemed worth living. As I have repeatedly been told by professionals, I had truth and right on my side, he had lies.

William was unwanted by his mother, to the point that when she discovered she was pregnant with him, she tried every trick she knew to abort him. All attempts failed and when William was born during an air raid in WWII in Romford, Essex, England, there was no joy in his mother's heart. William was badly neglected by his mother as a baby. If it were not for aunts and grandmothers, he would probably have died of malnutrition and neglect. When William had been five years old, his mother gave birth to another son, Stanley. This son was very much planned and loved by his mother. It was only ever going to be the two brothers for this family. Stanley, as he grew, caused William to constantly be in trouble with his mother and constantly being "boxed around the ear"; this would cause huge dramas with William 's hearing later in his life. It made no difference what William said in his own defence; he was always wrong and punished physically by his mother.

Where William developed his voyeuristic tendencies are impossible to guess. Is it feasible that he was born that way? I do not have any knowledge of whether it was familial or environmental. I do know that psuedologues have a deficiency in the logic part of their brains so they actually believe that the lies they are telling are the truth. It has most certainly made my life, as someone who cannot tolerate lies or liars in any shape or form, almost intolerable. My father used to tell me, 'It does not matter a single ounce what anyone else says or thinks; as long as you know the truth within yourself, you will always be fine.' It is a failing on my part that I abhor lies and liars so intensely that I feel it is my duty to prove the lies to everyone, or at least I used to. I am now much wiser than that. I now find karma is a far more effective way of outing the truth and comes to all who deserve it.

When William and I first started to have intimate relations, I thought he was trying to prove just how virile he was for a man 14 years and eight months my senior, by having sex four-five times/ day, every day. These sessions were not short; William could extend each session from one-three hours, depending on the time and circumstances, at any given moment. I was young and very up for as much sex as he was prepared to give but even I felt it was a bit of overkill on his part. People needed to work, clean houses, look after children, etc. It was unrealistic to expect to spend so many hours a day on only one pastime. I was to very quickly learn that William 's one and only interest was his sexual gratification. Nothing and no one else came anywhere near mattering to William unless his "macho act" was required to prove how big and brave he was to the world. This, too, would prove to be extremely problematic for the children fathered by him with me. It would take many decades before I was to become fully aware of the truth behind his violence.

I did expect that even if the frequency of sexual encounters did not diminish, perhaps they could be reduced in duration to suit the need of the time. Again, I would be proved wrong every time. William worked out very, very quickly that I was insatiable, sexually, when I was pregnant. This, of course, was tantamount to all of his Christmases coming at once. As previously explained, William was going through what turned out to be caffeine withdrawal whilst I was pregnant with Billy and also for a good period of time after he was born. William would be awake between 01:00 and 02:00 every night. He allowed me to fall asleep on the couch or even go to bed but as soon as he was ready, he would wake me up and I had to perform sexually to his satisfaction every night. This wasn't too bad whilst I was still pregnant but after Billy was born, William 's demands remained the same. The problem was that Billy awoke at 03:00 every night like clockwork and remained awake until 07:00. I had to then deal with the other children, the school lunches, runs and feeding Billy again. William would always sleep until incredibly late hours due to the caffeine issue, getting more than an adequate amount of sleep. I, on the other hand, was trying to operate on 2-3 hours of sleep per day.

Once it became obvious that I needed to return to the workforce when Billy was three months old due to a distinct lack of available funds and with William working on a dredge out of Fisherman's Island, something would need to change in my life. I was suffering from complete exhaustion before I even went back to work as Billy had proved to be a very difficult baby to manage. All of the night-time responsibilities had thus far fallen to me. According to William, he needed his rest. He never, ever, afforded me the same courtesy.

As previously explained, I was functioning on only a few hours of sleep per day and ideally needed to grab a few more hours once the children were settled for the night. William would not allow me to sleep as in his eyes, he had the right to have sex every day, he knew I would turn off sex once Billy had been born, the very least he would accept would be me satisfying his needs, every day, by wanking and/ or a blowjob, which could take anything up to an hour+. Inevitably, he would insist turning this into intercourse as the situation suited him and I would again head to work shattered and repeat every day thereafter. All the while trying to fit in visits to the hospital to see Jack, which William rarely, if ever, did on his own or in the evenings when he could very well have done so. William 's first, last and only thought was sexual gratification, whether I said no or not. I considered it rape; he considered it his conjugal right.

As already known, my health failed me and I had to give up work. William saw this only as an opportunity to return to his standard of normal sexual behaviour. It took him very little time to get me pregnant again, to satisfy his unrealistic sexual demands, without so much as a single thought that maybe what my body truly needed was rest. I had already learned that my needs and feelings were of no importance whatever where William was concerned. I was merely sex on tap to him. His own personal prostitute. William was very much into pornographic movies, S & M and tantric sex; what I felt about any of the above was of no consequence to him at all. But he would most certainly blame me for his inability to reach a climax if my performance and endurance were not up to scratch. Sex was never over until he had ejaculated, whether he could maintain an erection or not. It was my duty to go as far as I could to ensure his satisfaction. That was my main purpose in life, in William's eyes.

It was whilst I was pregnant with Isabelle that William went on a ship to the Solomon Islands. It ended up being very much longer than anticipated, with them floating at sea for 40 days as part of waiting their turn. He arrived home the day before my sister, Emma, was to be married in Toowoomba. At the exact same time, my uncle Dean and my cousin-in-law Jason had arrived at the house to visit on their way to the wedding. I had made them a cup of tea and they were sitting in the kitchen at the dining table, a single paper-thin wall away from the bathroom/toilet where William dragged me to perform a blowjob on him. He forced me to do this despite my complete and total embarrassment at having to perform such an act with a relative in the house. His only concession to me was that he would make it quick. I could not comprehend why he could not wait an hour or so until they were on their way but as far as he was concerned, he had rights and he had been away for some time and he would get what he wanted.

During those early days of the 1980s, William developed genital warts. I went to the GP with him and he prescribed him a solution to be painted onto the warts and the doctor told William that there was to be no sex until they had completely healed. Later that night, William demanded sex as usual, which I was reluctant to provide. I reminded him of the doctor's words.

'I am not going without sex ever,' he said. I reminded him that he would infect me, although he probably already had. 'Well, you can get treated if and when that happens,' he said. 'I will not give up sex for anyone.' He proceeded to force me to have sex vaginally, anally and orally every day thereafter. I should also mention here that William's daughter, Tracey, also suffered from genital warts in the early 1980s.

During this time period, William also developed, or perhaps revealed for the first time to me, some rather strange habits. I would be out or at work and would come home to find that he had been cutting the entire crotch out of my knickers so as to give him easier access for sex. My nightwear was constantly being unbuttoned or stretched in order that my breasts would fall out of them whilst I slept, for William's entertainment. In fact, it got to the point where I would sew nighties closed and just not wear what I was instructed to wear. William would arrange my drawers in order of the clothes that I was expected to wear. If I failed to comply, he would get extremely agitated and always took out his bad moods on the children. The only means at my disposal to effectively stop this behaviour was to do as specifically instructed and/or take him to the bedroom for sex. I was to later learn that the legal term for this is Sexual Servitude. This behaviour never changed until the time I left him.

When Rosemary was born, she was such a dreadful screamer that William started to send her and I to the lounge room to sleep. Or more accurately, for me to try to keep her quiet all night whilst William slept. This was after he had finished getting his conjugal rights, of course. Once Mitchell came along with all of his medical problems, it was I that was sent to the bedroom and William slept in the lounge. This was how life was to continue for the entirety of our marriage. William would never again sleep in my bed. I begged him for a reasonable explanation as to why we could no longer sleep together as a married couple. He had a million reasons but not one of them made sense. He did, of course, expect sex every day of his life and more than once a day if he could get it. On the rare occasion when he told me he was going to actually sleep with me, if he got no sex, he would be off to the lounge again. He managed to ruin a good few couches, camp beds and inflatable beds during this time until I asked Billy for help to get William a single ensemble when there was a spare room created by children leaving home as soon as they could; their excuse was always to get away from Dad, ironically.

It had been whilst I was pregnant with Rosemary that I began to notice changes in William 's behaviour. I would be lying in bed, he thought asleep, when I would see him hovering around Brianna's bedroom door. When Rosemary was a baby, I would often fall asleep on the couch during the day from lack of night-time sleep. One such weekend afternoon, something woke me up and instead of rolling over and going back to sleep, I felt compelled to get up and go and check on the children who were playing outside in the backyard. As I came down the back steps, I could see the children in the yard but I could also see that there was no William or Brianna in the yard. I also noted that the laundry door, always open during the day, was closed. The only way to lock this door was to close the outside bolt and use the padlock. However, when I went to push on the door to see if William and Brianna were in there, I could not budge it. Brianna was indeed in there with William but no amount of banging or yelling was about to open this door. I went around to the laundry window but due to the fact that I had put a curtain on it, it was impossible for me to see in. I continued banging and yelling, to no avail, until William was good and ready to open it.

I was beside myself with stress as to what was happening behind that forcefully closed door. The only way to achieve that would have been to push something, furniture or white goods, up against the door. Once finally out, I went for William in no uncertain terms but he went straight into one of his stories that was impossible to debate. I then went and used every single tool in my armament to try and establish the truth of what had been happening in that laundry. I was never going to be told the truth. I had been outwitted by a liar.

Perhaps his threats were more convincing than my nursing skills. We were under a microscope by children's services and I felt that I had to have proof before I could go to any authorities with my suspicions. I did not trust anyone in authority after the way I had been treated by the Mater Children's Hospital and children's services to date. I most certainly did not have any relatives that I trusted enough to take this to. I would forever remain vigilant and talk to Brianna at every single opportunity in the hope of tripping her up on her story but I could not get what I needed.

Other strange behaviours began to develop as well. We had a bilateral stereo/record player that had been very popular in its day. He wanted to take it where he could not use the power cord and wanted to check whether we had enough batteries for it to function. He sent me to one of his drawers to where the batteries were kept to get them. I opened the drawer and found tons of gold and silver change. I excitedly went to tell him that there was heaps of money in there and I got abused like I had never been before for daring to touch his money. 'But you sent me to that drawer, why would you have so much money stashed away when we are always so up against it?' I asked. The more appropriate question would have been where he had gotten it from. I knew that money was constantly going missing from my purse and I knew it was him but I was astounded to see just how much he had collected.

'I was saving up to buy you a gift,' he said. I am still waiting for that particular gift.

Was he depressed after having to give up going to sea? He was only ever too sick to go somewhere or do something when it came to school events or shopping. William was more than happy for me to manoeuvre two overflowing trolleys of groceries around the shopping aisles, down ramps, load everything into the car, drive home and then help unpack the car—hail, rain or shine and all whilst heavily pregnant. We did not have a garage/carport of any sort to cover our car in those days. Once all the shopping was sorted and put away, I was expected to have sex with him whilst the children were at school and hopefully those at home would be quiet. When they were not, it was always my responsibility to make them quiet so that he could get what he wanted. I knew by this stage that I had married a sex addict but the stress this was causing in my life and to my health was starting to really mount up.

It was whilst pregnant with Zach, after the accusation that Tracey had made against her father came to light and also having lost Zach's twin early in the pregnancy, when I started to experience quite severe heart palpitations. My doctor wanted to wait until after the birth to see if they would settle down. They did not and if anything, they were worse. I was put on to Digoxin to help prevent them. It was never truly investigated; I was not sent to a cardiologist at that stage for any hope of finding a cause—just take this pill and it will help. It did not and I eventually ended up on a massive dose, which I am still taking today at age 60.

No medical issue that I developed was cause for William to have to go without sex. It became for me an "exercise in pain endurance" and the only way to save my children from abuse, or so I thought. After William had been caught and charged with driving without a licence in 1987, he absolutely refused to even try to get one to help alleviate the pressure on me being the only driver. His excuses were childlike and ridiculous and many, many arguments ensued. I got to a stage where I had put up with enough of his crap and I started to bite back. I ended up giving as good as I got. This would earn me the reputation of "being as bad as Dad" in the eyes of some of my children. They had absolutely no idea what I had to endure or give up to try and protect them so as much as it upset me to my core when they said this, I always ended up letting it go.

Why was he so insistent on not getting a licence, especially when there were many, many days when I would be in and straight out of the house from early morning until late at night? We even bought a video camera to record all the things William missed out on because he was "too ill to go". What was he hiding, why did he need all that time at home without me there? Not long after we moved to Sunnybank Hills, when Zach had been just a month old, I was asleep on the couch and all the children were in the backyard playing, or so I thought. Something compelled me to go and check on them. I checked on Zach first, it was only he and I inside. This was a much larger house and I got to the backyard to find everyone there, except William and Brianna—again. I found the storeroom door locked and, as before, no amount of banging and yelling produced any results until William was ready. Again, with the lame excuses and again I questioned Brianna to the nth degree, to no avail. What could I possibly do if Brianna would not speak to me? I could believe what I wanted but without more than conjecture and speculation, what was I to do? I had been trained as a nurse to use key words to uncover the truth, especially with children. I had saved several children during my general training from abusive families. Why could I do nothing to help my own?

William had been making my life hell from December 1990 but things seemed to escalate even further since the move. I told him point blank that sex with him was repetitive, boring and way too long. He either tried to shorten it or we would not be doing it at all. He was not happy but neither was I. And still I was being forced to perform sexual servitude to try to protect my children. I thought I was but it has become apparent that my efforts may well have been in vain given the information that I have received since having left him. But I would give my life for each and every one of my children and what I went through was demeaning, embarrassing and well beneath me but I would do it all again if, even for a nanosecond, I believed it would protect my children.

Moving to this new house seemed to ignite William's voyeurism. He was constantly found peering at me from behind the door or crouched down at the end of the bed, bobbing back down very quickly when I moved in my sleep and scurrying with the wildest excuses when I would get up to go to the bathroom. I seemed to be awakened by my sixth sense to the fact that I was being watched constantly. Although the new house was much bigger and better than anything we had previously lived in, I did not feel right. It felt as if we were living in a goldfish bowl. Our house was very long and all on one level. The neighbours on all three sides were double-storeyed and it seemed to me that we were always being watched. This was not helped by the fact that one neighbour had full access to four of the bedroom windows, most of which were my daughters' bedrooms. This made them and me extremely uncomfortable. Coupled with the fact that I was being watched all night left me with a very sour taste in my mouth about the move to these new premises.

I tried to immerse myself in gardening, one of my favourite pastimes, but there was just so much to do for the household and the family that I really was trying to wear myself out; as a result, I was less inclined to realise when William was in a voyeuristic mood. It did not work and I just continued to become more and more stressed and exhausted. Every time I tried to broach the subject with William to discuss just how uncomfortable his "night-time antics" made me feel and that perhaps he needed to seek some professional help, he would totally deny any wrongdoing and it would always cause him to start an argument in which I was to blame and if there was an audience of children, all the better to make himself appear to be in the right whilst I was always in the wrong.

Within 12 months of us having moved to Sunnybank Hills, William was at war with one of the neighbours. This automatically meant that I was too by the mere fact that I was William 's wife. According to William 's story, the neighbour was at fault and I was duty bound to believe my husband and defend him. How could I ever know as he always ensured that I was nowhere in sight when he wanted to start something? Besides, I would always be too busy caring for children or completing household duties to know what was going on outside the front door.

In the winter of 1993, Clayton and his then wife, Elise, were visiting. Clayton asked about a particular item and so we were going through the many places it could have been. Of course, as always, it was me who had to go and fetch and I came back on one occasion with an old canvas bank bag full of items. As I was pulling things out one by one, I took out a very thick letter addressed to William from UK. I knew immediately whose handwriting it was as I had seen it on the overly loving Christmas card, I had read from William 's ex-sister-in-law, Maureen, in 1984. As I opened it and began to read the love letter she had written to MY husband, the truth that he had indeed cheated on me in 1984 with her in England must have been obvious by my facial expressions as William leapt up and angrily and nastily snatched the letter from my grasp and took off down the hallway with it. I headed in the other direction to my bedroom and slammed the door.

Why would he have kept this letter for almost a decade? Did he actually have feelings for her? Did he actually want me to know the truth? Or was he just so self-possessed that he had truly thought it would never, ever come to light? If I had followed my intuition in 1984 and not relied on having facts to back up my gut feeling, my life would have been dramatically different and also that of the children I then had—Brianna, Billy, Isabelle and very-soon-to-be born Jasmine. I knew that he had cheated on Angela and probably not just the once she had found out about. But I gave him all of myself, I met his every demand even if I considered them to be totally unreasonable and/or illegal. Why did he constantly remind me of the same old catch cry, "why would I want hamburger when I have steak at home?" It seemed that despite my constant warning since the day we became a couple that if he ever, ever cheated on me, I would chop off his dick and shove it down his throat on my way out the door, he actually was convinced that he could truly have his cake and eat it too.

What was I to do now? I was destroyed. All trust and respect for the man I had married was gone. If it were just, he and I, then it was over, and I desperately wanted it to be no matter how much I actually loved him. Love was not enough, as I have learned in the long term, especially when it had always only been one-sided love, but at that time, there were so many more things for me to consider before I gave him his marching orders. I remained in my bedroom, except for toilet breaks, until the following day. I was distraught and could not stop crying or move the massive pain in my chest and abdomen. My children would come in to see what was wrong and if they could help me, but I have always been a compartmentaliser, especially of the worst parts of my life. They had done nothing wrong; they did not need to have this pain on them. So I just told them that Dad had made me sad but that everything would be okay. William could take care of the children for once, provide their meals, do what I did every other day of their lives. I refused to speak to William, how could I? I could not as yet see a way through this mess.

All I had ever asked of him was love, honesty and support. In return, no matter how difficult, I would be there for him until I died. I would do everything I could to make his life and the lives of our children as easy as possible. For the entirety of our marriage, I sacrificed my self-worth, my dignity and my health in order to meet his unreasonable demands but nothing was ever going to be enough. I truly wish that I had known this on that fateful day in 1993 as the outcome might have been different. Later in the evening, when I started to think more clearly, I realised what it was that I had to do.

Firstly, and most importantly to me, was what would be the best outcome for my children. My children have always and will always mean more to me than anything else in this universe. They are of me and I love them unconditionally. Their needs have always and will always come first in my eyes and my world. I would gladly and willingly give up my life for each and every one of them now as I would have then. What decision I made had to be for my babies, I was of no consequence in this equation.

William's grandfather, also William, had left his wife, with whom he had had seven children, for a musician and had started a whole new family. In 1993, William and I had seven children—Brianna: 15, Billy: 11, Isabelle: 10, Jasmine: eight, Bianca: seven, Rosemary: six, Mitchell: four and Zach: two. Was I about to allow William to do to our children what his grandfather had done to his? Absolutely never, not on my watch! William's father and his siblings had to go into care until their mother could get a job and sort a way to get them all back together again. Then William's father had spent eight years instead of four, completing his apprenticeship in order to be able to financially support his family. In truth, William's father was an extremely clever man and should have gone to university were his life's circumstances not what they had been. With children's services already such a formidable force in our lives, there was absolutely no way that I would ever risk the safety and wellbeing of my babies, no matter what consequences that had on me.

Secondly, the only real way that I could see to actually cope and protect my children if I kicked William out, would be to ask my mother for help. I could never, ever give her the satisfaction of saying 'I told you so'. She would have dined on that for the rest of her life. I could not take that amount of stress and earache after the traumatic life that she had ensured I led. The only constant and loving influence in my life had been my dad; I longed for the times when he had been at home. Because of the extraordinary relationship I had been allowed to have with my father by the universe, I believed that the father/child relationship was sacrosanct and I could never take that away from my children, no matter how painful it was for me. I truly believed in my heart that William would never hurt our children. I was blinded to his true behaviours and motives by my respect, love and admiration for my own father. I was unable to see what was truly at play in my own household. But because of my love for my father and my loathing of my mother, I made the decision that as it was only me being abused and mistreated in the marriage and only I who had been cheated on, I would go through whatever kind of hell he threw at me in order that my children not become the product of a broken home.

I would never be able to forgive him for what he had done nor the decade-long lie he had maintained and I truly believed that I would never again be able to trust him or respect him but there had always been, within me, along with my ability to put all things into their little boxes and move forward, an ability to act the part as required, a lesson I had learned by growing up with my mother. I went to sleep that night, still crying and totally devastated, but knowing that I had to continue to live with this man for the sake of my children. I had no understanding of how I was going to fake my way through but I had always been able to rise to whatever challenge was thrown at my feet and this was just another mountain that I needed to climb. Time to put my hiking boots on.

Nothing hurts more than being disappointed by the person you thought would never hurt you.

-Zane Barker

CHAPTER 17

LIVING A LIFE WITHOUT TRUST AND RESPECT

I awoke from the small amount of dozing that I had done through the worst night of my life, still totally bereft of the depth of unfeeling that William had shown for me as a human being, his wife and the mother of seven of his children, but just as deeply resolute that I could tolerate living with this man in order to keep my children from the stigma of a broken home.

Once the school-aged children were all settled into school for the day, the "white-washing" began in earnest by William. It really made no difference to me whatever he came up with; I was going to make him suffer a good bit more yet before I let him know my decision. I wanted the letter he had snatched from my hands, I felt entitled to see that at least. He claimed that he had ripped it up and flushed it down the toilet. I did not believe him then and I still do not believe that was the fate that had befallen the love letter that he had retained for almost a decade, but he would not give in and I decided to let it go. He was spouting so much nonsense, trying desperately to get me to allow him to stay. He didn't have anyone else, he needed me. I neither believed him nor let him know the fact that he should have been begging my forgiveness for an error in his judgment but it was not that at all. He had held on to a very thick love letter for at least a decade, that was not remorse. That was a sick man's way of reliving a past he had thoroughly enjoyed. The carrying on was becoming somewhat "ad nauseam" when he came up with what he thought might be a game changer— 'I will let you have another baby', he said, feeling rather proud of himself for having used the "ace", in his opinion. Why on earth would I ever want to bring another child of his into this world? What was psychologically wrong with this man? Could he not see that he had destroyed everything I stood for, every principle I held dear, every fibre of my being had been insulted at the highest level, he had destroyed me. But despite this destruction, I had decided, as I always have and always will, that my children were of the utmost importance and their best interests would always be my "master" in decision-making of any and all kinds.

I finally put him out of his misery but it would be a very long time before I actually came to fully accept the decision I had made. I would, henceforth, take every opportunity presented to me to remind William that it was he who had been unfaithful in our marriage, he who had been accused of sexually abusing his eldest daughter, he who had been accused of sexual harassment of his eldest son's 18-year-old girlfriend and that all I had done throughout our marriage had been true to both our vows and to the laws of the land, given 120% of myself to our children, our marriage and our home. So why was it that William could only ever find fault with me at every turn and also with our children?

The same vicious cycle in William's behaviour took very little time to show its ugly head again. William had his usual air of superiority in full swing, believing he had conned me into submission. Nothing had changed except me. I would never forgive him for the way he had treated me but I truly hoped that this rage inside me would calm to a tolerable level at some point. It never really did as every time I started to relax, thinking he seemed somewhat normal, the next bombshell would befall me and I would have to go back on high alert.

In 1994, I decided it was time to try to re-join the workforce in some capacity. I bluntly refused to start at the bottom with nursing and had spoken with my sister-in-law, Debbie, who worked as a shelf packer in Woolworths. I started to look in earnest and found a job application for a new supermarket that was to open at Sunnybank Hills called Franklins, for night fill. It seemed to be ideal as it would not interfere with my requirement to be at home all day for the children, the housework, the school runs, doctors and so on. I applied and got the job of night fill. I started at Franklins in July. The store had opened and it was chaos packing the shelves with all of the opening specials. But I felt worthwhile again; I was making a contribution to the world I lived in and was again able to communicate with the general public. I was no longer stuck in the extremely narrow band of my home world. That did not mean that William ceased to make my life a living hell. On one occasion, a shift had gone until 04:30 and there he was, waiting for me at the gates, arms crossed and the usual scowl across his face. Where the hell had I been, why had I not contacted him, what right did they have to keep me there until this time in the morning, and on and on he dribbled. Well, actually, William, I was working hard for the entirety of my time away from the house, I was absolutely exhausted and just needed my bed. He had to continue to ensure that I was fully informed of his disdain about this situation. He finally went to bed knowing that he would get his full 8 hours and then some but my alarm would sound at 06:45 for me to get up and sort the children, their lunches, get them to school and then return home to start the day's workload of washing, housework and anything else that required doing at any given time.

I relished the freedom that working gave me but between the pressure William was placing on me, as usual, and the wrongdoings, as I saw them between members of staff at work, meant that I found it impossible to remain in this workplace and I left after 10 weeks. I then applied for a night filler's position at Coles at Garden City and started immediately. It was a far more organised environment, which suited me much better. I worked in health and beauty. The expected carton packing rate per hour was 20 but I was working at the rate of 80/hour and I loved it. The older customers would bring me a bag of bananas that were dirt cheap or anything else that they thought I would like. I would grab boxes of bread, rolls and cheap chickens to utilise for making the children's lunches for the next week or so. My life had begun to look up in ways that I had not thought possible and it was amazing just to be me again, in my own right.

William continued to put pressure on me to perform sexually as well as working and all of my home duties but I most certainly was much less giving since 1993 but he, as always, found every possible way to make sure that my life was hell and also that of my children if he did not get exactly what he wanted. I had to protect my children so I would grin and bear the painful experience that was sex with William over and over again. No matter how much I begged for him to alter his ridiculously long and boring ritual, it remained the same. William treated me as a prostitute, having sex was all about him and I was just the battering ram to help meet his end goal.

In February of 1995, my then team leader, Quentin, was being promoted and moving to Coles at Pinelands. He knew what a hard worker I was and he came to me and asked if I would consider moving to that store as well. It was only a couple of blocks from my home so travel would be a lot easier for me. This Coles was a smaller store and they only did dawn fill—05:00-08:00. This would also work well as I would finish, get home and sort the children and get them to school. I was honoured to be so highly thought of by someone, anyone really, and I agreed to change stores.

I fell into the swing of the new store quickly but I was no longer working in health and beauty. I was all over the shop and it was much heavier work with cartons of cans and bottles to pack but I would not let any of that get to me. During late April and into May, I started to feel quite ill. I was totally in the dark as to why I was feeling so weak, tired and exhausted all the time. I pushed on but it was becoming increasingly difficult. I was left with no choice but to head off to the doctor. He suspected early onset menopause; with the symptomology I had been displaying, it had also crossed my mind.

It transpired that I was actually pregnant with my youngest child. I was shocked as it had been two years since William had tried to bribe me and thrown caution to the wind. I had moved on with my life and really was very happy having me time and that small amount of independence. I did not know what to think and I continued to feel worse and worse. I had to give up work in May.

This was, undoubtedly, the most difficult pregnancy I had endured but more so, I think, because of my age—38—and my poor state of health. I spent what remained of this pregnancy getting sick from one thing or another. It seemed it would never end. My chemist had provided one of my heart medications in too high a dose and I was too ill to realise for a week, they were falling over themselves with apologies once I worked it out. The same chemist recommended Echinacea as my immune system was so low due to constantly being unwell with one virus or another. This only served to make me much worse. I went back to the chemist and they then advised me to stop it but to try again after the baby was born in order to build myself up. William would never stop making sexual demands and he could not care less what physical state I was in as long as he got what he wanted. As I had to have a Caesarean section, I organised to have a tubal ligation whilst having the Caesarean so that this would definitely be the last baby that I would have. My body was letting me know, in no uncertain terms, that I was way too old to continue to have children. This was to be my 5th Caesarean section.

William's mother, Daisy, had died in 1994 and his father, William, died at around the same time I would have fallen pregnant with this baby, in 1995. I was convinced then, as I still am now, that this baby was a reincarnation of William's father. Things continued to worsen for me and all I could do was just survive until it was time for the baby to be born. None of my duties lessened during this most difficult of times and neither did William's insatiable need for sex.

Billy was a runner, middle distance, and he had made it to Districts for the 800m race. This was to be held in Ipswich, 30-40 minutes from home. William, Zach and I went to see Billy race and to time it for him. I had parked on top of a hill looking down onto the track, a perfect view for the whole race. After he finished, Billy came up to see us and just after he went back to join his team, I stepped backwards and my foot went into a hole in the ground. I dislocated my knee and it took me a long time to get it back into its correct place. I had always managed to get it back in all past dislocations but this one was bad and extremely painful. We were, of course, quite away from home and my not-so-wonderful husband could not drive. I had to get myself around to the other side of the car, get in and manage to drive all the way home before I could elevate my leg, get ice on it or get pain relief. I was in agony. I was only one month away from delivering this baby. This was a complication I did not require but it was proof that my immune system was indeed at its lowest point.

I was booked to have my Caesarean late in November, a Monday. I went in early on that morning. The preparations were all done and I sat waiting. Finally, William arrived and I was taken to the operating theatre. I had elected to have an epidural performed for the procedure. The anaesthetist made three failed attempts at an epidural and three failed attempts at a spinal tap. I was begging for a general anaesthetic by this stage. I was in agonising pain. So, they wheeled me in and off to sleep I went. I awoke in the recovery ward, nauseated and vomiting as usual. I was eventually returned to my room in the ward and fell asleep. I had not seen William again and although the ultrasounds had said I was having a boy, no one had confirmed this for me. One of the nurses had brought him in and laid him in my arms. All I could see was the top of his head. At the same time, they came in and picked up the phone and gave it to me. It was William and I had to ask whether the baby was a boy or a girl.

My last ever pregnancy would be no different to all the rest. I would be doing it alone. Brianna was 17, Billy was 13, Isabelle 12, Jasmine 10, Bianca nine, Rosemary eight, Mitchell six and Zach was four. None of them were babies who could not fend for themselves and they had my girlfriend with them. Why on earth could William not stay with me until I was back in the ward? Why had he to rush off in such a hurry? Where was the hot date he had to get to? As always, I was alone with a new baby and that is how it would be from here on in. Why would I have even contemplated that William 's behaviour patterns would have changed just because he had committed so many offences against me and been found out?

My fallopian tubes were so badly damaged that they had to be removed almost in their entirety. It was a miracle that I had become pregnant at all. The anaesthetist showed her face to apologise for all the trauma she had caused with the failed epidurals and spinal taps. Too little, too late, as it turned out; I have lived with absolutely agonising pain in that region of my spine, which has continued to worsen as the years have worn on. It has come to the point where it causes me such great amounts of pain that it has totally hindered my abilities to live a normal life.

I went home early after this baby was born, the back pain was excruciating and I could not take it so I requested to be allowed to go home. Besides the pain, William was less than interested in visiting his new-born son or his mother and I desperately missed all of my other children whom William would not allow to visit. I had to have home visits from the Blue Nurses for wound care and also to do my baby's Day 5 blood tests.

We settled back into life at home, nothing was about to change on that front. As we lived in government housing and no longer had enough bedrooms for the number of children living in this house, they had decided that they would build an extension onto the back of the house, which would house the master bedroom, a walk-in-robe and an en suite. The work commenced on 15 January 1996 and was completed by 02 March 1996 when I moved into the new room with one beautiful new baby boy and slowly but surely, my life returned to the same old drudge that it had always been.

I made a very conscious and verbal decision that I was going to totally spoil my last baby. You will note that I have not mentioned my beautiful baby's name. This is a purposeful act and is at the specific request of my now almost 22-year-old baby boy. He requested that I not make any reference to him as he is so totally and completely ashamed of the actions of his father and his siblings and does not want any of his friends and associates to know he is in any way related to them. His disdain for them and their actions is extremely strong and he does not wish to be tainted by their vile attitudes and actions. He is nothing like any of them and would prefer that I did not even acknowledge his existence.

I wish to honour his wishes as best as I can but to pretend that he did not exist at all is not something I can bring myself to do. I cannot tell a lie. His existence has been my saviour. Without him, I would have given up long ago. He is a truly honourable man and he has my respect, my pride and my love.

Having children makes you no more a parent,
Than having a piano makes you a pianist.

-MICHAEL LEVINE

CHAPTER 18

GROWING PAINS

For the purpose of this book, I will call my youngest son 'Ben'. He was a true replica, as it turned out, of his older brother, Billy. They seemed to have so much in common but I still stuck by my theory that he was a reincarnation of his grandfather. Ben was keen to join everyone else, all of whom were so much older than he was. He crawled early and before he was seven months old, he was walking around objects and was almost ready to take off and run.

Ben had been due his 6-month immunisations but it had to be postponed as it was suspected that two of the girls had contracted whooping cough, despite being fully immunised. It was horrific for them and for me to watch them coughing and choking, trying to get air into their lungs. It seemed to be an endless condition for them. Although they were constantly being tested, it took some time to get a positive result even though it was so blatantly obvious that they both had the wicked condition.

The GP had finally received the positive result and called me on a Tuesday morning, requesting that I bring Ben straight to the surgery to be given his six-month immunisation. I did and by late Tuesday afternoon, he had developed a cough. As the days wore on, the cough became worse. I returned him to the doctor who believed it was a viral infection. By Saturday, he was so much worse and I took him to our second GP (who was on duty for this weekend), who thought it was an asthma type issue and requested I use the nebuliser on him. I begged him to cover him with an antibiotic but Nick was adamant that there was no infection and that the nebuliser would work.

By Sunday, I had not had any sleep for two nights now and Ben seemed to just keep getting worse. William and my friend, Kitty, had taken Billy to his football match (soccer to the uninitiated), which was on the north side of Brisbane. I was at home trying to rock a crying Ben to sleep, pacing up and down the hallway continuously. There came a point when I was coming back down the hallway and as I passed the wall clock, I felt compelled to look at the time; a cold shiver passed through me and I immediately knew that something was wrong with Billy.

Within 10 minutes, the phone rang and it was William to let me know that Billy had gone in for a tackle, landed on the ground and could not get back up. He was going with Billy in the ambulance to the Royal Brisbane Hospital whilst Kitty would head straight to me to take over with Ben and the other children so that I could get to the hospital. What should have taken Kitty the best part of an hour took her only 30 minutes and it was an immediate handover and I was off to the Royal.

Billy had fractured his femur straight through the growth plate, a Salter-Harris fracture. If Billy were to grow too much taller, he could develop a noticeable limp. He had been only 14 years old at the time. He was being sent to theatre to ensure that it was correctly aligned. We rushed back home so that William could take over with the children and Kitty and I would head back to the hospital to ensure I was there when Billy came out of theatre.

I was absolutely torn between my eldest and youngest sons, a position no mother should be placed in. Thankfully, Kitty had been able to see that I was in no fit state to drive again so she did the honours that evening. Billy was extremely groggy when he came out of theatre. There were three football injuries that evening that had all required a trip to the operating theatre. As Billy had never been in hospital since he was born, I tried to explain what would occur and what the nurses would do for him. I was not sure he took any of it on board but he was, at least, resting comfortably by the time we left.

Ben was not going to allow me any sleep for a third night as he was just getting worse and worse. I was up extremely early and made an appointment with the GP as soon as they opened. I got a very early appointment. William headed to the Royal to be with Billy and I headed to the GP with Ben. Stan suspected he had pneumonia and yes, antibiotics on Saturday may well have helped avoid him getting this sick. I was to head straight to the Mater Children's Hospital where he could be better treated.

An X-ray confirmed that Ben had pneumonia and the head paediatrician, Dr Rob Pitt, wanted him admitted to the hospital. I refused to allow this; I would care for him at home with the antibiotics prescribed. The doctor knew that I was a nurse as we had worked together at the Toowoomba General Hospital when I had been training. Rob guaranteed that I would be back with Ben, I guaranteed him that I would not. I returned home and the first couple of doses of antibiotic came straight back up due to coughing but I was one stubborn bitch; I would get Ben healthy without having to be separated from another son.

I had now gone four nights without sleep when I went to bring Billy home from the hospital. He was in incredible pain and due to the toe-to-hip plaster (40 kgs), he had to lay across the backseat in the car. It was a much slower than usual drive as he felt every bump and I tried to negotiate them more slowly or avoid them altogether. We finally made it home and the real fun began. One incapacitated son and one recovering from pneumonia.

Total exhaustion did not even come close to describing just exactly how I felt at this point. It was extremely fortuitous that we had an en suite that had fairly easy access as this was the only place that Billy could shower. It was an ordeal due to the weight of his plaster and the fact that it had to be completely covered and secured so that it would not get wet. I had a plastic chair in the shower for Billy to sit on and I would have to stand on the toilet in order to turn the water on and get the temperature right for him. Maintaining his privacy as I helped undress and redress my son was tantamount for a teenage boy but he was very patient with me. It did take a considerable amount of time to complete any endeavour that he required, however, and at the same time I was trying to ensure that Ben was improving every day as well.

I returned with Ben to the GP later that same week and he was well impressed with his progress as was I, but I had always intended it to be so. Despite an initial amount of enthusiasm from their father, William would never go without his sleep and would claim "no knowledge of how" when it came to looking after either of the boys' specific requirements. What he did do, frequently, was get jealous of the time I had to spend with them in caring for them and would pick a fight with me if I even looked like I was doing anything with Billy, in particular, which did not constitute actual care. For instance, a card game or a coin game we liked to play. As far as William was concerned, once I had provided the care, the rest of my time was his and his alone!

Brianna was 18 and a big help at this stage as she had been when I was pregnant with Ben. She had finished school halfway through year 12 and gone straight to TAFE to complete a Certificate III in cooking with a view to taking on a chef apprenticeship once she had finished the course. That had not worked out strictly to plan. She had applied for plenty of jobs in the hospitality industry but after a few knockbacks, she lost confidence and her enthusiasm for cooking waned.

Brianna had never had any extra-curricular activities despite my best efforts to get her interested in them. She had done ballet when she was quite young but that did not suit her and she asked if she could stop. I tried to get her interested in tennis and/or netball but she had fractured or jarred that many fingers playing at the school level and, again, I could not get her interested. She was a good swimmer and I had taken Brianna to classes when she had been two in Toowoomba and then again with Billy when he was about the same age. He had screamed the place down and refused to return. I persevered for a little while but he was learning nothing so I conceded defeat and decided that he could learn when he got to school. Brianna was just a casual swimmer, she showed no interest in formal training so I had to ask her to just let me know if there was anything she would like and despite the fact that I would check in with her every so often, nothing ever did appeal.

She worked in a Chinese restaurant for a while, then she worked for a supermarket chain called Jewel. She seemed to love working here and was definitely a people person. I took her to and collected her from work for every shift as she had no interest in getting a licence or a car at that stage. I had walked into the shops early one day to find her smoking, which I did not know about. Brianna had not started clubbing or going to pubs after she turned 18 but she had started when she was 19. William imposed the curfew that I considered ridiculous but was not allowed any say in. William would abuse her verbally and physically whenever she came home from being out. I was at a loss as to what the hell he had thought he was doing. He was treating her even more harshly than my mother had treated me for the same offences. Brianna was an adult now, she was my daughter but I was allowed no say in anything to do with Brianna, the daughter I had given birth to. Because I did not back him up, he would always start in on me. Tracey went out whenever she liked, came home drunk, spewed all over the carpeted floor in the room she shared with three other sisters, was under the legal drinking age, and she got treated like a princess. Who the fuck did he think he was to treat MY daughter in this way?

When Brianna got a boyfriend, James, William treated him like he was a piece of shit. The bravado had to be seen to be believed. He had absolutely no right to be treating my daughter in this manner but nothing I said had even the slightest impact on him. It was as if she was his sole property and he could do and say whatever he wanted. We argued on this point constantly. Brianna did get pregnant by James and on one occasion when she had come home past the curfew imposed by William alone, he was poking her so hard in the back all the way down the hallway that she almost fell over with every new poke. I have, in fact, only been told by Brianna in the last two weeks that at one point, William had smashed the side of Brianna's head and face into the metal double bunks that we had for the children. She is still suffering today, at almost 40, with severe pain in her jaw and it now clicks in and out, which it never did before this act. I asked why she had not come to me immediately and told me what he had done. Brianna stated that she had thought that Dad would just do it, or worse, again. She was blatantly too petrified of his violence to come to me. As I sit here now, I feel sick for what Brianna and possibly more of my children have endured at the hands of their father.

Given what I know now, especially in regard to narcissists and paedophiles and the fact that they use "trauma-based mind control" on their victims, it takes me back to the two broken arms that Brianna had in childhood. The first one had been when she was seven; of course, Dad had been playing with the children in the lounge room before school. Brianna had screamed and I had run. Dad had pulled her arm and it was obviously broken. William seemed to play up the fact, excessively, that because Brianna suffered from severe lactose/sucrose intolerance and was an asthmatic on and off corticosteroids, her bones were weak. It was only a greenstick fracture and I swallowed his excuse as it did hold some merit. I did not swallow it a second time when, a few years later, Dad was again playing with the children. This time, it was in a fairly narrow hallway whilst I was washing up the dishes from the evening meal in order to get ready to go to parent/teacher interviews at the children's school.

Brianna had let out an earth-shattering scream, Dad had stood on her forearm and both the radius and ulna were very clearly fractured and displaced. William had gone straight back into the 'Brianna's bones are weak' crap, it wasn't his fault. I felt sick to my stomach. I spent many hours at the Mater Children's Hospital whilst Brianna had been in the operating theatre to have her forearm bones realigned. I had spoken at length with the surgeon prior to the operation, asking whether he felt that Brianna's bone looked depleted in any way from the X-rays, as was suggested by William, and he assured me that her bones were perfect. I have, in my heart, always believed that William broke Brianna's arm on purpose definitely the second time but probably also the first time. I made my conversation with the doctor very clear to William and he was acutely aware that I believed the doctor. Without proof of any wrongdoing and children's services breathing down our necks, what the hell could I do? Again, I tried to get Brianna to talk to me about what was going on but she was blatantly too frightened of him to say. As a nurse, I have seen many children's fractures and I had never seen anything as blatant and calculated as this fracture had seemed to me. It would have taken considerable force to break both bones at exactly the same level on both the ulna and radius.

Brianna continued to work at Jewel until she was close to giving birth to her son when she was 20 years old. It was a very wet but extremely humid April day when my eldest grandchild was born. Yes, I said "my" and the reason for that will become obvious before too long. Brianna had gone into Logan Hospital the day before this to be induced into labour. Nothing was happening so I eventually left to go home to the usual grind of cooking, cleaning and so on. Ben had been only two at this point. I went to bed expecting to get the call to return to the hospital at any minute.

The call came just on 05:00 and I headed down to the hospital with a cup of tea. Brianna's contractions had started in earnest at MN but she was in agony now and not doing too well. My baby girl had never had a very high pain threshold and they were considering an epidural. It was eventually inserted and Brianna was off to sleep, literally. I was left to entertain myself. It was freezing in the labour ward and steaming hot and pouring with rain outside. The epidural had slowed the labour but by mid-afternoon, Brianna was fully dilated and ready to push. Not that she realised what was going on as she was still so dopey. I have joked for the last almost 20 years now that Brianna slept through the entirety of the birth. The midwives offered me the opportunity to deliver my grandson but I declined due to the fact that I had nine children and it might not be possible for me to do for all of them as I would do today. I said I would cut the cord. I regret having made that decision now with the way things have worked out. Steve was born and I cut his cord and bathed him. He was adorable and I fell in love all over again.

Steve was our first grandchild but William was very much less than interested in the baby in any way. Everyone else would be doting on him but William chose to ignore him altogether for some time. He had, of course, to show just how magnificent he was at burping a baby when Steve had issues and ensured that everyone knew just how brilliant he was. I am certain that he quite liked him really but as all of the attention was on the new baby, William had to re-assert his position of power. Steve was quite a difficult baby and toddler. Ben loved him with a passion but Steve would kick and scream, leaving Ben very clear on where he stood in the pecking order. Ben did not give up or stop being pushed, screamed at or lashed out at until one day, when Ben was four, he decided he was no longer going to tolerate this behaviour and he pushed his nephew rather hard into the screen door. If it had been open, Steve would have fallen down cement steps onto concrete. Ironically, as adults, Ben is still trying to be a good uncle and Steve is always finding fault with Ben.

Brianna had a second child, Ebony, three years later. I had been less than impressed that again, she was going to have to raise a child alone. Even though I had always told my children, 'Stay single and bring your children up the same way', I had not really expected her to take my advice so literally. But in hindsight, I wish I had done that exact same thing myself. I told Brianna, 'If you are going to do this, then at least have the good manners to give me a granddaughter.' As a toddler, Ebony thought the sun shone out of her uncles, especially Uncle Billy. They had a special bond and she would not go to sleep without a picture of him beside her bed.

Speaking of uncles, Billy would often go out with Brianna and Steve to assist her with the pram and belongings. Billy was four years younger than Brianna but was often asked if Steve was his son. He was excellent with Steve as he had been with all of his siblings.

Billy's future was beginning to look like it may not go as planned for him now that he had fractured his femur. The plaster was so heavy that he was unable to attend school and I would go to the school to collect the course work he had to complete and then return it when he had finished and collect the next lot. Billy was/is multi-talented. He had played club cricket as well as district cricket from the age of eight. He was also a middle distance and cross-country runner. He had been due to complete a 5km training run on the Monday morning after he had fractured his leg, no excuses accepted, the coach had stated. He had no choice but to accept this excuse.

Once the initial plaster was removed, Billy was allowed to return to school on crutches. He had woodwork at the end of the very first day back and he had slipped on sawdust and injured the knee of the leg he had fractured. He went to QEII Hospital this time and he had not re-fractured anything but had a huge haematoma under his patella. This was drained and he was again in plaster to immobilise the leg. It was a setback that would end any hope of Billy having a professional career in football; yes, he had been that good.

For the next couple of years, Billy tried to return to his beloved game but every time, his thigh would swell up incredulously and cause him agonising pain. I would ice and massage it but eventually, I took him to a specialist who stated that there was a bursa in the muscle (a fluid-filled sac or sac-like cavity) and he would require surgery to correct it. This was done at QEII Hospital again and as soon as he was out of the operating theatre, the physios had electrodes on his thigh to stimulate the muscles.

In time, Billy would recover from the fractured femur and he would walk without a limp. Luckily, he had done most of his growing by the time he had broken his leg. Billy was also extremely artistic; he had had some of his artwork imbedded into the overpass between two shopping centres in Sunnybank. He was also the school clown and "Jack the Lad". He had even given pole vaulting a go before he had fractured his leg.

His life seemed to be heading in a different direction now. He was an arrogant and cocky young man but what else could he be with a father such as his. William junior had gained employment as soon as he had recovered and started working at a Patisserie 1.5km up the road from our home, then he started working for Domino's Pizza. He also worked for a childcare centre. He was studying Film and Television at senior level and seemed to be doing quite well at it. Once he finished year 12, he went to TAFE and completed a Justice Course. As the year progressed, he informed us that he had decided to study nursing. You could have knocked me down with a feather.

The following year, he started at UQ—University of Queensland—for a degree in nursing. He had always been extremely clever but he seemed to excel at nursing. He worked at the Royal Brisbane Hospital once qualified, ironically, in the orthopaedic department where he had once been a patient himself.

He had a girlfriend he had gone to school with—Brandy. They ended up living together. Billy wanted to go and live and work in England, Brandy did not. She had a degree as a dental hygienist and it was quite difficult to transfer her skills in England. Whether it was just that or perhaps the fact that my son seemed to have fallen for someone else, but they went their separate ways.

As a mother, I have always found it extremely difficult when it comes to my children's partners. As a parent, we are expected to embrace the partners of our children with as much enthusiasm and zeal as our children feel themselves. I had no problem enveloping Brandy into our family at all. I loved her as if she was my own, she was a beautiful soul. But once the breakup occurs, we are again expected to side with our children and just drop those we have come to love. I personally had not anticipated the pain involved in this and it was a real trauma to suddenly not be able to have the same relationship with them as before. Indeed, to go from full on to nothing was extremely difficult for me.

Billy claimed he had met his soulmate in Janet. She was certainly very polite, educated but difficult to engage in a conversation. I set out to fulfil Billy's expectations of being the mother who could learn to love who he loved. Our common ground was nursing but it never really happened for Janet and I. She was very withdrawn, standoffish and so quiet, with me at least. She was always making special foods for me once I had been diagnosed with diabetes, and I do not think she ever fully understood just how appreciative I was of her efforts, which were way over and above. The thing that neither of them realised, although Billy should have remembered, was that I would sing Janet's praises to everyone but William would want to know what made me so special that I had particular foods made for me when he got nothing special.

Billy left to live in England in 2006. It was one of the most difficult days of my life saying goodbye to him and not knowing when I would see him again. We had put on a BBQ and had taken a million photos but when the time came to say goodbye and wave him and Janet off in the car, I was in bits. Again, I very much doubt that Billy has ever known how much I love him and how proud I am of him. I have always held him in the highest esteem and I had the utmost respect for him. I had also known that I was not, in the state I was in those days, quite good enough to be Billy's mum in his eyes and I certainly felt as if that was how Janet saw me too. My little "Fatman" was off to live in the big wide world and he had taken part of my soul with him.

Isabelle was a totally different kettle of fish but she and I somehow managed to get on extremely well despite the fact that we were polar opposites in almost everything in life. Isabelle has always had a rather wicked sense of humour, rather dry, unfortunately more like her father. Isabelle, also like him, has always called a spade a spade and one time, when Dad was eating a hamburger, she had told him, 'You are eating like a pig, Dad', and another time, she came out and told him, 'You are getting right up on my nerves, Dad.' She did not save this treatment only for Dad, although he was the most frequent recipient. My mother had come for a visit on one occasion and we had been enjoying afternoon tea, having a laugh, when Isabelle announced, 'It is time for you to go home now, Grandma, I think you have been here long enough!'

For whatever reason, and the total opposite is the case these days, but Isabelle also looked up to Billy as if he were a God. She would never allow herself to surpass his abilities and always kept herself in check. There were 15 months between them and Isabelle loved her big brother. I never truly understood why she acted the way she did towards Billy but, as stated, the leopard eventually showed his true spots and she did a complete 180.

Isabelle was a musician; her instrument was the euphonium. She was extraordinarily good and I spent many long hours travelling to musical performances and enjoying the respite from the normal grind of life. At one of these performances at Chandler, I had walked in and used the men's bathroom without even realising. Once Isabelle got to high school, she did rather well but she ended up being very much less than impressed when she had to use a very old euphonium hired from the school due to the fact that we could not afford to buy her an instrument of her own. Isabelle was stubborn, which she got from me, and eventually refused to continue with music. She, like her best friend at the time, would have ended up at the Conservatorium of Music. William had, or so he claimed, won a scholarship to the

Queensland Conservatorium of Music himself (exactly when was unknown) but had disliked having to play and learn the older styles of music and had given it up. William was a percussionist, a drummer and had played in a band when he had been younger.

Isabelle was very interested in childcare and started doing a Certificate II in childcare before she had finished year 12. Isabelle, like her mum, finished school on Friday and started work on the following Monday at a childcare centre opposite Garden City on Logan Road. Many promises had been made regarding on-going employment but as it turned out, all they had wanted was holiday cover and ended her employment in the New Year. I was livid for her.

Isabelle started a diploma in childcare at TAFE in Alexandra Hills soon after. She still has a few modules of that course that remain incomplete to this day but as one of the lowest paid careers to be in, Isabelle moved on. She worked in many different positions in many different places but has worked for the Queensland/Australian government now for well over a decade. Her skills are finely honed and very much appreciated in the workplace. I could not be prouder of my "Japanese Doll" for all that she has fought to achieve and I love her so dearly.

Poor Jasmine suffered a level IV intellectual disability that resulted in severe learning difficulties, for whatever reason—maybe because of the cord around her neck three times at birth or maybe when she had, as an infant, been upended out of the bassinet by Tracey in the bedroom she was sharing with her three older sisters. I knew in my heart, from the outset, that Jasmine needed extra help. For Christmas and birthdays, I always bought Jasmine educational toys and books. Preschool was not an issue despite me bringing my concerns to the teacher; I was told she was fine and they could not see any problem. Again, when Jasmine went to year 1, I voiced my concerns and was again told that I was seeing things that did not exist. When we moved to Sunnybank Hills and were forced to change the children's schools, the issues became very obvious.

From year two onwards for Jasmine, school also involved a lot of remedial assistance from extra teachers at school and also from me spending great amounts of time at the school with the teacher and Jasmine learning all the tricks they had in their arsenal to help the learning process and then at home with homework and everything in Jasmine's life in order to assist her. It became my life's mission to ensure that Jasmine would be able to cope in the world without me. It had been explained to me by the remedial teachers that the intellectual disability that Jasmine suffered from was hereditary. This was strongly demonstrated by William 's inability to spell, which was rather severe, and was an indication of a learning disability as a child. Jasmine, therefore, had inherited this disability from her father.

She was a beautiful child but learnt very quickly how to be blameless amidst such a large family. It was an art that dissatisfied all of her siblings greatly. It took many years for William to actually realise what Jasmine was truly like and things changed rather drastically for her after that.

Jasmine commenced a diploma in aged care at a nursing home in Mt Gravatt whilst still at school. This involved me driving her there and collecting her in the afternoons and also many meetings with both school and nursing home staff to set things up and follow-up sessions to check on Jasmine's progress. She was fantastic with the older generation and once shown how to do something excelled at it but it was the theory she would always struggle with. I did everything I could to assist her. Once she had finished year 12, she started working at a nursing home in Sunnybank Hills and attended Yeronga TAFE to complete a diploma in aged care. She was floundering and after many meetings and even more assistance from me, Jasmine had to let it go.

She worked in childcare at Yeronga for some time and also worked in a café at Macgregor. She has always managed to cope with whatever life has thrown at her. She is rather resilient even though she has trouble comprehending many things still. I have always given 150% to my gorgeous Babushka and she has always given her best to everything she has undertaken. My heart swells with pride at all the achievements my "Bush" has made in what has always been a difficult life for her.

Bianca also had some learning difficulties but not to the same extent as Jasmine. With Bianca, she could study 24/7 but when it came to exams, she had enormous trouble even passing. The poor girl's mind would just go a complete blank; the same thing had occurred with William, or so he said. Bianca never had the remedial assistance that Jasmine had received, which made it more difficult for her and also placed extra pressure on me to try and assist her to come to a comprehension of facts but also to try to find a way to assist Bianca to overcome her exam block.

Bianca had always been an extrovert and loved to perform. Her organisational skills were to be marvelled at. Her ability to organise her siblings for the performances that were performed for William and I were quite incredible and she definitely displayed leadership qualities rather early in life. One of Bianca's favourite forms of entertainment for William and I was to choreograph dances to songs she particularly loved. Billy Joel was a favourite, as was one particular version of the Three Little Bears. I had always felt that there was a special bond between Bianca and I from the start. We did seem, at least, to hold very similar beliefs, likes and dislikes. We also, as Bianca grew, shared a liking for the same music and many other things in life.

Bianca wanted to be a surgeon, that was all she dreamed about. I lived in fear that with her fear of exams, I may not be able to help her enough to make that dream a reality, but that would never stop me from trying. During her senior years at school, Bianca had two friends who were extremely clever and were also taking the time to assist her with study and strategies. When Bianca had completed year 12, she went to TAFE to complete a laboratory technician course. She hated it and was not coping at all. I tried to assist and advised that if she could complete this course and pass, she would then be able to gain entry into university and start her journey towards her desired career. She could not continue. Bianca undertook a course at the Mater Hospital in pathology collections. I was like a cat on a hot tin roof when the results of her exams were due. She had passed and passed well, over 80%. This was just the incentive Bianca had needed, to do it once and so well; she would now carve out her future. Bianca worked for the Mater from then on as a pathology collector and was accepted into Griffith University to do her nursing degree, which she successfully completed. I was fit to burst at her graduation ceremony, thinking of the incredibly hard road that Bianca had taken to get to this point in her life. It was all I could do not to burst into tears. Bianca had chosen paediatrics as her specialty and went on to work for the Mater Children's Hospital, followed by the Lady Cilento Children's Hospital.

Rosemary was a totally different kettle of fish from all of her siblings. She was almost a genius; she could read and do maths at the age of two. The afternoon-round-table homework bee was often assisted by Rosemary giving her older siblings the answers to their questions, and she was always right. She was, however, excessively hyperactive and a total nightmare to control, behaviour-wise. One of our doctors would literally freak out when Rosemary had an appointment. Poor old Nick, he would always be listening to you intently but his eyes were always on Rosemary and what she was getting into in his surgery room. She was recommended for assessment with a Dr Biggs at the Royal Children's Hospital when two. She had an EEG performed but she was refusing to show the doctor what she was capable of as we had dared to bring her here and put her through this trauma so the doctor did not get to see the real Rosemary, unfortunately. Despite this, he stated that, in his professional opinion, she could easily have completed year two at this stage. He recommended medications she was to take to calm her down. These did not last very long as they actually made her a good deal worse, she even tried with her tiny hands to strangle her father. I made the decision that there would be no medication, that Rosemary would be my burden to bear in life.

I did try different diets that were claimed to have a fantastic effect on lessening hyperactivity—they did not work. I was, at times, cooking three to four different types of food for just one meal. There would be the family meal, the special diet for Rosemary, the special diet for Mitchell's needs and then, if the evening meal was Chinese, I would also have to do something different for Billy who bluntly refused to eat Chinese food. Life was extremely difficult with Rosemary and sadly, it was set to stay that way.

When Rosemary started school, I fully informed the teachers of exactly what Rosemary was like but as parent/teacher interviews arrived, I was absolutely shocked to learn that they were not having any problems with her. She was so clever that she would have her work done in the blink of an eye so the teachers would have Rosemary doing extra jobs—taking messages to the office or anything else they could think of to keep her fully occupied. It seemed to be working, at least in the first few years. As Rosemary got older, she developed even more individual ideas and decided that she was not actually required to conform as every other person in society did. Her grades started to drop due to Rosemary's lack of interest in school. She was barely into high school when she decided that boys were far more interesting than schoolwork. Rosemary was a rule-breaker at school and at home. She would be truant from school as often as she was there. She had a boyfriend by the time she was 14, against family rules, and was having intimate relations with him, against the law. Despite ongoing meetings with the school to try and control her wayward behaviour, nothing worked. Rosemary would not be deterred by a mere rule or law, she would continue to do exactly as she wanted, and stuff the rest of the world. She finished year 12 with average marks when she could have been such a gifted student had she utilised her inbuilt abilities. Rosemary was always determined to get what she wanted and she worked for Hungry Jacks to save money to obtain those things. Even though I did not believe in "Schoolies Week", Rosemary told us that she was going and that there was nothing we could do to stop her. It was the story of her entire life really, nothing had changed.

She worked for an electricity provider, a very good position. She then went on to work for the Australian Taxation Office and has been there ever since. She has completed a degree since working there and is climbing the corporate ladder rather swiftly.

Mitchell was also extremely intelligent. It seemed that the universe had compensated Mitchell for his physical disabilities with a super intellect. He did it hard at school and was teased and bullied due to his disabilities and he did have a temper, which concerned me for a time. The teachers, however, felt that he coped admirably with things, given his restrictions. Mitchell was an achiever and tried to partake in every activity. He was unable to go to swimming lessons, however, and only got to experience a swimming pool at home but they were only small pools compared to the ones all the other children learned to swim in.

William and I were convinced that Mitchell would probably opt to have a colostomy eventually as his issues were quite severe, hampered enormously by his lactose/sucrose/fructose intolerance. He found it difficult to be on a diet totally different from not only his siblings but his peers at school, so there would be occasions when he would partake of the wrong food and pay a very expensive price for this dalliance into the unknown. All of my children, down to and including Mitchell, were also severe asthmatics. This was just another mountain for all to climb and for me to monitor and keep them all as well as possible.

Just before entering high school, I wanted Mitchell to be able to defend himself against any bullying that might occur as a "Vegemite", the nickname used to refer to those who have just started high school. I organised for Mitchell and Zach to have a free trial of Taekwondo to see if they liked it. Mitchell loved it, Zach hated it. Mitchell took to martial arts like a duck to water, he was an absolute natural. As William had dabbled in Kendo when younger, he decided that it should be he who went with Mitchell. I agreed in the beginning, although I equally had a sound knowledge of martial arts as my brother, Jonathon, was a black belt in Karate.

It most certainly boosted Mitchell's confidence, which was incredible, but as he had very few issues in high school, he flourished on both levels. He also succeeded with every grading that he completed. He also worked after school hours, first at Woolworths, then at Dick Smith's, followed by a restaurant on the north side of the river. Mitchell completed year 12 and went to Queensland University to study and successfully complete a degree in network engineering. He has since been working for data recovery companies and seems to enjoy this work. It is a testament to the determination of my beautiful "Action Jackson" that everything he has achieved and continues to achieve is with the extra impediment of being partially colour-blind. My heart skips a beat when I think of all that my boy has been through and yet is truly an honourable gentleman!

My little Noddy, Zach, was such a gorgeous little tyke. He was so shy; it was incredible just how quickly he could sense a stranger arriving at the house and even more amazing just how quickly he could disappear. He and Mitchell were a double act. I think Mitchell did the entertaining whilst Zach made his great escape in reality. Zach had latched onto Mitchell almost as the surrogate twin that he had lost. It was cute but there were so many things they could not do together due to the two-year difference in their ages. One thing they both did was climb into bed with me, every night. I was usually piggy in the middle. Not so great when one was wet or sick.

Zach would have been just as happy not to go to school at all. He was more than happy to be at home with William and I. I do think we made the mistake of sending him too soon as he really could have benefited from that extra year of maturity before starting the slog. Zach was never the most brilliant knife in the drawer but he was incredibly clever in his own way. He was very tall and very skinny and naturally loved basketball. "And 1" were his idols and all he dreamed of was playing one day. We bought a freestanding basketball hoop for him and he loved it. He was rather good, very skilled and agile.

As he entered high school, he started hanging with a group of young lads whose behaviour was not considered appropriate by the school. Zach seemed to be picked to get into trouble every time he turned around. He was so easy to spot amongst all of the students by being so tall, fair-skinned and red-haired. Talk about an easy target. I have no doubt that he was probably, at least sometimes, guilty of that for which he was accused but it seemed to be getting to the point of harassment in my opinion. So much so that I considered taking him out of the school when the CCTV surveillance could not tell the difference between a Sudanese student and Zach. Really, that had been the final straw for me. But to prevent Zach from totally giving up, we did not move him but would never use or recommend this high school again.

After completing and graduating year 12, Zach started a TAFE course at South Brisbane. He was not happy, was not doing well but again I tried to encourage him. Zach had been a rap singer/songwriter for several years at this stage and trusted the wrong people, who stole his work and let him down badly. I tried to encourage him but nothing seemed to help. Zach had worked at Hungry Jacks so that he could pay his way to Melbourne to see "And 1". Isabelle and her friend took him down. He no sooner returned than he stopped going to work and ended up getting the sack.

He eventually got a job working for a metal fabricating business and, although it was very early starts, he seemed to enjoy it and the independence it gave him. He was saving furiously in order to go to Thailand on a holiday with Clayton and his family. They went to Thailand but once they returned, Zach refused to go back to work and quit.

He was without employment for some time after that until he and his girlfriend, Charlie, went travelling and working around Australia. They travelled all over the country—New South Wales, Tasmania, Victoria, Sydney and others. He never seemed to have much money though and I was always so worried about him. He rocked up at home just before his 21st birthday. We put on a small party for him but he was after money to survive. I could not give him anywhere near what I would have loved to but I gave him all I could.

He and Charlie eventually settled back in Brisbane and Zach has had a series of employers since. He also completed a business course and has been back to Charlie's home in Taiwan several times and also sent Charlie to visit her parents on her own. They have now bought a brand-new car and a brand-new apartment. They seem to be doing really well and I am so very proud of my Noddy.

Last but by no means least, is Ben. It has been stated repeatedly since his birth that I left the best until last. This is so true in many ways. Ben could charm the birds from the trees and always has been able to. We had our difficult moments in his first year but since then, he has really not looked back.

Many of his siblings seem to consider that he was spoilt rotten and resent him for it. The thing is that whilst I may have made a conscious decision to spoil my last ever child, Ben has never had an expectation of being spoilt and he always showed an enormous amount of appreciation for whatever he did or received. All of my children were spoiled but choose to have incredibly short memories of the truth. That, however, is in no way Ben's fault.

I had always wanted to return to the workforce when Ben went to school but I was not well enough at that stage. Ben loved school and did extremely well. He, like all children, could be lazy and was not super keen on homework. His favourite place on earth was the Science Centre at the Queensland Museum. I have still not been there; Isabelle would be the one to take Ben all over the countryside. They were quite the team for many, many years. Ben's criterion for places to visit was always that he had to be able to learn something. When given the option of Dreamworld, Sea World or Movie World, he stated that the only one he could learn at was Sea World and that is where they went.

From when Ben had been very little, he wanted to be a pilot, a fighter pilot to be precise, and he wanted to fly an FIII. They would display their afterburners at the River Fire Festival every September and our home was in the direct flight path on their way to the Brisbane River so we would wait for them to fly over, then rush inside to see them on television. Ben went to Southbank on more than one occasion to watch it live. In the last year, the FIIIs were to fly before being retired even I went to see them.

Ben joined the Air Force Cadets at the age of 13. He did so well at the Cadets and absolutely loved the bivouacs. He loved the precision of the march-out parades and during classes even managed to correct a sergeant. I thought he would continue with the Cadets until he joined the Air Force or went to ADFA (Australian Defence Force Academy).

It came as a total shock to me when Ben told me that he did not want to continue with the Cadets. His love of music—he played both drums and the guitar—was taking over. Music was his life and all of his other subjects seemed to be suffering. He was also completing two school-based courses that took him off the school campus for two days a week. One was at Moreton TAFE for music and the other was at a steel fabrication factory just up the road from us.

Ben's world was totally blown apart whilst he was trying to complete year 12. More on the dramas that beset Ben and myself shortly.

You cannot bring Light to the Darkness;
You can only bring the Darkness to Light.

-MARIANNE WILLIAMSON

CHAPTER 19

THE GREATEST BETRAYAL

Throughout the years that I was a stepmother, I accepted the fact that I was a battering ram for Tracey's grief. As hard as I tried to be there for her, she had been too traumatised by her father and had never been allowed to grieve in the way that she had needed to grieve for her beloved mother, Angela, again due to her father's behaviour. It would not have mattered in any way who William had married; the outcome would have been the same. The mere fact that I had, in Tracey's eyes, stepped into the position that belonged to her mother and her mother only, whoever it was would have suffered the same fate that befell me. At least I can be comforted by the fact that I have saved someone else from enduring the sham of a marriage that I have and for that I am grateful as no one deserves the treatment that I have received. I do believe that my punishment has been greater due to the fact that I broke Tracey's rule of not having more children to her father than her mother did, by quite a long way. She was in so much pain that she needed to lash out at the person who was standing in a maternal position in her life—me. I would never give up trying to help her and living in hope that she would eventually come to terms with her loss and we could all move forward as a family unit. Tracey promised me that she would make me pay, one way or the other, and at that stage, I was certain that she actually believed what she was saying. I would always believe that she would grow up and find her own way in the world and perhaps even choose to find a way to get over her loss. A loss that had absolutely nothing to do with me.

My recommendation to William, which I truly believed as a nurse, was that both Tracey and Clayton required counselling in order to deal with their grief but this was always immediately rejected by William or fell on deaf ears. I did not feel it my place to go behind his back and seek help for them on my own so I was left with trying to go it alone. I had always observed how Tracey would tell Clayton all of her stories and she most certainly managed to get him rather stirred up, especially when she was in need of a fight and wanted Clayton to back her up. This happened rather frequently but never occurred when their father was at home, it only ever happened when he was at sea. Once William returned, he would always say that it was too late to worry about dealing with what events had occurred whilst he had been away. As a consequence of this attitude, Tracey and Clayton were, firstly, left to believe that their behaviour towards me was in no way wrong or unacceptable and secondly, that their grief over the loss of their mother was inconsequential to their father. Instead of taking her pain out on the person at fault—William —Tracey found it far more entertaining to take it out on me. Clayton was just a little puppy looking for love and followed whoever was rewarding him at any given time.

Clayton had been only nine when his mother had died. He had been incapable of fully understanding what had just happened in his life. He had always been a mummy's boy and was now left with no one except Tracey whose main aim in life was to make everyone else's life a misery. Clayton did not know if he was coming or going. He could not tell fact from fiction at that age and as he grew up with Tracey constantly ensuring that Clayton believed only her version of events and without the grief counselling that they both so desperately required, put together with the fact that Tracey was also a psuedologue (issues with the logic centre in her brain), both Clayton and Tracey have grown up believing that they are special and above any and all of my children but the worst thing of all is that Tracey has made absolutely certain that Clayton has grown up to believe total lies about his childhood, his father, his place in the world and especially me. It is the saddest thing when children are manipulated in such dreadful ways and Clayton was a classic case of this.

I had always believed that Clayton and I had had a reasonable relationship whilst he was growing up, with the exception of the period of time when he tried to sexually assault me but I tried not to allow that to overwhelm the rest of his teenage years. I had to find the fine line between always trying to be there for Clayton in ways that he may need and not allowing that to cross over into being too personal. I walked on eggshells most of the time.

When Tracey left home in 1984, Clayton seemed to come into his element being the eldest child at home. He took on the responsibility of being the man of the house and looking after his family. He had always been a great help to me with jobs and he loved his siblings, all of them. Of course, Tracey had wormed her way back into the family home in January 1985. She had failed to get her chosen outcome, had given up being in the big bad world and returned to try to control things from the inside, especially Clayton.

Tracey remained in our home for a year and when we moved to a new house in Holland Park, she moved in with a girlfriend. Again,

Clayton could take the mantle of the eldest child and he and the baby at that time, Bianca, became very close. He was the perfect son; he would wake me up with a coffee every morning and nothing was too much trouble for him.

Clayton decided, whilst his father was at sea of course, that he did not want to finish year 10 at school. It was only a couple of weeks until the exams started and he was piling the pressure on me to let him get a job. I tried saying that I would help him study for the exams, asked if he could wait until Dad was home from sea, but he was having none of it. He was convinced that he would not pass his exams and that there was no point in him being there. I finally agreed he could take one week off school to look for a job but if he did not get one, he would be back to school to complete the exams plus he had to clear it all with William.

Of course, he got a job almost immediately. William was happy enough for him to give up school. I was devastated for him after Tracey's antics regarding school; he was limiting his chances and opportunities in the long run. This did not seem to bother anyone but me so I had to let it drop. There were various jobs, taxation debts and times of no work when I would take him shopping and buy some basics so that he could survive as he no longer lived at home.

His girlfriend, Elise, was Tracey's friend, which only served to strengthen Tracey's hold over Clayton. Eventually, Clayton decided on joining the army. The period of time when Elise lived with us has already been documented but we had only just moved to Sunnybank Hills in October 1991 with a brand new baby when Clayton advised us that he and Elise were getting married in November. As the relationship with her parents was strained, the small reception fell to William and I. My sister-in-law had her mother make the cake, which was lovely. It had all been too much in way too short a time period with the baby, moving house, the wedding and then Christmas.

Clayton seemed finally to have grown up somewhat and also seemed to enjoy the army. Elise, on the other hand, was a pain in the rear. She eventually ended that marriage, but only after Clayton had fully paid for her university degree, had bought a block of land together and built a two-storey home on it in Jimboomba. She seemed to be constantly either at our house, on the phone with me or requesting my presence at their married quarters because she had heard something or believed someone was breaking in through the roof. She was incredulously difficult to deal with and had to be the centre of attention at all times. She claimed she could no longer live with what William had done to her. It must have been so traumatic when, for the ensuing years, she could not stay away from him or me. She claimed William had gone to a flat she and Clayton had before they married and that he had tried to seduce her again. I had dropped William off at the flat for the purpose of him completing some job she had requested that he do for her.

She faked an epileptic seizure after her first day at a new job in an extremely confined space in front of my children. The ambulance had been called and Clayton had gone with her. Apparently, they pulled in at the kerb further down the road and told her that she could stop the act now and open her eyes. I was the mug that had to take her to the specialist appointments. All she really achieved was to be unable to drive for two years. She blamed Tracey for causing her to have a possible miscarriage, more than likely just heavy periods. When she ended the marriage, we had not seen Clayton for some time. It was mid-1999 and I was shopping at Sunnybank Plaza when I ran into Clayton. He asked if we could sit down and have a coffee. He told me the whole sordid tale; again, I had been kept in the dark regarding all of it. How could I ever help people if they treated me like a mushroom?

I had to get home as William had an appointment at Princess Alexandra Hospital that afternoon, and didn't he cop it with both barrels all the way there. William did not deny having a pornographic movie on the television whilst I was in Toowoomba in January 1990, but he vehemently denied any wrongdoing on his part other than asking Elise to watch it with him. Was he mad? This was his son's 18-year-old girlfriend and I had not been present in the family home. It had also been almost exactly six weeks since William had heard, according to him for the very first time, about the accusation that Tracey had made against him of sexual assault. Why would any sane man enter into such behaviour? I had blamed the accusation from Tracey as being the reason he had started arguing with me from that moment on for no logical reason. It now seemed that assumption had been totally wrong or he would never have done quintessentially the exact same thing again so soon after. I was at a total loss as to the cause of my husband's apparent loathing of me for an action that he, himself, had been accused of and now to know that he had attempted to do the exact same thing only six weeks later. I was reeling, there was no one I could confide in, I no longer had the husband I had married and longed to get him back. It was beginning to dawn on me that the husband I had been dumped with since that December night in 1990 was in fact the real man and that he had fooled me up until that point in our marriage.

What I had also learned from Clayton that day was that he and his dad had walked to the corner shop about a week after the incident with Elise, and Clayton had confronted him about it. He had not denied anything about it but had put the blame onto the 18-year-old rather than himself, at that time, 49. Had he really believed his own lies? I also then remembered that when we had told Clayton of Tracey's accusation of her father, he had stated he had known all along that dad had done this to her. And yet I was never allowed in on this massive secret by anyone. This changed all of my views of Clayton from then on. What else had I not been told, what else was he hiding?

After this time, Clayton started to call in every night after work for his dinner before heading to his new home alone. Clayton has always been a huge eater and waits on the younger children to leave some of their dinner so he can swoop in like a vulture to clean the carcass. He, at no time, offered to help pay for all the food he was consuming, not to mention coffee. We had finished raising him; he had left home and needed to pay his own way.

Finally, William had asked him to contribute $30 per week towards the food he was consuming. We had both considered this to be extremely reasonable. It had been New Year's Eve, 1999, and we had been having a small party whilst Clayton sat on the couch pouting and sulking like a toddler for the entire proceeding. Nothing had changed from the eight-year-old Clayton that I had first met but then Tracey had made certain of that in order to achieve her own ends.

Clayton had to eventually surrender the house as he could not afford the mortgage repayments on his own. He lived with my brother for a while but Jonathon found it exceptionally difficult to live with such a tight wad. Eventually, Clayton decided to go to Thailand for a holiday. He enjoyed his time there and, of course, found a girlfriend. When he returned home, he was unsettled. All he wanted to do was go back to Thailand. He had his girlfriend, Agnes, come to Australia for a visit but she had to return. Jonathon had been astonished that Clayton had made her eat Aussie food like sausages and mashed potatoes, baked beans and sundry other delights that she found very difficult to eat.

Eventually, Clayton decided he was moving to Thailand to be with Agnes. On her visit to Australia, she had left her two children with her sister. Whilst she was here, her ex-husband had taken the children to live with him and refused to allow Agnes to take them back except for visits. Clayton initially worked teaching English but eventually got an administrative job in a hospital. He seemed happier than he had been here but he had walked out of Australia leaving a debt for his portion that remained after the repossession and sale of his house. We had been instructed to always return the mail to the Bendigo Bank with "Not known at this address" written on the front of the envelope. This went against everything I stood for. He had signed a contract with them for a house mortgage and Elise had repaid her outstanding half promptly. Clayton decided that such rules did not apply to him. I did as I was asked, reluctantly.

Clayton and Agnes had a daughter together, Rhianna. She was quite famous as her mostly white skin was prized in Thailand and she was in magazine ads. Clayton, Agnes and Rhianna came to Australia for a holiday when she had been two years old. They stayed with us. Rhianna did not take to us easily and William did not make much of an effort to get to know her. Clayton chose to come to me, not his father, to ask why Dad was not making a bigger effort with Rhianna. 'After all,' he said, 'Rhianna is his first real grandchild.' I was devastated at this statement but I chose not to say anything that would ruin their two-week holiday.

After they had returned to Thailand, I told William and the other children. William made out that he was furious but never, ever mentioned it to Clayton. As William had adopted Brianna, this made her legally his rightful daughter and Steve and Ebony his rightful first grandchildren. It was a real stab in the heart to me, which it was meant to be as I was adopted and had spent my life never being good enough. The hypocrite that Clayton was, however, expected me to fully accept him as a son and insisted that I refer to him as my eldest son (which he was not) and also expected me to take on the role of being grandmother to Rhianna when, by his rules, she had nothing to do with me in any way. I adored her and immediately and proudly announced to everyone that she was my granddaughter. He tried insisting that Rhianna would call William and I by the Thai words for grandparents, Yai and Da. This fell flat as, when Rhianna was a little older and they returned to Australia to live, she herself decided that I was Mumma and William was Dadda, which were the names Steve had given us, and I loved it.

Living in Thailand had changed Clayton, very much for the worse. He wanted everything on a silver plate, as usual. I had made it quite clear that they would not be able to stay with us long term whilst they got back on their feet. Brianna was the first and only sibling to put her hand up, despite the shit she had been handed by Clayton since she was two. Clayton had caused her to have the worst case of dermatitis she had ever had by using the cheapest washing powder he could in her washing machine. After staying in her public housing unit with Brianna, Ebony and Steve for four months without paying any rent whatsoever to the government, due after the first month, and paying no board to Brianna, Clayton thought he had been wonderful by handing her $40 for the entirety of the stay for two adults and one child. You wouldn't read about it and to think that he actually believed that was okay…total bottom feeder.

Clayton considered that we were free childminders as well. He never actually asked if I minded looking after Rhianna whilst he did what he wanted to do, go for a run, do something with his brothers. It was just assumed by him that it was okay. Well, actually it wasn't. Apart from complete honesty, I demanded good manners and Clayton would not know what they were if they flew up and bit him on the bollocks. It annoyed the life out of me that you could not turn around without Clayton being there. He collected Rhianna from school every afternoon and came straight to our place. If Agnes was working on the weekend, he would roll up each day and if he felt like a run or going to the shops, he would say to Rhianna, 'You stay here.' Never once was there a 'Would you mind watching Rhianna for me, Mum?'

He had my own son Zach recording conversations I had with William about how angry I was with how Clayton was treating us. I had no sooner finished talking to William one afternoon when Clayton rocked up at the house, for the second time in the same day. I was livid when I discovered that, as he had been instructed to do by Clayton, Zach had let him know what I had said, chapter and verse. My rights in my own home and my privacy and freedom of speech had been totally violated. I went to my room and locked the door. Clayton kept trying, way too hard in my opinion, to prove that I was wrong about him and that he was fantastic.

Why did he need to keep such a close eye on everything I did, what I felt, what I knew? It was becoming sickening to be so closely monitored. It was beginning to seem like the apples did not fall too far from the trees in this family. Clayton was becoming way too voyeuristic about my life. I was losing trust in him. He was always off having secret conversations with Dad and/or his siblings—according to the Rules by Clayton, half siblings—especially when we had family gatherings. There had been a Mother's Day event where Agnes had written a load of Thai writing in my card. She explained what it translated to; as she did not have a mother, she asked if she could have the honour of having me be her real mum. It was an honour and a privilege, as to me, family was not only blood but all of those who loved each other, supported each other and were there when times were tough—they were the real family.

There had been an occasion when Clayton, Agnes, Rhianna and Zach were going to Thailand for a holiday. They were calling to collect Zach and it had been extremely obvious that Clayton was in a feral mood and gunning for someone. It made no sense to me as they should have been happy to be heading off on a holiday. Clayton exploded and started abusing William. I took Agnes and Rhianna out the front and hugged them as they sobbed. Agnes kept repeating that she had begged him not to do this. Brianna was inside and Clayton was having a go at her too. Mitchell and his girlfriend made a hasty exit. Clayton was about to leap over the kitchen counter to punch Brianna but we all made sure it stopped there. To this day, I still have absolutely no idea what that disgustingly immature and uncontrollable display of the worst behaviour I have seen was about. And what made matters worse was that on their return, there was no apology from Clayton and no consequences to him from his father. It truly did not matter what he did, he was always going to be given a free pass unlike the rest of his half siblings, but that is for another chapter.

In the ensuing years, Agnes would talk to me more and more about Clayton's appalling behaviour and how she could not handle it. I tried to explain to her that he was becoming more and more like his father, which was not a good thing—far from it. I felt so sorry for her but also felt helpless in giving any usable advice except that she needed to get out whilst she was still sane, a barrier I was certain that I had crossed many years earlier. What Clayton wanted, Clayton would get or he would use his temper to ensure that he did.

As already stated, reconciliation with Jack occurred when he and his girlfriend, Heidi, had a son, Tomas. Whilst travelling to Nambour

Hospital to meet what I definitely considered to be "our grandson", Agnes made a grave error in judgment, in my opinion. She stated to William that Rhianna was his oldest granddaughter and that Tomas was his eldest grandson. That cut me very deeply as, apart from the fact that: 1. Steve and Ebony are our eldest grandchildren, 2. Agnes had asked that I be her mum, a role I took very seriously and 3. Jasmine and her husband, Richard, had had two children by then, Ashley born in 2008 and Emily born in 2010. They were the grandchildren of both William and I and even by the Rules of Clayton are entitled to full status as grandchildren. And it was now 2013, so there was no confusion over ages. What I knew in my heart was what Tracey had stated to me over and over all those years before. That **no** children of mine would ever count, only children of her mother to her father would count. Clayton had not only been thoroughly brainwashed by Tracey but now I knew that he and Tracey had brainwashed Agnes as well. All the while, the men were in the front seat of the car, Agnes and I were in the back; William sat silently, never once bringing up OUR four grandchildren. That had been a real AHA moment for me.

Clayton had always felt entitled to privileges that were completely and totally unreasonable and had assumed he would get them, especially given our family circumstances. It did, however, confirm that his view was that he was the only "important" member of our family left and as such was due entitlements. He believed that Dad and I should have given him $20,000-$30,000 to start him off in life. Why should he not have this when all of his mates' parents did this for them? He would tell all and sundry about this "right" he considered he was entitled to. When quizzed as to where he expected the money to come from, he was suddenly blank. In my eyes, if his father had not given up when he was told he could never go to sea again and had found a way, on land and out of air-conditioning, then whatever

Clayton received would automatically entitle everyone else to exactly the same sum of money. This would be a large amount for pensioners to produce, at the least $300,000 for all those who were at home, then of course, the same sum would need to be allocated for Tracey and Jack. Clayton never once considered his half siblings in his equations. Tracey was no longer a part of the family and the reconciliation with Jack had not yet taken place so yet another AHA moment! Only the children of his mother to his father were actually entitled to this money and as he was the only one in the fold, Clayton expected to get his entitlement and be the only one to do so.

He did, however, forget the Rule of Clayton and the Rule of Tracey when he wanted to have a dig at me. I did not treat him the same as I treated all of my other children. I had always showed them much greater amounts of physical affection; I just always treated him differently from the way I treated my own children. For God's sake, what did he want from me? Did he actually want me to remind him that he had tried to sexually assault me when he had been a teenager and I still in my 20s? Did he want me to say that I felt comfortable in the arms of my own children as they had never betrayed me in the way that he had? Did he want me to say that I was actually entitled to call Billy "My eldest son" and when I referred to Clayton whilst speaking to people, I always referred to him as "Our eldest son"? But this was not enough; he still wanted to be Mummy's boy in a situation where it was no longer a possible reality. Clayton had always wanted his cake and wanted to eat it too. And as William had allowed the children of Angela to get away with every wrongdoing they had ever committed, Clayton truly believed he had these rights and badgered me to give them to him.

He, like Tracey, must have told a good tale as he endeavoured to ensure that my children, apart from Brianna, were persuaded to see his world from his point of view. The advent of Facebook was a marvellous technological advancement but it also created a forum for all the nasties in the world to trick and manipulate people. Tracey had found her way in to start what she was desperate to complete, my destruction. She sent friend requests to her "half siblings". Of course, Rosemary and Jasmine fell for it straight off. They were reeled into her world of suffering like lambs to the slaughter. Others followed. Tracey also had her cousin, Beverly, befriend my children. Beverly knew nothing of me other than that her mother had had an affair with my husband whilst he had been in England in 1984 and I had been at home in Australia, heavily pregnant with Jasmine. Tracey knew my Achilles' Heel—my beautiful children—and set about destroying that bond. With Clayton as her underling and the one with face-to-face contact, how could they possibly fail to complete their objective?

*We are never so defenceless against
suffering as when we love.*

-SIGMUND FREUD

CHAPTER 20

DEATH BY MEDICINE

It has now and always been my most fervent belief that my life's purpose was to care for other people. I was barely able to understand the world when I had decided what I wanted my life to be. I wanted to be a nurse, I wanted to travel to Canada and I wanted to have 12 children. I fulfilled my need to care for people by starting to babysit from the tender young age of eight. Very much under my mother's supervision. Babysitting continued as I grew up and became a paid job for me. I used to babysit the children of James McSweeney and his wife when I was a teenager. James was a famous country and western musician in Australia.

I attended private schools and it was whilst I was completing year 10 that the Baillie Henderson Hospital staff went on strike in Toowoomba. Baillie Henderson was a mental institution and the private school students had been requested to come and help with the care of their patients. It was a truly amazing experience and cemented my goal to become a nurse.

To me, people are the most precious commodity this universe has and all deserve to be treated fairly, equally and with the greatest of respect. I had been informed by the charge nurse in a private ward when I first started there that these were private patients and were to be treated specially and with extra care. I got into a lot of bother by informing this nurse that I only had one standard of care across the board, the very best I could offer, I gave to all of my patients, regardless of their ability to pay for a service. To do anything less would make me less than human and I would have no right to be a nurse.

My beloved nursing served me well for the greater part until it was forcibly taken from me, but there were a few bug bears that would always serve to get my blood boiling. One was the total and complete incompetence in the efficiency of any and all outpatient clinics/antenatal clinics. Blind Freddie could organise these clinics better than I have ever seen one run since I started nursing in 1974. There were other niggles I had but by far the greatest and most obvious issue with medicine was the inability of doctors to look for the cause of an issue unless it hospitalised a patient and even then, was only taken to the point where a patient could be prescribed a medication and discharged until the next issue arose.

The first, last and only solution offered was to take a pill to control the symptomology without ever having correctly diagnosed why these symptoms developed in the first place. This, of course, was exactly how the pharmaceutical companies liked the system to work. After all, they were making billions of dollars off the backs of the illnesses of the general public. Why would the world need to know that cancer has been curable for a long, long time when there is so much money for them to make? Why would they not ban hemp when it can literally save the world, being used for everything from clothing to fuel? Ah, there it is, the magic word—fuel. If our cars could run on hemp, what would become of all the oil tycoons and the so-called super powers whose economy would go absolutely bust without an oil monopoly?

Sermon complete, for now, I have moved away from the point. The lack of investigation into the cause for diseases in my life has caused me enormous amounts of completely and totally unnecessary pain and hardship. As a child, I suspect my health was reasonable. I had a tonsillectomy at seven years of age, I had two plantar warts removed from my right heel at 10 years of age, I dislocated my patella at almost 12 years of age, I fractured my skull at 16 years of age and I had a laparotomy/appendicectomy at 18 years of age. The constants in my life were shocking headaches for as long as I have a memory and I always suffered from allergies and severe hay fever.

I have to wonder now if the severe headaches of my childhood and my outbursts of temper were not due to the excessive amounts of trauma caused by my mother and sister. With no one to confide in and being unable to understand why Mum and Emma treated me with so much disdain and yet wanted everything in return from me, I was constantly stressed, and with always having been put down by them both, I had never truly felt that I was ever going to be able to succeed at anything. But once I started nursing training, I knew I had found my true home. I had a purpose and I was good at caring for people. It was the only time since I could remember that I was truly happy, a feeling that I had never experienced before. The only other time I felt this happy was after the birth of each of my beautiful children. The alone time we had when William was too busy to visit me was the happiest I have been in my life. I so wish that I had been able to share that time with my dad; it was always my greatest wish to make Dad a granddad.

I remained reasonably well until I got married. The stresses of marriage showed themselves rather quickly due to the constant demands placed on me by William. Had he been prepared to meet me halfway with childcare, housework and washing, etc., I may well not have become so physically drained as quickly as I did. Having to also deal with children's services and a lying Tracey forced the stress levels through the roof. All my GP could say was, 'Mary is a rock; you can't break her.'

Having developed viral polyarthritis in 1982 and taking anti-inflammatories of varying kinds from then on was only the beginning. By 1985, I had chronic fatigue syndrome and in 1987 after the birth of Rosemary, I suddenly started having the heaviest periods of my life and the most excruciating pain. They would last for 10-14 days and I would often not get two weeks off before it would start all over again. For a great deal of this time, I could only leave the house for short amounts of time or I would haemorrhage everywhere. My GP did no investigations whatsoever. He offered me the mini pill, which did not make even the slightest difference. Eventually, at my request, I was referred to a gynaecologist who suggested I have a procedure called an ablation, which may or may not have an effect on the extremely heavy bleeding. It may also have made matters worse. I elected not to have the surgery. This continued until I had finished going through menopause in 2010. I was, of course, totally iron-deficient and due to my familial severe allergy to iron supplements of any and all kinds, my only hope was to eat tons of orange and green vegetables, which was no problem as vegetables are my favourite food and always have been and I found that they made me feel much better than red meat did in terms of absolute exhaustion.

The next major issue had come about whilst I had been pregnant with Zach. After having lost his twin early in the pregnancy and being under enormous stress from firstly, Tracey's accusation of sexual abuse against William, secondly, his abusive treatment to me after having confronted Tracey about her accusation and thirdly, his absolute refusal to allow me to clear "my husband's" name in a court of law, I started to experience heart palpitations. They were frightening and I was concerned that I was indeed under too much stress and may not be around for my children for too much longer. Again, I went to the GP. 'We will just monitor them whilst you are pregnant, they may well cease after the baby is delivered.'

Well, they did not and I returned to the doctor who started me on Digoxin 62.5mcg per day. Digoxin is an old people's pill and I was reluctant to take it but as that was all I was offered—no referral to a cardiologist for an actual diagnosis—I had to take them. I was then, only 34 years old. One Digoxin did not work and it was increased to two, then three, then four, at which point I was changed over to Digoxin 250mcg per day, still no referral to a cardiologist. I ended up taking Digoxin 250mcg + Digoxin 62.5mcg per day and that has remained constant until this very day.

I did get referred eventually to a cardiologist who had me wear a halter for 24 hours but the results were inconclusive and he told me to continue the same regime. So, the working theory was that I had atrial fibrillation but that has never actually been proved. Nonetheless, I had taken Vitamin E for 18 years and changed over to taking one aspirin tablet per day in an effort to prevent a stroke or myocardial infarction. I was suffering from severe gastro-oesophageal reflux and getting through tons of Mylanta. I was eventually put onto Somac, which I took every day.

After my youngest son was born, the deterioration of my health seemed to happen thick and fast. I had, for the first 44 years of my life, been hypotensive—always hovering around 110/70. Within six months of turning 44, I was hypertensive and placed on medication by the name of Karvezide, which also contained a diuretic. It was driving me mad with having to visit the toilet so frequently so he changed it to Karvea without the diuretic, which was rather short-lived as the blood pressure crept back up; again, there were no investigations as to the cause, just another pill to add to the growing regime.

My home life was horrendously stressful and getting worse. I so needed a break from William and the control he had over my every move. Even when I was out, if he considered that I was taking too long, he would call me on the mobile wanting chapter and verse of where I was and what I was doing but more importantly, when I was expected to be home as there was this to be done or that to be done. My life was not my own. I had no say about the things I did, the clothes I wore. My briefs were arranged by William in my drawers in the order that I was expected to wear them. If I broke his order, he would be onto me immediately as to why I was not doing as I was told. I had grown so very tired of him insisting that I went to bed either completely naked or, at the very least, have no undergarments on (winter or summer) and to lie on a certain side to give him easy access to masturbate at some ridiculous hour in the early morning all over my buttocks. Many times, that was not enough and he would start touching me and would forcibly ensure that I climaxed and I would then be responsible to ensure that he did as well. I had several nighties that had buttons in the front. There was no need for them to be undone as they went easily over my head but William ensured that he undid all of the buttons and then, once I was lying in bed, he insisted that my breasts be pulled out and remain exposed for his viewing pleasure whilst I slept. The sides of the nightie would be cutting into my breasts causing me a huge amount of pain but that was less than the wrath of William if I dared to attire myself comfortably. I got to the point that I could take no more so I sat at the sewing machine and sewed all the openings together. I also learned to buy pyjamas that did not have buttons in the front. None of these activities were ever with my consent but I had done as expected so I could be left in peace to return to sleep. This was a nightly ritual. He could care less about my health and my need for rest.

My mother died in 1999 on her 75th birthday. Because her death entailed arrangements being made for her return to Toowoomba from Ipswich and going to the funeral directors in Toowoomba and the church to organise the funeral plus ensuring that we all had suitable attire for the funeral, calling relatives and requesting they take part in the mass itself by doing readings etc, the six days between Mum's death and her funeral were some of the busiest of my life. William actually seemed to be acting almost like a normal human until the weekend after the funeral when he announced that it was now time for me to satisfy his needs as he had been so understanding all week and I owed him so much. I really could not believe his audacity. Did he want praise for actually looking after his own children or was it that he actually went to the funeral and did not start an argument with anyone, especially me? He was like a very small-minded little boy who had behaved in the lolly shop and now wanted his reward, it sickened me so much.

I was trying, for the umpteenth time, to offer the olive branch to my sister but, as always, she was having none of it. She had to keep up the lies about me in order to get the sympathy vote from Jonathon, who was busy sitting on the fence getting splinters in his bollocks. I always wondered about the extent of the lies Emma told that Jonathon never once made comment other than that he was sitting on the fence and that Emma claimed I had an issue with her. Even when I told Jonathon that this was not true, he refused to listen. Aunty Shirley had told him, at my home, what a bitch Emma had been about him and the lies she had told their family about him. It seemed Emma must really have had a vice on his more personal body parts or she had something criminal on him apart from his marijuana usage and he had to do as she said, because there was absolutely no other logical reason why an adult male, seemingly intelligent, would fall for so many lies. Mum finally woke up from the spell that Emma had held her in. Emma would never know what it was that Mum told me in the weeks and days before her death. The tides had turned as Mum had discovered the truth, as everyone approaching their own death did—they awoke to full consciousness. She chose to tell me the truth. Too little, too late, for Mum and I but it gave her peace in her final days and hours. And the fact that, even though she had wasted 42 years of my life believing lies and untruths, she went to her grave having fully vindicated me. Small comfort after a life full of trauma though. As my psychologist now states, the trauma caused by my mother was incredulous and it could take years just to scratch the surface of the damage it caused. It was my trauma at the hands of Mum that caused me to have OCD. This has been a curse to me and my children alike as they could never attain the standards that I set for myself. Even Mum, on one visit, said, 'You will never find dust under any of Ellie's furniture as it is moved and cleaned too often, unlike my other children.' She also stated that she had caused this to be the case as she had made me do everything whilst growing up and Jonathon and Emma had done nothing and as adults did not have a clue how to keep anything clean.

My health continued to deteriorate without any real cause, as far as I could see, apart from the totally unreasonable expectations of my husband. Of course, having so many children, there were day-to-day stresses with schools, health, finances, etc. but I loved every single second of being a mum and considered any hiccups as par for the course of being a parent.

William was very much not par for the course, he rarely left me alone. The exact moment the front gate would close on the last child leaving the house on any given day, William immediately wanted sex. It did not matter what time of day it was, what I needed to get done for that day, absolutely nothing came before William and his penis. If the sex had actually been exciting, it might have been okay. But when you are expected to complete an "exercise in pain endurance" every single time, and the sex itself was very much less than satisfactory, repetitive and boring, involving being forced into positions my body could no longer take, being blamed if he did not have the desired outcome when it was, in fact, he who would do everything in his power to prevent a climax until he had caused maximum pain to me, it was, by this stage in our marriage, just all too much. But William would take his frustrations out on my children if I did not provide what he wanted. I could not even count the number of times I agreed to be his prostitute in an effort to try and save my children from being upset or physically hurt. I have learned in recent years that this, by law, is called sexual servitude. Sounds horribly similar to prostitution in my book.

I developed irritable bowel syndrome, again a stress-related condition and an extremely painful one when you have a full-blown attack. These always occurred after particularly stressful occasions, arguments or William just being William. I finally made the decision, at age 50, to return to full-time work. I first succeeded in gaining employment at the Australian Taxation Office, a position that did not suit me. My daughter, Rosemary, already worked there and tried her best to help me but I was suffering from severe palpitations, dizziness and migraines and decided it was not for me. Rosemary went on to bigger and better things at the ATO and is still there today. Mitchell also spent a period of time working at the ATO until he finished university.

I applied for and got a job as a call centre operator at a computer repair company who only had one office but had hundreds of agents (technicians) throughout Australia, New Zealand and some of the islands around Australia. It seemed very straightforward but again the IBS was causing me issues. I found out very much later that William and one of the children had bets on how long I would last at this job, one had said two weeks and the other, two months. When I started, I was not certain it would be two days. The boss, James, was as narcissistic as William and the decision I had to make was whether I could work with one <u>and</u> live with one. There had been three new staff members employed, I was one, and there were also Matt and Julie. The second in charge, Martha, had been on holidays in her native New Zealand and returned the following week. James announced that it was "Curry Lunch", which the company paid for and all were expected to partake. I ate the mildest food that I could see and still had the worst oesophageal reflux all afternoon—what a nightmare! It took less than a week to realise that James was also a bully. I had only worked there for one month when James announced that he had found better premises just up the road and we were moving. He needed to have the current office repainted and I offered him the information for my son-in-law's company as he was a master painter. They got and completed the job and the staff were the packers, cleaners and general dogsbodies. Matt left the day we moved in, 31 August 2007.

I struggled to work full time and maintain the house on weekends. William had become the cook; very proudly, he would have dinner ready when I returned from work. It was typical English food, way too much gravy and way too many carbs involved, causing me to consume way too much Mylanta just to maintain an equilibrium. My weekends were spent cleaning, washing, ironing and anything else that was required at any given time. I was absolutely exhausted by Sunday evening and had to start another full week of work the next morning. This cycle was not helping my health. I used to run up the stairs at work in the mornings but it was becoming more of a drag myself up as time went on.

Just before Easter of 2008, I developed a UTI. This was completely and solely due to William's filthy dirty hands and the places they ventured when we had sex. He was well known by our children for leaving them infected every single time he would accidentally scratch them with his sharp nails. This infection had started on Saturday evening but I just kept taking paracetamol for the pain and carried on with household duties. I had gone to the doctor on Monday afternoon after work and he had prescribed a brand-new treatment for UTI, which I started immediately. By Wednesday evening, I knew something was very wrong. I went to walk down the hallway to go to the toilet and collapsed onto the floor and fainted, banging the side of my head, unbeknownst to me at the time. My son, Billy, had been called apparently. All I wanted to do was go to bed and sleep. They insisted on taking me to the hospital where I had an IV inserted and they gave me IV Gentamycin, which seemed, in the next few hours, to work a miracle. I felt almost normal. They had sent off urine to the laboratory but the results would not be back in a hurry. They allowed me to go home and advised I was to continue with the medication prescribed by my GP.

It was the following day that I found the lump on my head from the fall of the previous evening. Over the next two days, I seemed to be getting worse. My GP called to say that not only was my UTI not susceptible to this new wonder drug, it appeared that I may actually be allergic to it. I was then put on another antibiotic and off work for a good while. My doctor told me that I had come within a hair's breadth of developing septicaemia! I knew how sick I felt but all of this because my husband was a filthy bugger and bizarre sexual dominant.

Whilst I had been away, our team leader, Curtis, had left to go and live in New Zealand. I had missed saying goodbye to him. Brett, a young guy who had been employed a few months after me, took over his role. I was still far from returned to normal when I went back to work and when I needed to go to the toilet, I had to go immediately. I was working the late shift, 17:30 finish, and it was incredibly busy. I got up to run to the toilet as quickly as I could when James demanded to know what I thought I was doing. I explained that I would be as quick as possible but he refused to allow me to go at all. It was only him and myself left in the office at that time of the day. My doctor was very much less than impressed by the actions my boss had taken and how it had affected me.

It was during the period of 2007-8 that my doctor put me on antidepressants. I vehemently objected as I did not believe I was depressed but rather that I was under way too much stress. Either way, he insisted that I take Lexapro and there would be an improvement in the way I felt, especially as my boss was blatantly a narcissistic bully. On another occasion, later that year, a lady had come into the front office asking for directions to the Centrelink office in South Brisbane. I did not personally know but Brett did and set about offering assistance as I went to look on Google Maps in order to help this lady out. Again, I was the only female member of staff in the office and James chose this occasion to beat his chest, bully me into submission and prove what an absolute arsehole he truly was. The woman was still there when James started shouting and demanding to know what she wanted, why were we not just getting rid of her, this was *his office*, he said and 'what I say goes'. I lost what very little respect I had for him that day. When I told Martha the story, she told me about several occasions on which James had done the exact same thing to her in the past.

I wanted out but was too much in need of the stingy wage that this job gave me. I tried to tolerate the narcissists in my life and was failing miserably. I was becoming more and more stressed and yes, probably more and more depressed. My health was just going downhill fast. By this time, I had long since been diagnosed with Hashimoto's disease, osteoarthritis, heart arrhythmia, hypertension, oesophageal reflux, irritable bowel disease, depression plus the conditions I was gifted at birth with—scoliosis, a malformed patella, which caused my knee to dislocate, sciatica, which I had suffered since the day I fractured my sacrum when 21 weeks pregnant with Mitchell, psoriasis, bilateral carpel tunnel syndrome, calciferous tendonitis of both shoulders, bilateral focal ulna neuropathy of the elbows and bilateral De Quervain's tenosynovitis and bilateral tennis elbows. The list was continuing to grow and so was I. Obesity was very quickly becoming a major issue.

When I was 22 and completing my midwifery training in Brisbane, the period of time that Brianna and Emma were both in Brisbane, although excruciatingly stressful, had also been wonderful as I saw my beautiful baby girl every day and was able to take her out and about on time off. It had been a great time. But once I became surplus to Emma's requirements and she returned with Mum and Brianna to Toowoomba again, I had been devastated, I had felt so totally alone and empty. All I had been surviving on were coffee and cigarettes with a salad at night; I was putting on weight. A doctor in Coorparoo had been recommended to me as I did not have a clue about anyone in Brisbane at that time. I went to see him and explained my problem, all about my life and my daughter and he looked at me and said, 'You could do nothing but inhale fresh air and you would still put on weight! Until you are happy, this will be an ongoing issue for you.'

I thought he was a nutcase and asked which cereal box he had found his medical degree in. But as God is my witness, no one has ever since spoken the truth to me more clearly in my life. The number of times since that day in 1979 has that doctor been proven right! If only I had truly taken his advice on board, I may have made better decisions in my life and things may well have been different. Morbid obesity is still an issue to this day.

I was on Lexapro for a good while and thought I was fine so insisted that I come off them. It did not help that I had a husband who considered that I was totally incapable of ever being as sick as he was, based on the one and only fact that he was older than me. The more medications I had to take in his eyes was implying that I was worse than him and he would never have that, so why did I need so many pills when I was fine. He was the sick one. Ironically, one of my daughters also made me feel guilty for taking so many pills. Every time I was off to the doctor, especially if it was a new issue, she would say 'no more pills'. She was very big on polypharmacy. I was torn between trying to be the healthiest I could be and staying sane in two worlds that were mega stressful for me. So many times, I thought that I would just explode, literally. Throughout my full-time work, William 's sexual demands never once diminished, considering he "was so sick". I found it a miracle he had the strength but then sex was the one and only thing in his life that he was never "too sick to do".

I had started to try a new tactic in my life. I had booked a family holiday at Caloundra for Christmas of 2009. I had been madly saving and preparing all year. It would be the first actual holiday I had been on since October 1980, not that there would be any change in the workload but at least I would be able to smell, see and touch the ocean. I have always felt that I have seawater in place of blood in my vessels; the affinity was so strong and always has been. I had hoped that William may actually even behave as a normal human being for a change. Before we left for our holiday, my doctor insisted that I have a test as he suspected that I was a diabetic. I laughed in his face and said he was mad as I loathed sweet foods, had never added sugar and ate a healthy diet. He was crazy but was not going to be dissuaded so I took his silly tests, then carried on with my life. It had been an amazing holiday. We were in a cabin in a caravan park and Brianna, Steve, Ebony and Isabelle had rented another cabin. It was the first time I had been in a swimming pool since I had married. Of course, I had to go and purchase a bathing suit first. Billy had come with us and stayed for the first night. Then Mitchell and his girlfriend came up and stayed. Everyone else came for Christmas day. Before we even left Caloundra from this holiday, William and I had gone and booked for the following Christmas for a top floor apartment and paid the deposit there and then. I had truly enjoyed this week and looked forward to making a habit of it. William had been his usual self, refused to sleep with me and refused to sleep in the room that had two sets of bunks with Ben. Instead, he chose to curl up on the small couch each night. I let him get on with it. I was enjoying myself too much to give a shit.

January 2010 became the defining moment in my life. I finally returned to the doctor and was told that I was a Type II diabetic; my glucose tolerance test was 7. In my opinion, it was too close to call. Did he give me time to try to correct it, bring it down? Oh no, like everything and everyone in my life, it was all or nothing. It was a long, long time since I had worked in a medical ward and how to work with diets, etc. was well behind me. He prescribed me Diabex XR 500mg daily. He handed me the script along with a script for Crestor (a Statin), stating now that I had been diagnosed with diabetes, I had to take these as well and, 'You also have Fibromyalgia.' I had long since been presenting him with symptoms I could not explain, ever-worsening fatigue and ever-increasing pain that were making my life almost unbearable. Now I had been hit with a double whammy. I asked what sort of diet I would have to follow; would low carbs be okay? He said he was happy with that. I left his office and drove the rest of the way home exhausted from my day at work and devastated at the turn my life had just taken. William really could have cared less but I had expected nothing more from him. This was just another attempt on my part to move him further down the pecking order, in his mind. I had never needed someone to help me come to grips with this more than I did then. But, as usual, my husband was not the kind of person who could be relied on for anything other than his own self-interest. Why did I keep hoping that one day he would actually be there for me when I needed him?

Isabelle kicked into gear and started to research everything to do with diabetes. I went off to work the next day and for the rest of the week in a complete blur, feeling like I was living a nightmare that had come to life. On Saturday, Isabelle had me at the chemist purchasing a glucometer and joining the diabetic associations for my state. I had to be on a low GI diet and she started purchasing books to help me come to terms with diabetes and the new dietary regime. I really was at a loss and still not coming to terms easily with this new condition and yet more medication. Isabelle had my back and was a superstar with helping me at every turn.

I got a call one afternoon a couple of weeks later from the nurse at my GP surgery to organise an appointment to complete a patient care plan now that I was a diabetic, but only after I had gone back to the doctor to ask a lot of questions and explain how he had made me feel. 'You are diabetic and have to take these pills,' he had said. On this occasion, he stated, 'Well, I guess we really should do a care plan, I will have the nurse contact you to set a time.' I had an appointment to see a dietitian and a diabetes nurse at the QEII Hospital. I saw the dietitian and she asked what I had been eating, I explained and proudly told her that I had already lost 5kg. Her reply was, 'I very much doubt that is true with the food you have been eating, it is just not possible.' I never went back to her. I saw the nurse at the QEII, a lovely lady but again, as an ex-nurse myself, there was little she could do for me as I already knew all the actual risks and complications of diabetes so I have never seen her again. My only true ally since that day has been Isabelle, even though she always believed that I never really had diabetes and should not have been put on the medication so quickly. I would not have survived without Isabelle's strength to guide me, especially with what was to follow.

Exactly one month to the day after I had been diagnosed with diabetes and fibromyalgia, I was heading home from work but was going by QEII Hospital to pick up William where he had gone to have an X-ray of his chest. He was waiting at the bus stop, as arranged, as I came around the busy corner. I pulled over to collect him when a nurse came running out, calling his name. The X-ray had revealed a tiny apex pneumothorax and they needed William to come back inside. I had to continue on to the primary school and collect my grandchildren and care for them until their parents came to collect them after work. I rang all the children that I could contact and just had to wait. Clayton arrived first and he went straight to the hospital to be with William. He came home later that evening stating that he was no longer to do anything, vacuuming, hanging up washing or any activity that involved him raising his arm until the pneumothorax had time to heal.

I immediately became a full-time worker at my place of employment and a full-time worker at my home whilst trying to also fit in exercise, walks and using an exercise bike to try to lose weight. I had to come home and do washing, cook dinner, do the housework, go for my walks and try to find time to relax a little. It was a recipe for disaster and it had already started brewing. As the team leader at work, I had responsibilities to the staff and I took my role extremely seriously. As the year moved on, I noticed the staff pulling away from me and I was becoming more and more stressed both with work and my home life. Isabelle had taken me to Melbourne in June 2010 and we had VIP tickets to a cocktail party and a show with Jamie Oliver. We always went to dine at his restaurant, *15*, whilst in Melbourne. It had special significance on this visit as Gareth McKay, one of Billy's best friends and former chef at *15* in London, was now head chef in Melbourne. Isabelle and I were treated like royalty and received a complimentary bottle of wine.

There were some of my children that considered I was being completely selfish by leaving Dad to fend for himself when he was so ill and could not do anything at all! His pneumothorax had well and truly healed by this time but William, being the malingerer and hypochondriac that he was, was playing this up for all it was worth. It takes approximately six weeks for a pneumothorax to heal itself and one so small would more than probably have healed a whole lot sooner than that but milking things was William's style, even though he would have been given the exact same information by the doctor at the hospital in February. It was now June and I had left prepared meals for both the evenings that I would be away.

My return to work was less than pleasant; not a single member of staff even asked how my short holiday had been. I was already an emotional wreck but trying to lead a team whose respect I had lost, for no reason that I could think of, was sending me over the edge completely. I had instigated training sessions to ensure that we were all on the same page and offering the same service to all our customers. This was all with Martha's knowledge and consent. I attempted to start the first session with two staff members, one not the sharpest tool in the shed and a very slow worker, the other, a family man who seemed lovely but told me straight that I had to expect that they would talk about me behind my back and treat me with contempt as all children did to their parents. As I was in the leading role, in his eyes, I was equivalent to being a parent. I was not certain how things were done in Malaysia or if this was what he tolerated and probably encouraged in his own children, but I was already in a dark place and this just sent me right over the edge and into the waiting abyss.

I made it home but was shaking, crying, had chest pains and felt as if I was dying. I took the next day off sick as I truly was but I insisted on writing a full report, in the form of an email, to Martha. Isabelle tried to get me to stop, to try to calm down as it was she I sent the draft to before forwarding it on to work. She was right and most of me knew that but I was in such despair that I very much doubt I was even in control of my faculties at that point in time. William had even asked Jonathon over to talk to me about going bankrupt so that I could give up work. It was in the back of my mind but I had spent my entire life with a certain set of morals and ethics and it seemed like I would be giving them up in some way if I followed that path.

I rang to tell Martha that I was still sick and would not be in the following day; if anything, I was much worse. She refused to allow me to take the day off work, insisting that I be there at my usual time the following day and that she would be in early. I was not sure that I would be able to perform my duties in the state I was in and fully expected to be sacked anyway. As soon as she arrived, I was called into her office and she turned on me rather viciously. I found her manner totally unacceptable but as she began to see the true state I was in, she softened and told me that I was to take the next two days off—stress leave, fully paid—and she wanted me out of the office before anyone else arrived. I obliged as I could not concentrate but I had seen her real side and would never forget it. I returned to work after the stress leave and was again sent home for the day. I went back and although it took all the strength and stubbornness I could muster, I slowly and very quietly fell back into the routine of work, which would never be the same again.

Unbeknownst to me, at that time, I had developed PTSD along with depression. I had gone to my doctor and explained what had occurred and, without ever suggesting that I might need to see a psychiatrist or psychologist, he put me on Cymbalta, a different antidepressant without bothering to advise me that once on this medication, it was all but impossible to get off it again. He was either lacking knowledge or just not communicating effectively, but also failed to mention that Cymbalta was one of the three leading treatments for fibromyalgia. It did take the edge off things but I still had to live with a bone-idle narcissist at home, trying to do everything there, and with a narcissistic bully and a vindictive immediate superior at work, the type that would stab you in the back as quickly as look at you. It was definitely the type of poisonous cocktail that would kill me if it were allowed to continue. I had to make some huge decisions. Obviously, William had told the children all about my "episode", as not too long later, Billy had come to me to say that he and his siblings wanted to offer to help pay off my debts by contributing a small amount each month to the payments. I thanked him for the generous offer but I would have to decline. I had managed to get into this mess trying to do the best by my children and trying to satisfy my husband's demands and I would work out how to get myself out of it. I am incapable of being beholden to anyone, it makes me feel sick to my stomach.

It was almost unbelievable at that point to know that I had been debt-free in 2000. After Mum's estate had been finalised, I was able to clear my debts and purchase a slightly newer car. I had, at first, given my XD Ford to my son, Billy, thinking it would be great for him. It was a wagon and was well-maintained. It had rather good alloy wheels on it too. But it did not have power steering and was considered too big and cumbersome by Billy. My youngest son, Ben, would have so loved it. He has often said it is a pity that I had not had him at the time I had Billy because he would have fulfilled my dream to restore it to its former glory. But there was also the fact that my brother-in-law, Adam, had called me not long after the estate had been sorted and told me that as Jonathon was bankrupt and had to surrender his entire inheritance, and that it was considered my responsibility to give him some of that which I had received. Both he and my sister worked—he in the Air Force, she in a bank. They had a lot of money and several properties and yet expected me, whose husband had not worked since 1986 and never would again, to help my brother when they could have actually handed him his entire share out of their own pockets and not even blinked twice!

These were the types of occurrences that were sending me deeper and deeper into the abyss. I gave Jonathon the car—the mags alone were valued at over $500. He used it for a while and then gave it to his son and that was basically the end of the poor thing.

I bought Billy an old Datsun, at his request, which he sideswiped on another car. He also had a bad habit of leaving the lights on so buying batteries was a constant in my life and anything else the vehicle required, tyres, etc. Billy did not pay me back for any of this; that was all on one credit card. Eventually, I was asked to buy him another car, an older Mitsubishi Magna. This one was for $2000 and I asked that he pay me back for that one. It was on my other credit card. Again, there were ongoing expenses but true to his word, Billy did pay me back all but $50 of the principal but nothing for the incurred interest or ongoing expenses. When the car died, a friend of ours took it and it cost him very little to get it up and running again but Billy was very quick to drop things and people. His level of interest was very short-lived. That was the beginning of the end for me though, I was left to pay both debts and their interest plus whatever else was added through sheer necessity or William 's demands.

I made the decision that I did, indeed, need to declare myself bankrupt for the sake of my health and my sanity. Once that was finalised, I decided to resign from my job. My final day was 17 December 2010. Of course, it was all a bed of roses and nobody wanted me to leave but William was making my life hell, still playing it up a treat that he could do absolutely nothing and needed me to be there for him so I was left with no choice. When I resigned, Martha wanted me to just take unpaid leave for as long as I needed and come back when things had improved. I said that I considered a clean break the best course of action for me. On my last day, the staff put on a farewell lunch, which was lovely. It was all frivolity and photos and Martha asked if I would work for her from home for four hours per day. They were affiliating with a similar company and wanted me to handle that body of work. I agreed to this but was still uncertain that I wanted an ongoing relationship with this company after the way I had been made to feel over the years I had been there.

We went on our holiday, which I thought was fantastic, but as always, had to return to the humdrum and crap of home. It was always such a let-down. I was due to start work for Martha on 04 January 2011 but the phone connection with the company was not functional and we put it off for a week so that the issue could be sorted. By 11 January 2011, we in Brisbane were facing a major flood crisis and the area where the office was situated in South Brisbane was right on the river and everyone in and around the city had to leave. James and Martha were trying to keep the business going from home. My services were again not required. It was a relief!

Eventually, I did get to start working from home but the deal with the other company had fallen through and I was not required for that work. I was more than happy to call it quits but Martha claimed she had plenty of other work to keep me going. I started with two hours a day, this increased when I was covering someone off sick or on leave. I was growing tired of being treated very poorly. My pay slips stated that I was receiving sick pay and holiday pay allowances and as no contract had ever been drawn up for this work, I believed I was entitled to public holiday pay as well but never received it. This was brought to Martha's attention many times.

Things were changing in the workplace, James was retiring, Martha was taking his place and new people had been employed. A lady, only one year my junior, Lottie, whom I had thought very highly of whilst I had worked there, had been made the team leader. I had, at one point, been invited to come in to the office for a lunch but then the invitation had been rescinded. I had emailed Martha to discuss where I stood in this new regime as I had hoped to return to the office as had been the opinion she had voiced before I left. My calls went unanswered but later in the day, I received a vicious email from Martha, she had reverted to kind. My reply was swift; I was no longer able to offer the company my assistance, effective immediately. One of the worst periods of my life was finally over. They would then, as they had done to every single previous ex-staff member, bad mouth and defame me. I was well off out of it. That was 3 June 2011 and my life and my health were not far from going through the abyss into the depths below.

We are all now aware of the scientific proof that 99% of all diseases suffered by human beings are caused by stress. Only a tiny 1% has anything to do with genetics. It has also been proved that our DNA is nothing more than a blueprint and that our environment dictates the life we lead. I draw the attention to an article written by Dr Carol Dean, who is an experienced medical and naturopathic doctor.

Dr Dean was the lead author on the seminal paper, *Death by Medicine*, published in 2003. She is also the author of the book, *Death by Modern Medicine*. She received the Arrhythmia Alliance Outstanding Medical Contribution to Cardiac Rhythm Management Services Award in 2012, by the Heart Rhythm Society in UK.

The following passage taken from an article written by Dr Dean seems eerily close to my own health scenario:

The scenario that I like to talk about is very basic. You will recognise it immediately in either yourself or your family members. You go to your doctor. You're under massive stress. Massive stress means you're losing magnesium. You're burning magnesium out of your body because it helps support your adrenal glands.

It helps keep you away from anxiety and depression. It helps relax your muscles. If you're all tight and stressed, your magnesium is being lost, [which makes] the muscles of your blood vessels tighten. That tightness is going to cause increased blood pressure. Your doctor...will say, 'Oh, your blood pressure is elevated. We'll give you a diuretic.' A diuretic will drop the fluid level in your body to take the pressure off your blood vessels, so your blood pressure will drop. But diuretics also drain off your magnesium... A month later you come back, and the doctor finds your blood pressure's even more elevated.

Yes—because you've just lost more magnesium! Your doctor then puts you on a calcium channel blocker. Now, they have that part right. They know that without magnesium, your calcium is going to become elevated and will tighten up your blood vessels, so they try to block calcium.

But they don't know that magnesium is a natural calcium channel blocker. Your doctor may also put you on an angiotensin-converting-enzyme (ACE) inhibitor, another blood pressure drug... So, you go away with three drugs now.

After two or three months, you come back and have blood taken to make sure that drugs aren't hurting your liver... All of a sudden, your cholesterol is elevated. All of a sudden, your blood sugar is elevated. What does the doctor say? 'Oh, we caught your cholesterol. We just caught your blood sugar. We can put you on medications.' But they didn't catch them; they caused them.

Oh, to have had such information on board, even from 2003. What a difference it would have made to my health journey.

Dr Dean goes on to explain the importance of magnesium for the health of the entire body and the numerous biological functions it performs:

Providing body energy by activating adenosine triphosphate (ATP)
    Activating nerves and muscles
    Serves as a building block for RNA and DNA synthesis
    A precursor for neurotransmitters such as serotonin

Improves the digestion of fats, proteins, carbohydrates

This mineral is extremely important for the cardiovascular health, as the imbalance of magnesium and calcium may cause a heart attack and sudden death.

The heart contains the highest amount of magnesium in the body, specifically in the left ventricle, so a deficiency of this mineral impairs the function of the heart.

There is no easily available commercial laboratory test that can accurately check your magnesium status in the tissues. Namely, only 1% of magnesium in the body is distributed in the blood, so a serum magnesium blood test would be largely inaccurate if based on a simple sample of magnesium.

It is also very interesting to note that Dr Dean adds:

The early symptoms of magnesium deficiency are headaches, fatigue, loss of appetite, nausea and weakness.

If not treated on time, these symptoms may be aggravated, and the person will experience other signs such as seizures, personality changes, abnormal heart rhythms, numbness and tingling, muscle contractions and cramps, and coronary spasms.

As a teenager, my mother had me taking magnesium phosphate tablets in an effort to help my constant severe headaches. I had never been informed of the importance of magnesium to the body and I never had this explained to me by any doctor. I also never learned of the importance of magnesium in my nursing career and if my mother had been told of any such information by whomever she purchased the magnesium tablets from, she most certainly never passed that information on to me.

My life was doomed to end up as it has because of the levels of trauma and stress that I have endured since the day I was adopted. The doctor I had seen way back when I was 22 turned out to be the only person who spoke the truth to me and I did not heed his advice because I, like all other nurses and doctors of that time, had been indoctrinated by the establishment and what they believed to be true or rather what they wanted us to believe to be true to line the pockets of Big Pharma...

Don't be apologetic for moving away from something
that was unhealthy for you.
It's a beautiful thing when you
recognise you deserve better
And an even more beautiful thing
when you steer towards better.

-LLOYD BARKER

CHAPTER 21

THE END IS NIGH

Once I was finally free of work, I turned my attentions to my garden. I, again, did a complete refurbishment of all the gardens. It was my passion, and Steve would work beside me, which I loved, but most importantly, it was my escape from William. He was becoming even more bone idle and still maintaining that he could not do any work as he was too sick! He was also become weirder by the day.

Whilst I had been working, I could finally afford to try to help myself, for once. I had spent so many decades putting my needs and basic rights last that it was a true novelty for me to start to think about me. William did not approve and seemed jealous, of what I do not know. For example, I started to buy slightly better than the cheapest of hair products. I even dared to buy some that claimed they could thicken hair and as the top of my head was all but bald, I thought I deserved to try it. It was actually working but William did not agree that I deserved this apparently and started to add water to it. For what purpose I have no real idea but it was getting more and more watery every time I shampooed so I ended up using a permanent marker to ensure that if there was a change, I would know about it. I always purchased Avon shampoo, aftershave, deodorants, talcs, shower gel and/or Brut products for William. Never once did I expect him to use cheap shit. He would have refused anyway. So, his reason for the shampoo would remain a mystery to me forever because he always denied any wrongdoing.

Another instance of totally bizarre behaviour on William 's part was my shower gel. I had been using the cheap big bottle from Aldi for some time but had developed the most awful case of chaffing, which developed into dermatitis. Nothing I tried seemed to be helping it. On one of our trips to Melbourne, I decided to buy the small travel essentials of bathroom products as we would only be away for two days. The only shower gel available in this size was Radox. After my first shower in Melbourne, I found a notable improvement in my condition. After the second shower, there was an even bigger improvement. After returning home, I had enough left for one more shower and again there was further improvement. I was sold and went to the shops the following day and bought a larger bottle but not the big pump one as I wanted to be certain of the facts first.

With each day came more improvement and I was just so happy to be free of the pain, itch and embarrassing walk when I was in public. When the pump bottle was on sale, I snapped it up as it was far more economical than the smaller ones. After a while, I noticed my blue shower gel turning green and usually only about 1/3 to ½ of the bottle would be gone. This always seemed to happen when I did not have a backup bottle and would be forced to continue to use it. I had gone to have my shower one evening and noted an extremely offensive smell about the shower gel and it was even greener. It smelled putrid but, having been a nurse for many years, it smelled like urine. I brought the bottle out to the kitchen and asked Isabelle to smell it; she also said it smelled like urine. I looked straight at William and all he could say was that the en suite was too humid. The new master bedroom, en suite and walk-in-robe were all fully insulated and at least 5-10 degrees cooler than the rest of the house. So that story was definitely not based in truth. But as truth was a totally unknown concept to William, all I could do was throw good money into the bin and start a new bottle. As if to prove his point, the same thing kept happening to every pump bottle I purchased thereafter.

For the future, I only used the smaller available bottles of Radox. William still did not seem happy as he had a 2-in-1 shampoo/conditioner, all branded, whilst I used separate shampoo and conditioner bottles, so I had to start buying the same for him. It was like living with a child in the guise of an almost 70-year-old man and it was causing my stress levels to rise ever further. If I did not remain vigilant and alert, I would fall from an even greater height as he always found a way to burst any bubbles of light that I found in life. It was best that I walked on eggshells permanently in the hope of fewer shocks.

Our holiday was booked for Christmas and we were going to be on Level 1 so as to avoid William having to climb four flights of stairs. It was a more sparsely furnished apartment compared to the one we had the year before but we were going to be there for nine days. A couple of days at the beginning and the end by ourselves. I was trying desperately to understand William and work with him. I was still unaware that he could never be worked with and there were way too many secrets and lies that would get in the way.

Nonetheless, I set off for our holiday with the best of intentions and hoped, yet again, to really enjoy myself. It was becoming a habit for me to go swimming in a pool again and I absolutely loved it. Although we always held a family Christmas gathering the weekend before we went on holidays and used that occasion to give gifts, most of the children still came up on Christmas Day to help devour our food and utilise the swimming pool. This year was no different. Billy only ever came to see us Christmas morning and then was off to spend the day with Janet and her friend, as was their tradition. Janet's family celebrated Christmas on Christmas Eve and Janet always spent the actual day with her friend. One would have thought that, like the rest of the world, once she was firmly attached and married, she would do alternate Christmases with her family and with her partner's family. But Janet did not do anything that did not suit her and that was the way it was going to stay.

The day Alfie and Catarina, Janet's parents, came to our holiday accommodation to meet us was the day before we were due to come home. William had not had a shower for the whole nine days! Why he cared so much about personal care products was truly beyond me. I went off to do a bit of last-minute shopping whilst he finally had a shower. I was truly happy to get home after that holiday and would never again make the mistake of going anywhere away from home with William for more than seven days.

William, more often than not, had a runny nose and was always complaining about it. I knew, as did anyone with the smallest amount of intelligence, that his issues were down to dirt and dust. I was not allowed to help myself to his room, even though I was his wife and the fact that he was in my room going through my belongings constantly. William almost never changed his sheets, opened his window and absolutely never dusted his room. For the entire nine days we had been on holiday, there had been absolutely no sign of any nasal problems at all but upon our return home, back came his issues. Even William finally conceded that I was right.

I told him I would be cleaning his room, from the ceiling down, the following day. I had stripped the bed, taken the curtains down and started the washing of the same when he came and announced that he wanted to go to Garden City, a very large shopping centre in

Upper Mt Gravatt. He wanted to buy a new pair of trousers. I offered to take him; no, he wanted to go on his own. I offered to drop him off and come back and collect him. 'Absolutely not,' he said, 'I will go on the bus as I need some alone time.' I thought nothing more of it and off he went.

I was busy vacuuming his mattress, dusting, cleaning windows, walls and every piece of furniture and blinds in his room. I was still going when he returned from his outing. I was head down and bum up as he walked past the door, saying he had returned. I eventually completed my current task and surfaced to see the trousers he had purchased. He had not bought any trousers. There had been nothing that he had liked? I found that almost impossible given the amount of men's clothing outlets in this large shopping centre and the fact that the January sales were well underway. I thought no more of it and completed the cleaning of his bedroom, 5 ½ hours I had spent to bring it up to what I considered a habitable standard.

It was not until two days later that I discovered the truth of William 's visit to Garden City. He had not been looking for trousers at all. He had purchased a new surveillance camera to use on me. I had just been getting comfortable in bed when I noticed a bright red light on the duchess. I knew immediately what it was and why he had not wanted me anywhere near his trip to the shops. I disconnected it and tried to sleep. Upon waking the following morning, I had a severe pain in my head. It did not go away. Every night, the camera would be set up in a different position and every night, I would cover it up or disconnect it. There was absolutely no point whatsoever in speaking to William about it as I had not only done so many times but had written a document stating I did not and never would consent. This fell on his deaf narcissistic ears. Every single day, the pains in my head got worse.

My birthday is late in January and I always got together with my girlfriend of 23 years, Kitty. The friendship had been strained for some time due to her becoming needier and needier of me and my time. I had so many issues going on in my life, which I would have given anything to be able to talk through with someone, but she always had so many things going wrong that there was never time for her to be there for me and the issues that I really needed help to sort out. It was definitely a one-way street where Kitty was concerned, all her way and no more so than that early February day when we finally caught up and went to our usual Yum Cha Restaurant. Before going in, we talked for a short while. She definitely had an issue and I was in desperate need of a true friend that day.

Instead, what I got was a teary complaining friend saying that she had no one in her life who was there for her. I stated, 'I am here for you and have always tried to be when needed.' Her reply almost bowled me over, 'Yea, but if I needed you and one of your kids needed you at the same time, you would always put them before me and I would be alone.'

What the fuck! I tried to remain as calm as I could. What my gut was telling me was to turn and get out of here as quickly as I could. Anyone who expected me to put them before my precious children knew absolutely nothing about me as a person even after 23 years of friendship and was so self-absorbed by her own life, melanomas, miscarriage and myocardial infarction—all of which I had been there to support her through and care for her daughter, Sarah, despite any hardships that caused me, especially with William who considered I was his property and his property alone and that Kitty took up way too much of my time.

That anyone, other than William, would actually expect me to put them before my precious babies was unthinkable and incomprehensible to me on every level of my being and in that instant, I was living the same nightmare that I lived every day of my life with my narcissistic psychopath husband. Up until this point, even though Kitty had always been very high maintenance, she had also been an outlet for me, one that I desperately needed in my life. That had just ended in the space of one sentence. But, always being the one who was expected to put everyone else first, I tried to appease her and we continued on to have lunch. Why? It was William and Janet's engagement party, to which Kitty had been invited, in less than two weeks. I did not want to disappoint my son by causing her not to be there. I wound things up much more quickly than usual and we made our way back to my car. Isabelle and I had purchased a new second-hand Triton Ute. It was just four years old and Kitty was extremely jealous, so I made it a very quick goodbye and I was off.

I had offered over and over anything I could do to assist William and Janet with the preparations for the engagement party, which was to take place in New Farm Park. Billy had finally brought over the tiniest boneless beef roast I have seen for me to cook for the party—what a joke! Catarina and Janet had been cooking for a week or more and I had not been allowed to contribute to my own son's celebration, except for a tiny plate of roast beef. I should, perhaps, have got the message when my daughter, Jasmine, had totally cut me out of any and all things wedding when she and Richard had gotten married. I had offered to host the wedding in our backyard with the beautiful lawn and plants and host the reception as well. I was told that they had decided to get married in the Registry Office and would be having the reception in their backyard. It is now blatantly apparent that my children have always thought very much less of me than I have thought of them. I would die to save any of my children and that never has and never will change.

It was extremely difficult for me to even be civil to Kitty at the engagement party but I did my best. Luckily, there were many people there that I could talk to but she tended to follow me around like a lost puppy. The worst part was when Billy was giving a speech stating just how long Janet, Catarina and other people had spent in preparing for the day. I felt subterranean when he included me in that list for a tiny bit of beef. Why would no one allow me to help them? I truly had no idea of the reason then or now. I don't believe in making assumptions as "assumptions are the mother of all fuck ups", but even to guesstimate, one would have to think that Janet had very set ideas and I was not included in them. The whole day only served to increase the pain in my head to an unbearable level. As Kitty walked despondently across the park to leave, I knew that was the last time I would ever see her.

She sent me an email to ask if we were going to do our usual Wednesday fortnightly meet up. I explained that I needed a break for a while and that I was incapable of not being there for my children. She knew, at that stage, that I always got off the computer at around 11 pm so she waited until after then and sent a rather nasty email back and unfriended me from FB. There had been an occasion when Outlook had changed things up that same year and it had sent an FB Friend Request to everyone for whom I had an email address. This had included Kitty and she had accepted, but I deleted it. That portion of my life was over.

My headaches continued to increase in intensity and there was not a single day when I was free of them. I went to my GP at that time. She requested a brain scan, which I had done at the earliest possible appointment. When I returned to get the results, she told me that they had found a meningioma on my right parietal bone but believed it had been there for a very long time. They also saw another mass that they thought could have been an aneurysm or some sort of mass and they had also found several polyps in my sinus cavity. As I did not have private health insurance anymore, I had to go onto the public waiting list. The public system did not consider me to be a priority one case—to be seen within 30 days. My doctor totally disagreed as did my children and they paid for me to see a private neurosurgeon who organised an MRI.

Fortunately for me, the MRI did not reveal anything other than the meningioma, which was considered as an incidental finding that had probably been caused when I had fractured my skull at 16 by fainting and falling down a flight of stairs at the Stock Exchange Building in Brisbane. The neurosurgeon diagnosed severe migraines and recommended three different medications that might assist with the pain. He would write them in his report to my GP and she would organise them for me. Of the three recommended medications, there was only one that would not react badly with the other medications that I was already taking, Lyrica. But it would definitely make me gain weight. I was stuck between a rock and a hard place. I needed some respite from the migraines so I agreed to try them.

Whilst I had been at the specialist's office, William was at home busy setting up the surveillance camera, again, this time with great amounts of blue tack. He positioned it between the large duchess and chest of drawers looking directly at my bed. I failed to notice it when I lay down that afternoon to try to get my migraine to lighten up slightly but I most certainly saw it when I went to bed that night. This time, I dismantled it and hid it, in several pieces. It has always been said that if you do not want someone to find something, then hide it in plain sight. I employed this theory and it was never found.

The next day, I organised with Clayton to contact William (Billy) and set up a meeting for the three of us using any excuse he chose to say to Dad. Clayton had been looking at bikes to buy his daughter for her upcoming birthday so he was going to come and take me out Saturday afternoon so that he could show them to me. We went to the Coffee Club at Sunnybank Plaza and were not sitting there too long before Billy arrived. He came towards me with a dreadful thunderous look on his face. 'This had better not be a waste of my time. I hope it is not about Zach.'

I was not important enough to warrant using any of his time apparently. I told him it was not about Zach. Drinks were organised, and crying and shaking, I explained that Dad had been using surveillance cameras on me, that I had told him many times that I did not consent, that he had apologised and promised to stop but never did, in fact he had bought a new one. I explained that I had even written and signed a document that stated that I did not consent and never would to being surveilled and being shut in my room every night was driving me crazy, I felt like a caged lion. I was not allowed to be me and had not been allowed that privilege for decades. I explained that I was at the end of my tether, that I felt like I was going mad and that I did not think I could take this treatment for very much longer. I needed their help desperately for advice but also on practical solutions as to how I could move forward in any capacity.

Billy sat, looking dumbfounded, but saying almost nothing except, 'You need to go and talk to Dad.' What did he think I had been doing all of those decades? I explained that Dad had long since stopped listening to me and did exactly what he wanted, when he wanted. Again, Billy said, 'You need to go talk to Dad.'

Clayton, on the other hand, said, 'I knew you were going to say that.'

How exactly, I wondered, unless he already knew about them. He then said, 'Just put both of the cameras on the kitchen bench and smash them up with a hammer in front of him.' Billy agreed with Clayton.

It is time to remind you that Billy is a lawyer. He is bound by a code of ethics and has been since he was admitted to the Bar. I fail to see the ethics in advising a victim to "destroy the evidence". I was devastated that neither of them seemed to want to help me get professional help for their father if our marriage was to survive. On to the bike shop we went. Clayton and Billy walked around talking whilst I wandered aimlessly trying to work out what I could do now to get some help. Why didn't I just take the cameras to the police station and explain my situation? The answer to this was that probably I was suffering so severely from PTSD and major depressive disorder by then that I did not know which way was up and which down. I was so disappointed that Billy had let me down so badly, I was inconsolable that evening when I went to bed. He has never once, since that day, spoken to me about the things that I endured at the hands of his father.

One week later, William was in the laundry hanging up all the underwear on the lines we had in there for them (his special little delight) when I decided that I would try to speak to him again. I told him that I had met up with Clayton and Billy and I told him the full conversation. I even told him that I would try to find a compromise if he would work with me instead of against me, but that if he did not do anything, then the marriage would be over and it would be he who would leave as I had never done anything wrong in our marriage. He did not say a single word to me, not one, he did not look at me even once and when I was finished, he just left me standing there as if I did not exist. Did this mean that he already knew about the meeting? It would not have surprised me particularly with what I know about Clayton now.

What William did do, from that moment on, was to make my life a living hell. If I had thought that his abuse of me had been bad since the night I had it out with Tracey over her accusation in 1990, I was about to find out that what I had already endured was child's play compared to what was coming. He found more and more ways to torment me but at the same time, he was turning my children against me with his lies. Unfortunately, I did not know this and by the time I put it all together it was far too late to salvage any relationship with four of my children. None of them would A. have a single thing to do with me B. would not explain to me why they no longer loved me C. none of them would allow me the right to defend myself.

Easter came quickly and we were having a BBQ with everyone asked just to bring their own meat and I would provide the salads and desserts. William had invited my brother, Jonathon, and his girlfriend, Bec, without my knowledge or consent. Due to the fact that I have severe hearing loss, William would call something to me, always whilst I was very busy and usually coming from the fridge in the garage and going up the stairs to the kitchen. He would cause me to stop on the stairs and say something I could not hear properly and then say, 'That's right, isn't it, Ellie?'

I could care less what he said at this point and would nearly always wave a hand and say, 'Whatever.' Little did I realise at the time but this was how he was getting me to seemingly confirm his lies to my children. What is so frustrating and disappointing is that they actually believed what he said even though they could see I was rushing about busy. Blind Freddie could work out that I had a hearing issue. My biological uncle had been stone-deaf. They all knew that it was hereditary but because William had hearing issues, mostly due to the fact that he had years' worth of wax build-up in his ears, I could not possibly have a worse hearing problem than he did and therefore my hearing, in his eyes, was fine.

Isabelle and Ebony had gone to a show at QPac at Southbank and it was on this day that Isabelle fell when they were coming out and fractured her elbow. By the time I got the call that afternoon, I was exhausted and got Clayton to go and collect them and drop Isabelle at the hospital. She required my assistance with showering, shampooing and dressing and it was sometimes a 3-ring circus trying to get it all done and we would be in stitches of laughter. William again displayed his traditional jealousy wanting to know whether I was married to Isabelle or him. What a child; I was doing what decent parents did. They help their children out especially in times of need.

My treatment by William continued to worsen throughout 2012. He began to refuse to allow me to go in with him when he saw his specialists at the hospital as he had slipped up one day—refusing to allow the doctor to speak and I had tapped him on the arm and he had viciously turned on me and said, 'Don't you ever do that to me again or you will be sorry.' The doctor now knew the type of person he was and without me there, as he had done so many times before, he could create the stories about his evil wife and how hard done by he truly was. In fact, he would also ensure that there was nowhere for me to sit near him after I had been made to drop him off and go find a carpark.

It was William 's 70th birthday that October and I had been emailing the children all year to organise something to celebrate this milestone and also Zach's 21st in September. Zach was away travelling with Charlie but came home for his birthday, which was a last-minute BBQ. It was decided that we would all go to the club for a meal for William 's 70th. Again, Jonathon and Bec were there, opposite me. It was a very strained evening for me as William was constantly making, not so subtle digs. There was no way to communicate with my children as the table was so long. I am not certain that I would have liked to have heard their conversation anyway by the reports I got on it later.

I had chosen to give up smoking, decades after I should have done. My reticence was solely due to the fact that William refused to give up no matter what incentive I put up. I had been at him for years about giving up together but he was having none of it. Earlier in the year, after having bought the new surveillance camera, he wanted to go and see the GP. I was told to wait in the car. When he came out, he had asked for a prescription for patches to help him stop smoking. He started to use the patches but he did not stop smoking, did not even try. I had asked Janet about the best way for me to give up, which seemed to give William the incentive to want to beat me to it. Janet had said that, as Brianna and I both wanted to give up, we should do it together in order to be a support to each other. She said it was far more likely to succeed with a support team behind you. As William knew so much more than I did, he continued to both smoke and use the patches. Of course, he eventually stopped the patches, stating that they made him sick. 'No William,' I told him, 'The nicotine patches are not making you sick, it is the nicotine poisoning you are causing yourself by continuing to smoke whilst using them.' But he was having none of that nonsense.

I had purchased the patches and the very first day I put one on had been the Winter Solstice—21 June 2012 at 09:00. I went out the back to water my garden and decided that I would succeed despite the treatment I was receiving from William, despite the fact that my PTSD and major depressive disorder were continuing to worsen by the day but I had my children for support and they would help me get through. It took William eight days to even acknowledge to me that

I had stopped smoking. He, of course, continued to smoke around me, which made my task more difficult but I was determined to beat it and I was so sure that my babies would support me.

A week later on Saturday, 10 days since I had stopped smoking, I sent all of my children a text. They all replied and my heart swelled as I read each one. I thought that I would text every Saturday to let them know that I was still going strong. I only received a few replies the following week and to my great disappointment, I only received a reply from Brianna the following week. I gave up, knowing that I was on my own with no support in the life situation I was in; it was devastating but I was not going to be beaten.

So, it turned out that the conversation at the table of William 's 70th amongst my children was why Mum had been sending them texts every week to say how long it had been since I had smoked, what did I expect from them, wasn't I doing it for myself and not them, etc. By all accounts, the ringleader was Billy, a former nurse who had been present when Janet had stated how important a support team was when giving up smoking, and Bianca, also a nurse. Janet herself was a nurse and yet none of them could pick up how depressed I was or that I truly needed support, or was it that they just didn't care? I was convinced that Janet would have been against Billy in this conversation but no, she was agreeing with them as well. I could not believe what I was hearing. I was feeling terribly alone without any family support after all that I had tried to teach them about the importance of family as they grew up. To me there was nothing in the universe more important than the love and support of a family. Mine seemed to be slipping away from me but at that point, I had no real idea why.

William developed further ideas on how to use surveillance on me, by standing in the en suite with the door open just enough for him to hold his mobile phone up to film me whilst I slept. What was the point of this exercise? His invasion of my privacy and personal space knew no bounds. All the children had put in to purchase Dad an iPad for his birthday. At first it was all exciting but the following day when he could not work anything out, he claimed, as always, 'They can take it back as it is useless and I cannot make it work.' After a few short lessons from Debbie and Bianca, he certainly seemed to come to grips with it very quickly as the iPad too was used as a filming device on me whilst I slept. He was caught red-handed every time due to me perceiving I was being watched, but with devices hidden behind his back, he would deny any such activity every single time.

Later that month, William had a specialist appointment at the Mater Hospital. As I was no longer allowed to go in to the doctor with William, I decided that I would drop him off and visit Bianca in an effort to explain my plight and seek some assistance. Bianca and her partner, Debbie, lived quite close to the hospital as they both worked at the Mater. I had not expected that Debbie would be home but she was so that was the end of any hope for trying to talk to Bianca. They were holding our pre-Christmas party at their unit this year so all discussions were about the arrangements for that, and very little seemed to be worked out. As far as I could tell, it was a front to stop me saying what she must have suspected I wanted to say to her. I fervently believe that Clayton had already forewarned her. They had always been very close after all; despite being brought up to understand that no subject was off limits and that we would openly discuss any subject with any and all of our children. We had always added that if there was something we did not know, we would make every effort to find the answer for them and finally, our only goal…well, I really do have to add here, *my* only goal, was to see and know that my children were happy with their lives. Despite being able to talk the talk, William proved himself to be an absolute liar so I will never know now whether we were ever on the same page. Whether he was or not, did not alter the fact that Bianca chose to tell Clayton, many months before she had told William and I, that she was gay.

I had always believed Bianca and I were the most alike and that we were very close. I missed her dearly when she first left home. I cried and cried and nearly every time she came for a visit, I would tear up when she was leaving, I missed her that much. But she also took over two weeks to tell me that she had left her partner of the time, which was a huge shock to me as I was unable to comfort her when she needed it. I was not certain what was happening but I was so low that there was no way I could work it out. Perhaps it was in front of me but I was blinded by PTSD and depression. Upon leaving Bianca's that day to go and collect William from the hospital, I had asked if Bianca and I could organise to go for a coffee the following week. She said she would check her days off and let me know.

That week came and went, as did the next and the next. This behaviour was totally and completely out of character for Bianca and I realised that Clayton or William had already spoken to her. Isabelle was going on a holiday to England and Europe with her best friend, Tin, from late November and it was fast approaching. As Bianca was intent on letting me down when I truly needed her, I told Isabelle everything. She could not believe how badly Clayton, William and Bianca had let me down and why had I not just come to her in the first place. The very last thing I had wanted to do was dampen her long-awaited holiday in any way and had wanted not to tell her until after her return but I knew that if I did not seek and receive guidance from someone, I would probably be in a mental institution by the time she returned.

She was fantastic, calmed me as much as I could be at that stage, asked if I could hang on until she got back and generally made me feel better than I had in a very, very long time. I knew that William 's abuse would go into high gear whilst she was overseas but I vowed to do everything I could to hang in there until she returned. It was an early morning flight that Isabelle had to get to Sydney to join Tin, who was flying from Melbourne. I cried most of the way home, knowing I was alone now until the early part of January. The sun had not even set on that first day of Isabelle's holiday when William found a reason to say, 'Isabelle is not here to save you now.' It was going to be a long five weeks or so.

Things with William went downhill from there. We were booked into an even more luxurious apartment for a week's holiday for Christmas in 2012. William asked several times whether he was allowed to come on this holiday. I had told him each time that I was giving very serious consideration to cancelling it despite the deposit that I would lose. I was in a real quandary as to whether I could tolerate his utter crap up the coast again. But before I had made a decision either way, William decided for me. He had called Mitchell and told him that he and I wanted to invite him to come up to Caloundra with us for our holiday. The very first I heard of it was when Mitchell called to thank me for my kind offer and to accept it. I was stuck with going up the coast. I would not disappoint Mitchell as well as Ben. William had been doing this sort of thing all our married life in order to ensure that he got exactly what he wanted but this, at that time, was a step too far. I would have cancelled the holiday and I think he knew that only too well.

I tried desperately to keep myself busy and stay out of his way as much as I could but all too soon, it was time for the Christmas party at Bianca's place. The only time I had seen her was when she had brought over the chicken and pork roasts for me to cook for the event. The drive to their place was particularly unpleasant and I was an absolute mess by the time we arrived. Many of the family were in the pool as we passed on our way to the apartment. It was an incredibly hot and humid day and I was sweating a treat. I put all the food down and stood under the air-conditioner vent to stop dripping as if I had just stepped out of a shower. Bianca, Debbie and Janet were all in the kitchen working. I offered and offered to assist them but they were not interested. Janet was starting to slice the meat and I said that it was not fair that Janet had to cut the meat when she did not eat it. I offered again to do that job, but no, again, I was rejected.

All I could do was sit there watching, feeling as useless as "tits on a bull". Clayton came in and came straight over to me and asked, 'What has Dad been up to lately?'

So, I told him how he had been behaving by leaving a full ashtray in the PC room or emptying it into the rubbish bin that sat beside me; I had not smoked since June. When I moved the bin, he would lean right under and empty the butts and ash into it. Then I removed the bag from the bin and moved it so far under the big corner PC table I had that you had to get on your hands and knees to access it but still he emptied his stinky ashtray into it. I was very nastily told by Bianca that this was neither the time nor the place for that conversation. Clayton and I went outside the front door of the unit into the alleyway until we were called for our meal.

They had two large tables set up with chairs and a separate table for the food. William was on the far side of one table and I was on the far side of the other. Almost no one spoke to me except for Brianna, Steve and Ebony. I had received hellos from everyone but there had been a weird atmosphere all afternoon and into the evening. Lots of photos were taken but none of them were with me. No one seemed interested in taking a photo with me. After the main meal was dessert. As I am a diabetic, Bianca had made a low GI trifle in individual bowls. I did not like it at all and could not eat it, she was livid with me and if looks could kill, I would have been dead on the spot. Following this were the presents. All the children were first, then our children, then us. Someone did take a photo of us sitting on the couch to show just how far apart we were.

Jasmine had asked Brianna and I if we would come to her house on the following Tuesday to help her with her Christmas cooking for their gathering with Richard's family. I was more than eager, anything to get away from William. We had not long gotten underway when Jasmine announced that they would not be coming to share Christmas lunch with us this year. They had come and devoured more than their fair share every other year and always took extras home. I, of course, asked why. Jasmine told me that Richard had told her that William had spent most of the Christmas party at Bianca and Debbie's telling him horrible things about me and how dreadfully I treated William and that he was no longer prepared to spend time with us so they would not be coming up. I asked what it was that William had told Richard, as it was all lies. She replied that Richard would not tell her because it was so bad but she believed Richard and that is why they would not be coming up. I replied that I could tell her the truth about her father. Her reply was, 'It would only be your word against his.' I told Jasmine that if she was a son of mine, I would have slapped her and walked out right then and there. I was apparently still good enough to do her cooking for her! I told her, 'Well, I will tell you this much, Jasmine, when I was very pregnant with you, Dad was in England screwing his ex-sister-in-law.'

Her reply was, 'Well, why didn't you fucking leave him there and then?'

I told her, 'Because he lied about it for almost a decade and by the time I had found proof, I had seven children with him.'

I was livid and couldn't wait to get out of there. On the way home, I also told Brianna that William had caused Clayton's marriage to end. She was blown away. I was so down I did not know what to do or who to turn to. I was Skyping Isabelle but I wanted her to enjoy this holiday, she really deserved it. She was verbally abused by Dad every single day of her life and I was not about to impose any downers on her holiday.

The days ticked by quickly and we were off to Caloundra. It was indeed a beautiful apartment and William, although it had two balconies, chose to mainly use the smaller one outside my bedroom door. And, of course, he would leave the full ashtray there for me to inhale. On Christmas Eve, he claimed to be sick and was shivering with cold. He had not brought any warm clothes with him. I had to head out for late-night shopping and went to Kmart to buy track pants and a dressing gown, the only warmer types of clothing they had. The next morning, he was fine, as he had been the night before, but he always turned on the malingering to get what he wanted and elicit the pity vote, something he had been doing at Christmas for more than a decade and also to inconvenience me as much as possible. But William had become so entrenched in finding ways to make my life difficult, I actually had come to expect it and accept that it would always be that way if our marriage continued. But that was no longer a done deal as he pushed me past breaking point and it was, now, merely a matter of time before it ended.

Christmas Day, 2012, was a rather larger than usual disappointment. Billy arrived on his bike for his visit. He did not appear to be in a particularly good mood and proved that by starting an argument over something I had said and stormed out. William followed him, which added more suspicion in my mind that there was a "behind my back team" working against me that did not involve only my husband. The day would definitely not improve from there.

Clayton arrived with Rhianna and his stepson, Pee, in tow, as always to devour free food. And that is exactly what they all did. For whatever unknown reason, Jasmine, Richard, Ashley and Emily, despite their claims about me and my integrity, showed up and devoured their fair share of food as well. I was thrilled to see my grandchildren. Rosemary also came up for a visit. But there was no sign of Bianca and I was heartbroken as she had come up on all previous occasions, even one year when she had been stuck on the highway for hours due to a multi-vehicle accident. That year I knew that nothing would stop her from coming to see us but just a mere two years later, my entire world had turned upside down. Even when she called, there was very little interest in speaking to me so I gave the phone to William who seemed to have a great conversation with her. Brianna had called and it was awesome to speak to her, Steve and Ebony. But the highlight of the day had to be the Skype call from Isabelle who was staying at Claridge's Hotel in London and explaining about the Christmas stocking that had been left on the door and then when they went to their 8-course Christmas dinner at Gordon Ramsay's restaurant, we got a course-by-course description. It was the next best thing to actually being there.

Personally, I could not wait to get home where I had a much larger environment in which to get away from William. Also, the sooner we got back home, the sooner Isabelle would be returning home.

During the days leading up to Isabelle's return, Rosemary and Michael came for a visit. I asked if she would be free the following weekend for a family meeting. She wanted to know the "ins and outs of a cat's arse" but I tried to insist that she wait until then. She kept goading and goading until I told her it was about Dad. She then wanted to know if Dad would be present and I said no, that I wanted to speak to my children. She replied, 'Anything you say would only be his word against yours.'

I saw red as, apart from this being the second time I had heard this exact phrase, I also knew where it had come from. So I said to her, 'I will tell you what I told Jasmine.'

Rosemary started to do her acting routine and said, 'No, I don't want to know.'

I said, 'Whilst I was heavily pregnant with Jasmine, Dad was in England screwing his ex-sister-in-law.' Rosemary started her usual screaming and yelling like a wailing banshee and stormed out of the house, followed by Michael but only after he had stood and given me the death stare.

I collected Isabelle from the airport and we talked all the way home. She had had a wonderful time in England and Europe and wished it could have been so much longer. She arrived home with four tattoos that she had done at London Ink. They were a map of UK, a Keep Calm and Carry On, a commemorative Union Jack with 2012 printed on it. Isabelle told me that she had these done whilst she had been in UK. What she had also told me was that when she was 18, she had told Dad that she wanted to get a tattoo and he had told her that if she did get a tattoo, he would kick her out of the house and disown her. This was the first I had ever heard of this about tattoos. William himself had one. Over the years, Bianca and Rosemary had tattoos and weird piercings done and to my knowledge, they had not been met with the same treatment as Isabelle had. When Zach had gone to Thailand, he had sat for 7 or 8 hours to have a tattoo on his right upper arm. What absolutely blew me away was the indifference with which William treated me when it came to decisions involving "our" children. I had no say at all, it seemed.

When we arrived home from the airport, he was in for a shock but now that I was aware of his sick and petty game plus the fact that four of the other children had them, including Brianna, he could not say anything. The tattoo that Isabelle had done across her back was written in Gaelic and I am the only other person who knows what it means. It is our secret.

The bombshell came when Isabelle had recovered from the initial part of the homecoming, the gift-giving, opening parcels she had sent home and going through all the photos, of which there were many, and had caught up on some sleep.

Isabelle said that she truly had a fantastic time but had also spent a lot of time thinking about what I had said to her before she left and her childhood and the one thing that she had remembered vividly and which had stuck out, for all the wrong reasons, was that every time I had been out of the house or asleep through the day, Dad would be behind a locked door with Brianna and that every time they came out, Brianna had been crying. WTF! I almost collapsed on the spot. I felt the vomit rising in my throat. Was that why he refused to get a licence, was that why he was always insisting that I had to go out and do this or that, was this why Brianna always threw a tantrum when I did not take her out with me even though she was a teenager? I had a billion thoughts running through my mind and I could not properly correlate any of them. I went to William and asked him straight, 'What were you doing with Brianna behind closed/locked doors?'

'I never was behind closed/locked doors with Brianna,' was his response. Denial had always been William 's default setting. 'More allegations; I have nothing to be sorry for.' Another default setting.

Brianna had come around and I made an excuse that she and I were going to the shops. I asked her straight, 'What did Dad do to you behind closed or locked doors when I was not around, love?'

'I do not know, Mum, I can't actually remember hardly anything from my childhood except for going to stay with Grandma.'

Clayton actually confirmed to me that yes, this did happen, or at least he knew all about it, when he next came around and I asked him. Again, Clayton had known what was going on; what had he done to stop his father, why had he never informed me of what he apparently knew to be occurring or was he condoning it? Or, as was suggested many times later, was he actually a part of the whole sordid saga all along?

The trust of the innocent is the liar's most useful tool.

-STEPHEN KING

CHAPTER 22

THE MAN BEHIND THE MASK

After Rosemary's academy award-winning performance, yet again, the growing suspicions that I held regarding what my children already knew, the new level of depression I had sunk to over this latest revelation and William 's subsequent blatant lies, I no longer saw the need to hold a meeting with my children. Bianca continued to avoid me at all costs, as did Rosemary. I rarely saw Billy anyway, Zach was still on his travels, Jasmine was not so visible these days and Mitchell was still my boy but was having issues with his own relationships, which kept his mind fully occupied and due to that, he had not been selected as a member of the inner circle, which was led by Clayton and possibly William.

Isabelle had asked me, with her back home now, if I thought I could possibly wait to leave William until after Billy's and Janet's wedding on 6 April 2013. She thought it best that we presented a united front so as not to ruin their big day. It seemed like a lifetime away but I agreed to try, now that I had her to turn to. But I said to her that if I was to stay any longer, I wanted to get a dog. She agreed as she adored dogs as well. I suggested we get a small dog and had seen a television vet claim that Jack Russell was the sturdiest breed. We were out having lunch when I suggested we get two so that we would have one each. Isabelle agreed but I would not be informing William as I no longer cared what he thought of anything. He was systematically turning my children against me with his lies and I was just treading water until this sham of a marriage could be ended.

I was what you may easily term a total wreck, and still had not smoked despite William 's continuing campaign of ignorance to ensure my failure. He was failing and not liking it, it had now been six months and he had not been able to make me give in. Coupled with the fact that I now knew another of his horrendous truths and believed that he was a paedophile, his abuse of me was growing exponentially with every day that passed.

I had asked him to bring the mop and bucket from my en suite and he made a nasty comment as we met up in the kitchen. He was off and screaming at me, I responded in kind. He slammed the handle of the mop into my forehead, causing my glasses to bang into my eyebrow. It really hurt and as I had my mobile phone on me, I immediately called Isabelle who was at work so that she could witness everything he said. She did and was horrified at his actions against me. It was the 3rd time in our marriage he had resorted to physical violence against me but it would be the last. This was early February 2013.

Things eventually calmed and I assured Isabelle that I would be okay and she could remain at work. From that moment on, I kept my laptop on the dining room table so that I could email Isabelle as soon as he looked like kicking off physically again. He sat on the front patio waiting for Ben to get home from school and Ben could tell by the look on his face that something was wrong. 'What have you done this time?' he asked Dad.

'I tapped your mother with the mop handle and she is making it seem bigger than Ben Hur.'

'Are you sure that is what happened, Dad?' He claimed it was but when Ben came in to see me, he could see it had been much more than a tap and he told his father so. But William still maintained his version of events despite the fact that Isabelle had heard all but the initial exchange. Ben still says that my glasses were bent and that I had a mark on my forehead even though it had been many hours since the incident when he returned from school.

The damage was done. I became a true insomniac; I was living in fear for my life. I did not truly know what this monster was capable of. I had bought a doorstop to stop him coming into my room at night. There was a lock on the door but he would use his filthy dirty long fingernails to unlock that in a second. I spent the next few months only ever dozing; I could not risk sleep whilst he was in the house.

I had sent a text to every one of my children to advise them of what Dad had done to me. Their support was overwhelmingly evident by its massive lack; were these the children that I had brought up? It was during this time, with Bianca's strange behaviour toward me, that I got on the phone to her. It did not even sound like Bianca's voice and the words she was saying could not possibly be coming from her heart because mine was breaking. The severe abdominal and chest pain continued to escalate as I realised that Bianca had been turned against me. I was inconsolable from that day on. I felt physically sick and wanted to die. She told me that I deserved everything I got, but why, what had I done, no one would tell me anything. The truth was that the only thing I had done wrong had been to marry William. I truly believed that I would not be able to continue to live without my beautiful "Krink".

I begged William to tell them the truth as none of them would now listen to me. He claimed he had, which, of course, he had not. His web of lies was now so entrenched in my children that all I could do was crumble and watch it happen. I was numb after the realisation about Bianca; I kept sending texts and emails asking to meet up so that we could sort things out, especially with the wedding coming ever closer. She was too busy and uninterested to entertain me in any way. This was not the person I had always known as my daughter. I was incapable of comprehending the depth of depravity that William had sunk to—to be able to turn my children against me so completely—but I also knew I never would understand as I blatantly lived on a totally different plane of existence to the one that he inhabited. Was it my mental illness that was preventing me from seeing what was happening in my life or was it that William's abilities as a narcissistic psychopath, voyeur and psuedologue were too far beyond my comprehension as an empath? I did not know the answer to that question and at that point, did not know where to turn to get that answer. All I knew then, as I still know now, I need, want and love my babies just as much today as I did at the moment of their birth. Nothing has ever changed for me. Despite many years of tapping, mindfulness and meditation, to name but a few, as I write this, I feel that same sick feeling in my gut, the same emptiness in my heart and severe abdominal pain that is the longing to hold my babies and grandbabies in my arms and to tell them how much I love them.

I have never, and now believe that I never will, stop waiting for them to come to me. Every single time a car pulls up, every time the doorbell rings, every time I go to collect the post, receive a text or my phone rings, just for a second, I hope it is from one of my babies. Now that it is almost time for me to leave Brisbane forever, I am having such anxiety attacks that I am abandoning my babies and grandbabies. Even though I have spent the better part of a year culling, selling and giving away my most precious reminders and triggers of my past life, I have come to a point where I can no longer pack as it will accommodate the move away from my beloved children. It has been scientifically proven that it only takes between two and three years for an average intelligent adult to realise the lies of the narcissist/psychopath. A special lady who I met when I first came to live in Loganlea said to me that they will come back, hers had after three years and she had been in the same situation that I had. I hung onto those words but three years came and went, four years came and went. But I will never give up on the intelligence that I know my children have. At some point, they have to work out they have been lied to and brainwashed by very sick people and as, thus far, not a single one of them has ever asked me about that which I have been accused of, surely, I should be given the opportunity to defend myself. Is that not a basic human right?

I had asked Rosemary in 2012 if she would do my make-up and hair for the wedding, she had said yes. In fact, she had said, 'You are very lucky that you are the first to ask me as I will only do one apart from myself.'

I think I was meant to feel privileged that she would be helping me in this way. I had been informed that the mother of the groom had to "fit in" with the mother of the bride so I could not do anything regarding an outfit until I knew what Catarina was going to be wearing. I had already purchased new suits for William and Ben. But Billy did not really want his father to wear a suit as Alfie did not own one and was not accustomed to formal wear. William was insistent that he would be wearing his suit. Once Catarina had purchased her dress, which was black and white, I had to try and fit in with that. I felt that black and white left me nowhere to go. I had been researching online and had found two outfits I particularly liked. As they had to be shipped from USA, I needed to get a decision from William and Janet as to which they preferred. Luckily, they agreed with the one that I most liked. It was fairly formal and I had no real idea what Catarina's dress looked like so I had no idea of knowing whether I was going over the top. I also ordered silver shoes with 3¼ inch heels from USA and spent many hours walking around in them to get reused to walking in heels. To cover myself, I also bought a pair of flats in the same colour as my dress, which was peach.

William and Janet's wedding was to be a 3-day event in Noosa. Initially, everyone was to meet at a restaurant for lunch on Friday. After a horrendous journey full of arguments and wrong turns in Noosa, we were unable to find a park within miles of the venue and time was continuing to slip away. I was driving our vehicle and Clayton and his family were behind us. Eventually, someone had to ring William junior, (Billy) and say that we thought it best if we went straight to the accommodation (which William and Janet had paid in full for all of the family members). It was to be a beach wedding followed by a boat ride up the Noosa River to the reception venue on Saturday morning. A taxi was booked for us to be taken to the wedding. The accommodation worked really well for us. It was upstairs and downstairs and could be used as separate units or as one for a larger family. So, William, Ben and Zach had the downstairs and Isabelle and I had the upstairs. On Friday night, Brianna brought Ashley and Emily to see me, which was lovely, but as no children were allowed at the wedding, I would not see them the following day.

Rosemary and Michael and Jasmine and Richard were all staying in the same complex but none of them had come anywhere near us. Bianca and Debbie were actually holidaying in Noosa and I did not know where they were staying but she made no effort whatsoever to come and speak to me in order to try and make Billy's wedding day more family-oriented. I also was no longer going to have anyone do my hair and make-up as I was well and truly being ignored by Rosemary. It was heartbreakingly difficult to know that most of your family were so close and you were not welcome to visit them.

The day that I had dreaded for so long arrived, that I had even offered not to go to so that all who thought me such a criminal could enjoy their day. It was, as I had suspected, going to be the most difficult day of my life. We arrived at the spot where the wedding was to take place and finally got to speak to my son, Billy, before his wedding. He seemed to care less. I took a seat where instructed and just waited for things to get underway. As I was seated there, Bianca, Rosemary and Jasmine all came and gave me a peck on the cheek and said how nice I looked but that was it. They just as quickly moved away and stayed away. I had been given the "kiss of death", or at least that is what it felt like at the time.

The wedding went off without a hitch and was followed by photos taken on the beach. My heels were constantly sinking into the sand and I almost fell over so many times that I had to take them off and go barefoot. Once the photos were done, we were all directed to the two waiting vessels that would sail us up the river to the reception. Once there, we were directed to a large waiting area outside the room where the reception was to be held. Plates of food were being brought out but they were devoured just as quickly. As I was a diabetic, I needed to eat at certain intervals and it had been many hours since I had eaten breakfast. I was feeling very nauseated, light-headed and very hot. I did not want a fuss made but if I did not get something to eat soon, I would need to leave and find some food. Finally, Mitchell's girlfriend, Shelley, went up to the staff and explained the situation and brought out a special plate of nibbles. I was so appreciative and very soon felt much better. Even though Billy and Janet had gone to the trouble of having several pages printed up as part of their invitations, one of which was about any special dietary requirements, no real arrangements had been made to accommodate those with the same. Billy had known for three years that I was diabetic and he also knew that Isabelle was allergic to shellfish. For all the airs and graces and false shows of concern, especially given all the doctors and nurses that were in attendance, there was absolutely no concern shown of any kind regarding dietary needs.

When the wedding party finally arrived, there was more fun and frivolity to occur in this same room. There was dancing and a load of talking. If they had just bothered to mention the time that their wedding meal would be served, I could have made other arrangements to accommodate my medical conditions. But I guess that would have been too easy really. We were finally all shown in to the tables and it seemed to still take a good while before the food was served. All of our family was seated at one very long table. Of course, Bianca, Rosemary and Jasmine were way up the other end of our table. In my experience, and I have been to many, many weddings, the parents of the bride and groom normally sit at the bridal table on either end to show them the respect for having brought up these children.

It was such a difficult day. I was pleased to see some of Billy's friends that I had not seen for a good while but I had no idea what they thought of me at this point or what they had been told. Although William had sat beside me for the entirety of the meal, he had started to move around once it was finished. For the first time since a toddler, Bianca came and sat on her father's lap as if to confirm that I was on the outer. The speeches had been interesting, to say the least. The most William could say about me was to speak of the time when he had broken his leg and I had been his carer; I was very disappointed with that. Then there were tons of more photos, they were definitely far more interested in their friends for this. All the young people were going on to a club so we walked back to the apartment. It had been an extremely lonely and sad day for me but I also knew in my heart that it would be the last full family occasion that I would attend and that was even sadder.

The following morning, before heading back home, was the 3rd leg of the wedding—coffee and croissants in the park. Not everyone was there but many were, quite a few very hungover. It was not too long before William decided that we should be off. I was happy with that as no one was speaking to me anyway. I said my goodbyes, to those I could, and we made our way back to Brisbane. William and Janet were off to South America for their honeymoon.

Upon returning home, Isabelle and I starting preparing for the arrival of our two puppies, which was due to occur on 19 April 2013. I was sewing blankets and pillows and covers for their new beds. Isabelle had gone mad having special bowls made with their names printed on them, Hamish and Angus. It was a complete case of overkill but this was my distraction from the abusive and extremely invasive life I was leading and I was pouring my heart and soul into it. As the puppies we had chosen were born in Glenn Innes, a 4-hour drive into New South Wales, the breeders, who were off on their holidays, had asked if we could meet them at Aratula, a small township west of Brisbane. They were to also deliver another of their puppies to a new owner there as well. We were so excited to collect our new boys, they were so tiny and fluffy.

It most certainly cannot be said that we received the warmest of receptions on our return home but neither Isabelle nor I cared. We settled the boys in, showed them around their new home and set about setting up a routine. Isabelle had bought a huge playpen for them to spend time outdoors each day, giving me the opportunity to do some work and get them used to the new arrangements. It was a huge pen and had a cover over half of the top to provide them with shade. As it was made from metal, the air circulated beautifully. Isabelle tried it out but we were too busy wanting to be with them to worry about it. On Monday, when Isabelle returned to work and after they had finished their breakfast, I set up the pen, put in their water bowls and put the boys in there. I was trying to complete my housework. William was, as always, sitting on his arse on the front patio. It tuned out that Angus was a screamer. He was not impressed by being encaged. As Angus was my dog, I most certainly understood his plight more than he was capable of ever understanding. I, however, as a mother of nine children, had an awesomely effective "off switch" so this did not bother me. On the other hand, William was constantly telling him to shut up and swearing at and about them. The pen lasted two days before William was ready to kill him and I never bothered to put it together again.

When Isabelle had first come back from her overseas trip, she had booked a 7-day cruise for herself and me to Cairns and back. It was in early June. Her intentions were extremely honourable; she wanted to give me something to look forward to where I would not have to worry about abuse and surveillance cameras. It was a posh suite with a balcony and a lovely bathroom. It also had a sitting area and television. We sailed on 8 June 2013 and returned on 15 June 2013. Our biggest issue with going on this trip were our precious new puppies. We could not leave them with William as his cruelty to dogs in the past ensured that they would probably not still be alive on our return if we had chosen him to care for them. We really did not have anyone and after much discussion between Isabelle and I, we asked Rhianna if she would babysit them for a week, we would pay her for it and her mum, Agnes, could help her. We were fully aware that Clayton was not a lot different from his father but we put our faith in the fact that we had entrusted Rhianna and not Clayton to the task of caring for our beloved boys. Early on the Saturday morning that we were to sail, we gathered everything the boys would require and headed down to their new home for the week. They seemed very happy when we left them there and hurried back home to be sure we were back in time to get our pre-arranged transport to the ship.

The minibus was not a second late and we were off, leaving William standing there with a smirk on his face. I knew he would be up to no good during the following week. We had to call in at a hotel in the city to collect other passengers for the cruise, a family from New Zealand. As we approached the ship terminal, the excitement grew for both Isabelle and I. As we were among the VIP passengers, we were in the first group to be loaded on to the ship. The meals were open from that time so that we could eat lunch and rest in our cabin. I sat on the balcony watching all the luggage being taken aboard and all the other passengers coming onboard. It was dark by the time the 2,000 passengers were aboard and we started to leave the port of Brisbane. The ship, Pacific Dawn, had to be turned around first and then we were off and sailing. Once we were out into Moreton Bay, we were really on our way for our cruise.

That was the first night that I fell asleep almost instantly and slept so soundly that I got a real shock upon waking up the next morning. It had shown fantastic foresight to pre-purchase travel sickness pills before sailing, as I was having some real issues with nausea that following day and I spent most of the morning lying down. Using the medication worked a treat and I began to really enjoy the freedom, being able to see the ocean all the time was the most incredible part of helping me calm to a point where I could finally start to make some real decisions. There was a variety of different age groups on board from young families to old couples and groups. What struck me and, in fact, stuck out like a mountain the size of Everest in the middle of the ocean, was the number of older couples who were blatantly in love and actually enjoyed each other's company and were sitting in groups discussing both previous cruises and further plans. The way they cared for each other was a thing of beauty and I had never experienced the true affection they shared, something that I never received from William at any point in our marriage. I knew this was something that I could and would never experience in my life. I was hanging on to a marriage that really should never have survived this long, and actually would not have done but for the fact that I was still in love with William despite all the abuse he had put me through and I had married for life, to me that did not mean when it became too difficult, I would throw in the towel and walk away. With professional assistance and medications, William could have been helped to deal with his mental conditions and although he may well have and probably should have been convicted of his crimes against both me and our children, I could probably have put up with almost anything. The fact that I suspected he was a paedophile and not only against my first daughter and his but possibly against more of our daughters, was my breaking point but, until this cruise, I could not let go of the love I still felt for this damaged individual.

The cruise truly was a wonderful break for me and the longer it went, the more I enjoyed it. I could well have become very used to living in an environment where everyone was friendly and there were smiles for all. The peace I felt sunk deep into my bones and it was certainly a feeling I hoped could be maintained once I was on land again.

Of course, altogether too soon, Isabelle and I were back in Brisbane. We were with the first group to be disembarked and so arrived home extremely early. We were barely there long enough to have a cup of tea when Isabelle and I headed down to collect our precious little boys. They were extremely pleased to see us and it was said that they had been well-behaved. We paid Rhianna and she was very grateful. Isabelle was to learn later on that Clayton had been hitting the dogs almost constantly. We knew that something had changed as their behaviour was so totally different to what it had been when we had entrusted their care to those whom we thought could be trusted. We should have had Clayton done in for animal cruelty.

William had indeed had a busy week. He had been taken, by Clayton and Bianca from what I could ascertain to get a new bank account set up and get his 18+ card as prior to this, he did not have any photo ID. It had very blatantly been organised for the week when I was not around. The need to be so underhanded and do things behind my back proved that any last threads of trust or respect had completely evaporated in that instant. The marriage, in my eyes, was completely over and done!

A house divided cannot stand.

-Matthew 12:25

CHAPTER 23

THE GREAT DIVIDE

The following Monday, 17 June 2013, I sent a text to all of my children stating that it was time for Dad and I to go our separate ways and I would truly appreciate that what was the most difficult time in our lives should be amicable and conducted with decorum. I knew it would be anything but with the way my children were already treating me and had been for many, many months now but it was and always would be my goal that, as William and I were the parents to 12 children in total, we could find a way to be amicable through the hard part of the process so that when it came to important milestones and events in our children's lives, we could all come together as a family without fighting, bickering, name-calling or ignorance. I expressed these wishes over and over to William and Clayton in person and to all the others through emails, all of which I still have. I could not then and still do not understand, why it is that seemingly intelligent adults cannot actually read and comprehend the English language. And further to that, if they have misunderstood or misinterpreted the written word, why then they did not come and speak to me, their mother, and ask what I meant, explain to me what they are accusing me of and why they can so suddenly stop loving the one and only person in this universe who has always loved them unconditionally and never, ever used violence against them. They chose a different path.

I had informed William later that night of the text that I had sent to all of our children, he again had not a single word to say to me. I had asked for amicability and decorum in our separation but I had known in my heart that he would do everything within his power to ensure it was anything but. I was also equally confident that he already knew that I had sent a text and was fully aware of its content.

On Tuesday, 18 June 2013, William had an appointment with his GP to get test results for his right ear. I was informed that I was to drive him and remain in the car waiting. The journey back home was filled with a tale of woe. He claimed to have been diagnosed with a cholesteatoma, which is an abnormal, noncancerous skin growth in the middle section of the ear behind the eardrum. It can be a birth defect but is most commonly caused by repeated middle ear infections. Cholesteatoma is a serious but treatable ear condition. Bone erosion can cause the infection to spread into the surrounding areas including the inner ear and brain. If untreated, deafness, brain abscess, meningitis and *rarely*, death could occur. This information is courtesy of Wikipedia, many thanks. William's version was far more dramatic. He only had 18 months to 2 years left to live. He would become deaf, blind, be unable to eat and the whole side of his skull would cave in as his bone was eaten away. He went on to paint as grim a picture as he possibly could. Blatantly, he had this issue and had known about it for more than 20 years. It had first been discovered when he was seeing a private ENT specialist in Annerley. The surgery had been booked to do the reparation; in those days, I ensured that we had private health insurance. When William had found out that the anaesthetist would charge $300 over the scheduled fee, he refused to have the surgery performed. Again, approximately a decade prior to this time, William was being seen by the ENT department at Logan Hospital and had been diagnosed with this condition and again William had refused to have any treatment for it. It most certainly suited him now that it had advanced to be able to play it up to the maximum. William was in possession of a smartphone and could very easily have looked up cholesteatoma before coming back out to the car! I am absolutely certain that he contacted every one of the children and told them his tale of woe.

I did not realise at the time, but came to understand much later, that William 's description of his impending death was made to look as bad as it could possibly look for both my benefit and for the sympathy vote from his children. I now understand that he honestly believed that I would not leave him if I actually believed he was dying. He seemed to forget that he had been guaranteeing me that "he would be dead soon" since he was 45. I was hardly likely to go into hysterics over this revelation. I was as familiar as everyone else with the "boy who cried wolf". I received a text from Jasmine stating that I was not to do anything or make any decision until she had the chance to come and speak to me. I was a big girl and I had every right to make my decisions based on the information provided to me. The fact that my entire married life had been a continual series of "Secrets and Lies" had finally become evident enough to me now and I had made my decision. I had to look deep within myself—the wife, the nurse, the empath—and ask if I was capable of caring for this man who had abused me and my children for 32.5 years as he was dying. Essentially, was I prepared to wipe his arse? The answer was an emphatic No.

Billy called a family meeting for Saturday, 22 June 2017. I did not really see the point of the meeting as I had communicated everything that they needed to know via text and emails. To my mind, it was just a bit of chest beating by Billy and Clayton. William was obviously concerned about what I would do with the information I had on him once he really believed that I would leave despite his best efforts to get me to stay. He came and sat at the dining table one day and said to me, 'I have been thinking and there are only three things that you could have me done for, the rest you cannot prove!'

When I asked him what he thought about me telling all of the children the actual truth, not his excessively distorted version that painted him as the victim, he replied, 'It would only be your word against mine!' Bingo! He had just proved all of his children to be liars as they did not come up with that exact statement on two other separate occasions without having had discussions with their father with me being the topic of conversation. This was something they all repeatedly denied to me. Now I knew the truth of their lies. I was astonished but realised that all he and they were concerned about was whether I would ensure he ended up dying in jail, where he truly deserved to be for the crimes he had committed. If he had actually loved me, which is what he had claimed consistently despite his actions telling a completely different tale, he would probably have made some sort of effort to apologise for all that he had done and caused and would have promised to seek professional help and marriage counselling or whatever else it took to save our marriage. But he did not. Instead, he systematically, with the help of Clayton and Tracey, turned my children against me and seemed to relish it. He also had Clayton take him to visit the grave of Angela, his first wife, and made absolutely certain that I knew exactly where he was going. The only way that marriage could work for William was on his terms, without any compromises on his part ever! Angela's acute myeloid leukaemia had been caused by the stress he had kept Angela under and the crap she had had to wash off his work clothes when he had worked for Queensland Rail. Just as I have been inflicted with asbestos from unpacking his suitcases, doing his washing, etc., when he worked on the ships. The fact that I have even been on the ships and in the engine room and the laundry of the ships with the dryers blowing asbestos fibres everywhere, is the reason I have been diagnosed with COPD and am also registered with the Queensland Asbestos Association. So, both Angela and I will have died at the hands of a man who loved no one but himself.

The meeting occurred with very few of my children there. Clayton attempted, for the second time, to coerce me into not claiming Dad's insurance money upon his death. The first time this subject had arisen had been when Clayton had sent Zach to coerce me into not making a claim on his insurance money. It was not enough that when William had first received his asbestosis diagnosis that he had contacted AMP stating that he was now terminally ill and wanted to claim his $20,000 in full. It was, of course, declined by them. That was William's 2nd attempt to claim that money. When the insurance policies had first been taken out by William and I in 1992, they were for the purpose of having enough money for funeral costs and help cover any debts to make life easier for the other party. Both William and Clayton were particularly money-hungry bastards but for Clayton to try to coerce me out of a lousy $20,000 was incredible.

I asked Jasmine what it was that she had wanted to speak to me about but she claimed it was all too late for that. I was asked about the items that I had purchased with my $9,000 superannuation pay-out when I had retired at age 55. I had already listed off in an email the items that I would be unable to take with me and asked for a small payment for each as they were only 1½ years old. I made the error of stating that "I" had bought the Gazebo in Bunnings. That was all my lawyer son needed to start his abuse of me. 'There is no such thing as "I" in marriage, there is only "we".'

I tried to explain a few other things to him and again he was off. 'How dare you speak to me like that, I have three degrees and I know a lot more than you do.'

Bianca had eventually shown up after work and in no mood to entertain me. I mentioned that they had gone behind my back whilst I had been on the cruise to get William organised with everything he would need to be on his own. Bianca claimed, 'We did not go behind your back at all, you told us about Dad's need for a bank card, etc.'

'No Bianca, I did not tell you any such thing.'

She insisted and whilst William sat at the other end of the table not saying a single word just smirking, I stood up to leave the table and as I passed Bianca, she tried to grab my arm and I reefed it from her grasp, telling her to leave me alone. I keep records in triplicate and I have the memory of an elephant. Why did my children think that this would have changed? The truth was that I had written an email to Billy, and Billy ONLY, and I had requested that, until further notice, he keep the contents of that email strictly to himself. He had not! The information that Bianca was now claiming that I had told _them_ was actually from the email I had sent to Billy in May 2013 when I had applied for a disability support pension due to my health. Now at least I knew for certain that I could no longer trust Billy.

Nothing was really gained from this meeting. Clayton was very blatant in saying to the others, 'Let's go to the Coffee Club to continue this conversation.' I was in a dreadful state but there was no going back now. William was behaving like the spineless prick that he had always been and I could not wait to get out of there. I was the elected house inspector. The very first house I saw I loved and felt was perfect as it was so private with a 6-foot-high metal fence all around, a huge double garage and double carport, three bedrooms, a huge undercover outdoor area and a separate laundry, across the road from a shopping centre, a street away from Ben's school and extremely close to buses and trains. Its two drawbacks were an extremely small kitchen and the bathroom needed repairs. This was Isabelle's first foray into private rental and she wanted the dogs to be allowed inside the house. This was absolutely never allowed in this country. She had gotten the real estate to agree to allow them to sleep in the laundry but Isabelle was not satisfied and wanted more. We were automatically rejected for the property, I was devastated.

I kept looking and so many were just crap so we decided to look at the smaller houses that had cropped up in the streets behind the family home we were leaving. I went to view one and whilst it was a three-bedroom house, it only had one bathroom and the bedrooms were small, but it had a large backyard for the dogs. We applied for it, sent through all the paperwork required and we got it. It was only two blocks from our previous home and a short walk from Brianna in the next street. We were moving on 19 July 2013. I sent an email to all the children to advise them of our move date and also to organise a working bee to clean the place out so that Dad was not left in a massive mess. William stated immediately upon hearing we were moving that anything that was not taken was going straight to the dump. Most of the children still had at least some belongings in the storeroom, garage or shed.

I had called Jonathon to organise a time to go to his place to speak to him. I went over one evening when both he and Bec would be at home. I told him the whole truth about William, what my life had been like and what he had done to me and what I now suspected that he had done to Brianna. I asked that he not try to sort anything out as he had claimed he was going to do when he had first heard Tracey's accusation of William in 1984—he had intended to kill William. I told him when I was moving and what the new address would be. I offered him the air-conditioner that had belonged to Mum that he had installed in my bedroom. He said that he would call over on the day we were moving to collect it.

When I arrived home, Isabelle advised me that as soon as she had walked in the door that night, Dad had told her, 'Mum has gone to see Jonathon.'

She had said, 'Yes, I know.'

He had added, 'Well, that's the end of fucking fishing.' He had then walked away. The light was beginning to come on in my brain, especially as the day to move arrived and Jonathon popped in to collect the air-conditioner and William totally and completely ignored him. What could Jonathon have possibly done to warrant this total turnaround in William 's attitude towards him? He had supposedly considered Jonathon a best friend and certainly used and abused him when it came to things that William wanted. He had found out William 's truths. Once anyone found out William 's truth, he disowned them. The problem was that when I found out his truth, in 1990, I had been his wife and he could not get rid of me or totally ignore me so he chose to start abusing me in a big way and the more truths I found out about him, the worse the abuse became. It seemed so obvious now but I had been unable to work it out before—you cannot know something until you know it.

Just to backtrack slightly here, the weekend before we were to move had been the working bee. Bright and early on Saturday morning, Rosemary, Michael and Mitchell had arrived to collect their belongings, mostly from the shed. Rosemary was even speaking to me and I was delighted. One may have even said that she was chatty. They sorted what they thought was all of their stuff and were off. Of course, Clayton was there, nothing ever occurred in my life without Clayton being present. Billy arrived. He was busy packing all the pavers into the back of his car followed by the white pebbles; there was no offer of recompense. William was basically just walking around giving orders, many of which he should have consulted with me about first, according to the law of Billy! He did not, however, actually lift a finger to help in any way. I was working like a beaver and got quite agitated by this. 'For God's sake, William, could you not actually do something to help instead of just barking orders?'

Zach had been working quite closely at the time and he said to me, 'But Mum, Dad is not allowed to do any work or lift anything heavy.'

'What are you talking about?' I asked Zach.

He replied, 'His lung thing that stops him from doing anything.'

I smiled at Zach and said, 'Oh Zach, the pneumothorax was totally healed six weeks or so after it happened in February 2010, he has been perfectly capable ever since but has chosen to fool you all.'

Zach had looked at his father and said, 'You lying bastard.'

William made the decision that Billy could have our shed and that it could be dismantled and laid on the back lawn; therefore, causing all the remaining shed items to be placed on the uncovered part of the back cement. Later in the day, when there was an absolute mess everywhere and everyone had left, I did my best to drag as much as my aching body would allow me to under cover, even lifting boxes of items up onto the outdoor tables so that they had some cover overnight. I worked until my body gave out.

It was thundering rain by the following morning and anything that had not made it under cover was totally saturated. Jasmine and Richard arrived, announcing that they would only be transporting Dad's rubbish to the dump! When they arrived, I was emptying the buffets and dividing the items up. Jasmine was in a feral mood and it was all directed at me. She was almost yelling at me at times. I could not take her attitude any longer and I retreated to my room, crying and shaking, to try and sleep to quell the increasingly worsening migraine. Rosemary and Michael arrived whilst I was there to collect the last of her things, which had been amongst those left out in the rain. Of course, she started a rampage of abusive language, all of which was directed at and about me. She completely and totally blamed me for every single bit of it instead of the people who had actually caused it to be in the rain.

The remainder of that week was difficult, to say the very least. I ensured that my bedroom, walk-in-robe and en suite were immaculate and that we were fully ready to go on Friday morning. We were up with the larks and at the service station to collect the Ute we were hiring to assist with the move by 07:00. Richard had offered his services with the help of his friend, Zach; Isabelle had accepted. I would have preferred they were nowhere near us but at least on this one occasion, Richard displayed a conscience, which was much more than any of my other children did. I had gone next door to the neighbour who had been there throughout the entire time I had lived in this marital home. He had lost his beloved wife, Nora, whilst I had been working full-time and was now a very lonely old man. I wanted to say my goodbyes to him as it would be impossible to come and visit him without being seen by William. I had to choose my words very carefully as I did not want William to mistreat Noel the way he had so many others when they knew the truth about his behaviours and actions. The moment I walked back into our front door, William was in my face wanting to know exactly what I had said to Noel about him. I had finally worked out his secret and why he had treated me so despicably poorly for all these decades. I felt so sad that I would not be able to see Noel again; I could not take the risk of William causing him any more suffering than he had already endured.

The move was all accomplished in an orderly fashion and when I was doing the last load with the hired Ute, I looked around the house to which I did not believe I would ever return but William said nothing to me as I came out the front door so I replied in kind and said nothing back. Our marriage had ended, no pomp, no ceremony, no last hoorah, not even the slightest of efforts on William 's part to improve things or the offer to try to seek help, no apology for his atrocities against me or even to ask me to stay—just over.

Feelings of worth can flourish
Only in an atmosphere where individual differences are
appreciated, mistakes are tolerated,
communication is open,
And rules are flexible
The kind of atmosphere that is found
in a nurturing family.

-VIRGINIA SATIR

CHAPTER 24

HOW DO I MOVE FORWARD NOW?

For the first week of living in a new and different property, it was a flurry of unpacking, sorting things the way they were best suited in the very small spaces that we now had to deal with, settling the dogs into their new environment but mostly there was, within me, a tentative peace that I really was free of William at last, mixed with stress as to how I would cope long term and what this brand-new life might throw up on my journey along this path.

I had always hoped and prayed that William would find a conscience and tell our children the truth about the situation he had kept me in for decades. On the contrary, as I would learn later, he would destroy all that was precious to me and continue to try to brainwash my children against me. Zach had still been living at home with him when I left and was, one might say, somewhat antagonistic towards me at first. I could not understand his actions as we had always been so very close. He told me sometime later that he had been able to watch Dad as he had tried to turn Zach against me as well. He was intelligent enough to see the game his father was playing. He told me that he was actually pretty good at it, but not quite smart enough to fool my Zach. What does that say for William, Jasmine, Bianca and Rosemary?

Days became weeks and I busied myself with the gardens and cleaning the house. But it was not enough to stop me from constantly falling into the abyss. I knew that Ben was very depressed but I did not have the wherewithal to help him at this time. We argued frequently, he wanted help from me that I was incapable of giving to him because of the darkness that surrounded me. He had fallen into his own abyss when he had gone to Dad's on one Friday night when all the siblings had been there for dinner. He came home so dejected as no one had spoken to him, not even his father. What had this poor kid done to them? He was in his senior year of high school, undertaking two extra-curricular courses and trying to deal with having to leave the family home. William never made one single mention of Ben, where he would live, when and how he would see him, would he need to pay child support to help Ben until he turned 18. Nothing, nada, zilch about the youngest of his 12 children. Everything was about William and trying to brainwash his children against their mother. There was no other way that Ben could feel other than totally rejected by his family when he, himself, had done absolutely nothing to deserve being blacklisted from his blood.

It hit me extremely hard as this was the child that I had allowed to be born after William 's secret about his affair with his sister-in-law had come to light, just to ensure that my children did not grow up in a broken home, that William did not get the free ticket that his grandfather had taken, that my mother did not get to throw things back in my face and that I could fulfil my lifelong dream to have 12 children of my own. Ben had not asked to be born and most certainly did not deserve to be abandoned in this most heinous of ways. How alone and lonely must he have felt when I, his greatest supporter, could not do for him that which he needed so desperately because of what his father had done to me. I was devastated and fell further and further into my own abyss.

Every day when I arose, I would try to make it a positive day, but every day something would occur to bring me down. One such day was a Sunday when Isabelle, Brianna, Steve and Ebony were going out to the shops. They were calling in at Dad's on the way. Steve called me and said, 'Mumma, you had better get ready for some visitors as everyone is here at Dadda's and I am sure they will come to see you soon.' Oh, the innocence of children. That is most certainly what I had requested over and over to everyone, but not a single one of my children came to see me that day or since, with the exception of Billy, extremely rarely, until May 2014. Down I would go again, despite my best efforts to try to remain upbeat. If I had ever been given, from any of my children, the reasons they perceived that I no longer deserved their love, then I could have started to deal with it. Without having ever been told a single reason for my ostracisation, which was totally suspicious and reeked of they themselves knowing their actions were totally unwarranted, left me with the equivalent of "dead children" with no grave to place flowers on, to mourn on the day I lost them, no closure as to the "why" I had lost not only them but my beloved grandchildren.

William's birthday was 11th October and when Isabelle had called in on her way home from work to wish him a Happy Birthday, he stated that he would have liked to have heard from me. I saw this as an opportunity to open communications towards getting my estranged children back—nothing more, nothing less. He, naturally, was excited when I called him and asked me if I would come and visit him. His birthday had been a Friday and I agreed to visit the following Wednesday, in the middle of the day so that no one else would be around. I started getting extremely jittery and nervous but as I would walk over hot coals with even the slightest hope of re-establishing contact with my beloved estranged children, I would undertake whatever to achieve this goal.

I pulled into the drive feeling extremely tentative and immediately realised that my gorgeous garden was being totally neglected; my heart sank after the thousands of hours I had spent creating a place of peace and beauty. I walked in the front door and started shaking to be back in this "house of horrors". I immediately felt like I needed to turn around and run. I did not as I was here to try to establish a way to get my babies back. I tried desperately to calm myself enough to take a seat and be able to state my case. I was not there for small talk after the hell this man had put me through. I asked him straight up, 'What are your expectations of us meeting up?'

He stated that he wanted me back. I asked for a family meeting with all of my children present. 'They will never accept that,' he said. I could and should have ended it there and left but I so wanted to get my children back. When asked why he had not told our children the truth of why I was left with no other choice than to leave him, he stated, 'There was fault on both sides and that is what I told the children.'

That made no sense to me as they were all self-proclaimed intelligent people, and it would have taken a lot more than 'fault on both sides' for them to totally abandon me. William could not maintain eye contact with me whilst he said any of this fabricated truth. Nor did he even hint that he loved me, missed me, found life difficult without me or any other sign of a normal "man in love", he most certainly did not respond to ask what my expectations were of our meeting but he was on home turf. I was going to have to try a lot harder so I invited him to our new home for dinner. A chance to see where his youngest son lived and spend quality time with him.

William was his usual arrogant macho self as there was yet another young lady there, he felt duty bound to impress, Ben's girlfriend, Tracey. They had never met before and boy, did William slip so easily back into his role as the "master of all he surveyed"! He was a bloody guest in our house but acted as if he was the lord and master! He had spent way too much time lingering in my bedroom and I could not wait for him to go home. I offered to take him shopping, which he stated he would like, and we agreed on a day. That too was a display of William 's charm offensive at its best, or from my point of view, his worst. When we arrived back at his house, I offered to help unpack the groceries. It was then that I noticed the missing clock from above the front window. Jasmine and Richard, many years ago, had given William an anchor clock as a gift, which he had really loved. It had broken; how, was anyone's guess, and I had asked Jonathon to replicate the clock. I had paid him for the actual clock but he would not take more payment as he had all the wood, varnishes and everything else he needed in his workshop in spades. I asked where the clock had gone. As cool as a cucumber, William replied, 'Oh, I smashed it up with the hammer and threw it in the bin.' What sane man would do that? Did he think he was hurting me? Or perhaps Jonathon? Or perhaps just being the vindictive little man that he had always been? I had never believed any differently before or since that day but it was just so true that leopards never changed their spots.

I was becoming more and more distressed and making little to no headway with getting any closer to being in touch with my children. As it was now so close to the end of the school year and Ben was completing his last year of school, I decided to make this last bit of effort. The darkness was all but engulfing me but I have always put my children's needs before my own and I would not change now. William had called and asked if he could come for dinner again. He had bought the main component and told me to just do salad and chips. I so did not want this to occur but felt I had no choice after the path I had set for myself and I owed this much to Ben after the total upheaval he had endured. William had purchased a huge marinated salmon filet. He had arrived earlier than I would have liked. He had no choice but to smoke outside in this rental property, which he did not like at all. I was using the sprinkler on the backyard and for the final section, he was unable to go outside for a smoke. When I went out to turn off the water, he said, 'Thank fuck for that.' He had been unaware of exactly where the tap was—right behind his back where he sat on the dining chair just outside the window—and when I came in, I asked if he had spoken to me. 'Oh no, I was just telling the dogs that you were turning off the water.' Lies just flowed from this man's mouth like water flowed over Niagara Falls.

The meal was the same bravado as Tracey was again present. On this visit, William had even had the audacity to ask where we were going on our holiday this year. I could not believe it. 'I had to cancel it as I cannot afford it,' I told him. Jonathon and Bec visited often and Bec begged me to seek the professional assistance of a psychologist as I was now sliding so far backwards into the abyss that any progress I may have made since leaving the marital home was totally gone. I went to my GP to organise professional assistance and as she was blatantly not up to the task of working out her patients' true diagnoses or needs, I was referred to a family therapist and had to await a call for the first possible appointment.

As hard as it was for Ben, he managed, by the skin of his teeth, to complete and pass year 12. He looked so handsome on the day of his Formal, I was so proud of him. I took him to his father's so that he could see just how handsome he looked. Clayton and Rhianna were there when we arrived. As I was walking down the road from the car to the house, I waved at Rhianna and said hello. Clayton completely ignored me, spoke to Ben and was off. I will not state here what I called him, after all I had done for him throughout his life, it was extremely painful to be treated as a bit of shit on the ground to be stepped over and avoided. Brianna, Steve, Ebony and Isabelle were there. Many, many photos were taken. Isabelle was driving him to collect Tracey, where many more photos were taken before Isabelle drove them to Southbank where they were being collected by a beautiful horse-drawn carriage. It was two days later when Ben graduated from high school. William had been invited but as always there was the age-old excuse for everything—I am not well enough to go. Ben was truly pissed off that his father could not make this tiny effort for the last ever time. My 33 years of having dealt with all the aspects of school for all of our children had come to an end. We returned to show William his certificates and miraculously, he seemed perfectly fit and healthy, all normal fare for me. Ben had, through stress and depression, failed to complete his courses and lost his guaranteed job from one of those courses. The blame for that lay squarely at the feet of his father and all his siblings. Every single one of them had been fully supported through their entire schooling, at least by me, and not one of them could acknowledge the huge achievement made by Ben who had lost his family, his father and his siblings and still made it. Unlike them who had received the accolades, Ben actually deserved them and was given nothing but a sizzler lunch by his mum. What a truly sad indictment that was in the end.

A mere two weeks later, Ben turned 18. Brianna decided that she would give Ben an 18th birthday party at her house as she had known that no one would come if it were held at our home. Isabelle and I were busy doing everything we could to assist Brianna. Isabelle had ordered the most expensive birthday cake any of my family had ever seen and I had to collect it from Salisbury in the factory on Friday, 29 November 2013 at 12:00. I had my first family therapy appointment at 13:30. It would be tight but I crossed my fingers and went for it. I collected the cake with no worries. It was when I got back home that the trouble started.

No matter which way I turned it or how much I removed from the fridge, the box and the cake were just way too big to fit in the fridge. I thought of the 600+ litre upside down fridge that I had left with William and called him to ask if it would fit in there. I had measured the dimensions of the box. He answered the phone and was in a funny mood. I asked, 'Could you please measure the inside width of the fridge as Ben's birthday cake will not fit into this one?'

'Why should I?' he asked.

'Well, it is extremely hot and there will not be too much of a cake left by tomorrow night if it is not refrigerated,' I replied.

'What's the rush?' he asked.

'I am running late to get to an appointment.'

'What appointment is this?'

'Just an appointment, William, are you able to help me or not?'

'Well, I could say no, you know,' he said, and I hung up. He had once again proved that he was absolutely nothing more than a sperm donor; it takes a lot more than that to be a father.

I rushed to my first appointment with Margaret, with whom I hit it off immediately. She had been a psych nurse for many, many years and had then gone on to train as a family therapist. That first session was explicitly about how I would be able to get through Ben's 18th birthday party without actually falling apart and embarrassing

Ben in front of all his mates. His siblings were attending, except for Clayton. Jonathon had refused to attend so as to avoid any conflict with William. It was a tumultuous hour and a quarter during which Margaret got to hear about the cake saga as well. She said that she had a Styrofoam box that she thought would be big enough and ice bricks. I said I appreciated the offer but I would work something out. I left there feeling empowered and good for the first time in months.

When I got home, I started the mowing and Margaret rolled up with the Styrofoam box and ice bricks as promised. I was overwhelmed with her generosity. A woman whom I had only met a couple of hours earlier was showing me so much kindness and compassion. This was something my own family could not do for me. When Ben got home, I told him about the conversation with his father and asked if he would try. He rang him and he said yes and that the fridge was big enough. We could take it around straightaway. Steve, Ben and I set off to travel the two blocks to the house. Steve and I remained in the car as Clayton's car was parked out front. To be treated with such disdain once was more than enough for me; I could not take it again. I hoped Ben would be in and out as quickly as possible.

No sooner had Ben entered the front door than William came rushing out to my side of the car. I put the window down, and the barrage started. 'Why didn't you answer your phone, I called you over and over?'

'I was in an appointment and had my phone on silent. I had told you earlier that I was running late for an appointment.'

'And who was the appointment with?' he asked.

'That is not relevant, William, I had an appointment.' He kept going and going, with his grandson in the front seat beside me. I eventually gave in as I could not lie. 'I saw my psychologist, if you must know.'

'Oh, so you have told them everything about me?'

'Yes William, I have told her the truth and she is going to help me.' I was disgusted with what he said next in front of our grandson and started to back the car up. The moment Ben got in the car; I was off.

All the empowerment that had been achieved only a few hours earlier was all but gone. How could I get through Ben's party in one piece so as not to ruin his big day for him? I would do anything to ensure it went well and would have to just do my very best. It was a long and sleepless night for me but the day had arrived and all I could do was the best I could muster, given the circumstances, to get through it. It was absolutely no surprise to anyone that William decided, yet again and for only about the millionth time, 'I am too sick to attend.' The gutless wonder, to let Ben down so badly in the space of two weeks was unforgiveable to me. Ben, however, has never and will never forgive him. He told me just the other day, 'I do not like Dad at all.' Not one of our children had an 18th or 21st or, in fact, any birthday without their father being present, except for Ben.

The time came to head to Brianna's for the party. The cake had been collected from William who, by all accounts, was perfectly well but putting on the usual 'woe is me'. It was a finely honed act that fooled almost everyone, except the one he was married to who could pick a malingerer a mile off. If you were going to claim to not be able to get your breath and be coughing and spluttering, you were probably best to be medicating yourself correctly, which he never did, probably should not have a lit cigarette on the go almost constantly, which he always did. The biggest dead giveaway of all with a patient who suffered from COPD and asbestosis—there was absolutely no sign of cyanosis and pulse and all other observations were perfectly fine, then you were very clearly bullshitting!

I had the shakes good and proper by the time we arrived and the tears were barely able to be held at bay. Thankfully, there were plenty of Ben's friends there to distract me and Tracey had my back. She was very aware of how I was feeling and kept a very close eye on me. I took up a position right outside the back door beside the food table, not so that I could eat but so that I could hide in the corner and slowly drink a bottle of wine. I almost never drank anymore but this night I was going to need it very badly.

Slowly, my children began to arrive with their partners. Jasmine said hello to me, Richard said an obligatory hi to me. I asked if I was allowed to speak to my gorgeous grandchildren, Ashley and Emily, I was and I did but as children, all they really wanted was to run off and play, especially as we had bought our dogs with us. Rosemary had trouble saying hello, Michael gave a grunt. William and Janet both said hello and gave me a kiss. Zach and Mitchell were their usual loving selves. The party was underway but the one I had stressed about the most, Bianca, would not arrive until she had finished work and when she did arrive, she walked straight past me without so much as a glance and had not brought her partner, Debbie. I could not contain the waterfall any longer. I went into the lounge and cried; I could not stop. Tracey had followed me in to comfort me, I would forever be grateful to her for that. I finally managed to compose myself and went back outside. None of my children spoke to me; they were huddled in the same old gossip group, looking as if they believed they were better than everyone else there. We did the cake and everything was going really well. I had resumed my position and continued to drink. I watched as Ben went and spoke to each one of his siblings, one by one. Bianca was not there for long and again walked straight past me without a single sign of recognition and was gone. When Ben and Tracey had eventually returned home that night, he said to me, 'Mum, it will be back to normal soon, I have spoken to all of them and I do not think it will be long before they come and see you again. Bianca told me that it was more complicated than it seemed, but I am sure my talk with each of them will work.' What disappointment Ben was to feel when things seemed to go from bad to worse.

My therapy sessions were frequent from that time on as it had torn my heart out to be treated with such disdain after having spent my entire adult lifetime giving totally of myself to my children, always having put their needs before my own, I had always been proud that I put all of my children on a pedestal, I was so proud of the people they were and the adults they had become. Now all I felt was emptiness and shame that they had fallen for the brainwashing of their father, Clayton and Tracey. I was the one who had cared for them from the moment of their conception, NOT Dad, NOT Clayton and most certainly NOT Tracey. How could I move on from this with no idea of what I was supposed to have done that could warrant this treatment of their mother? After this apathetic display by William, I told him I never wanted to see him again and that I did not want to hear from him either. He considered himself absolutely wonderful to have given Ben $50 for his 18th; I had given him a $400 watch and a lovely pair of cufflinks for his formal/graduation.

Christmas came and went; it was a non-event that first year from my point of view as I had no funds to buy gifts for anyone other than cheap meaningless things. Due to flybuys points, there was plenty of food and Isabelle, Brianna, Ben, Steve, Ebony and I all enjoyed a nice meal together. William and Janet had come over on Boxing Day for a visit and had offered to come and collect Ben to take him down to Clayton's on his birthday, 28 December, for a BBQ. Apparently, all they could talk about was me and Ben was stuck in the middle of it. We ended up arguing after he arrived home, inebriated.

I tried again, as it became 2014, to focus on the garden, the house and the dogs. Unfortunately, the old gentleman who lived next door turned out to be a real pest and had decided that he did not like us and was going to get rid of us. Within the first two weeks of living there, I had been warned by two different acquaintances who lived on the same street that this man was a paedophile and to watch him closely, especially when my grandchildren were there. One week to the day that we had moved in, a woman knocked on my front door, introduced herself as the neighbour from two doors down, invited me to become part of the community garden scheme they were discussing with Council for the empty land on the corner, and generally kept me talking and talking. The dogs were barking and I had moved from the front door past the car to where I could see that it was the next-door neighbour with his arm over the fence doing something with the boys. She eventually left after seeming to have received what she had wanted. Later that evening, Angus had to be rushed to the emergency vet's and was diagnosed with haemorrhagic gastroenteritis. That exercise cost more than $1,000 and, more importantly, we almost lost him. I will never be convinced that the neighbour did not feed him bad food as he had already made it perfectly clear that he disliked the dogs, that they could not possibly be Jack Russell pups as they were black and white when, in fact, black and white was their dominate colour, but they are actually tri-colour. His part Jack Russell was brown and white and she ate what he ate and therefore it was good enough for all dogs. He was told to desist in feeding our dogs but I have photographic proof that he continued to do so. As the fence was only 150cm high, we sought and were given permission to put up temporary fencing to a height of 180cm in front of this to try to prevent the neighbour from defying our requests; it did not. The irony of the situation was that the female neighbour never ever spoke to me or acknowledged me in any way ever again and there was never a community garden and still is not, to this day.

Also, during the first week we lived there, he informed us that part of the fence between our properties was being replaced the following week. He told us that we had no need to concern ourselves with it as he was great mates with the owner and his father and it had been worked out between them seemingly without real estate involvement. We should have been informed by the real estate of any upcoming works to be performed on the property. No workman had any right to come onto our property without first knocking on the front door and introducing himself/themselves and advising us of the purpose of their being at our property. Neither of these things had occurred and even though I was hanging washing on the line, never once did he even have the manners to acknowledge me. Isabelle and I had fenced off an area for the boys so that they would be safe and not able to hurt themselves or escape the property. I was sitting at the dining table writing when I sensed someone close. I looked up to find the neighbour IN our backyard, with his dog, leaning over the barrier to touch our dogs. I was home alone and froze. I called my daughter at work immediately.

Living with this person constantly staring into our home at us was doing very little for my mental well-being. I had even purchased an outdoor blind that I attached to the Al fresco area in an effort to try to prevent him from causing us to live in a fishbowl. As time went on, there were heated words exchanged. He disliked it greatly when I watered the garden between our properties and came onto our property through the side gate and cut my brand-new hose that had a 15-year warranty on it. Again, I have photographic proof. He had stated that he made neighbours move that he did not like and we were on the hit list. This filthy dirty old man could be seen and heard in the evening drinking beer and urinating at the front of his property. This was equally as bad as living with a paedophile, narcissistic psychopath who was also a voyeur and psuedologue… It could not go on; I was all over the place.

During our time living in this house, Jonathon, who had always believed that he knew better than anyone else, came for a visit. After making him a coffee, he asked if we could sit out the back as he had something he wanted to tell me. He had called William and recorded their conversation. He had specifically asked if he had used surveillance cameras to film me in my bedroom. William had said, 'Yes, I had every right to.'

Jonathon had said, 'No, you don't, it is illegal without consent and knowledge.'

'She had stopped having sex with me and I had every right to work out what was going on.'

'No William, you did not.'

William had replied, 'She was masturbating.'

Jonathon had said, 'She is allowed to, you know.'

William was apparently too thick to realise that his idea of sex was not mine and even though he was told this on a weekly basis, he would never change for anyone, especially when he very wrongly presumed, he was the world's greatest lover. Jonathon continued to try to question him, 'Did you sexually abuse Tracey and Brianna, William?'

'No, of course not.' The conversation had ended rather quickly after that. Jonathon put a copy of the recording onto my PC.

'We have him now, Mary,' he said. 'I will organise a meeting for you to meet Andrew and Phil and start proceedings against him.'

'I will meet your friends but I am not certain that this is the right way to go, Jonathon. I have absolutely no idea why my children will not speak to me, what it is they perceive I have done to lose them so how would this help me get any closer to finding out their truth?'

'But William is guilty of so much,' said Jonathon.

'Oh, believe me, Jonathon, for what he has done to me, Tracey, Elise and Brianna, he deserves to be in jail being raped and mistreated just as he has done to all of us.'

Jonathon took me to Andrew's house; we were there for hours going through the shit life I had led at the hands of William. I spoke to Phil on the phone in New South Wales. They were looking into many things and we would communicate via email and phone and decide what we would do and how we would tackle it. Jonathon trusted Andrew and as my only prior personal knowledge of solicitors was when Brianna had been just a baby, I could only play this out and see what happened. It just so happened that Billy had interviewed for a job with them but was too scared to take on the position, according to the way they told the story. Billy never, ever once, apart from his abuse, had actually given me any legal advice or even advised me to seek professional family law assistance. Did he not have a duty of care ethically to make sure that I knew my rights, at the very least?

Isabelle, Ben and I spoke and I started looking for possible houses to rent. We really just needed to stay on the Beenleigh trainline for Ben to get to college and with good bus links for Isabelle to get to her government job in the city. We had decided to go further south and Ben and I saw one house in Loganlea that we thought would suit our purpose and took an application form. Isabelle could see all the picks on line and it was rather dirty, which would keep me occupied, but we applied for it and we got it.

I had been packing up for weeks and so after signing the contract on 19 March 2014, Ben and I immediately started to bring boxes down to the new house in Loganlea. We continued to do so every day so that it was mostly just the big items that needed to be moved on Saturday, 22 March 2014. A lot of Ben's mates had come to help with a trailer and a Ute or three; Jonathon had brought his trailer and we had again hired a Ute for the day. Zach had also come to help us move. William, he said, had been calling him all morning trying to find out where we were moving to, Zach would not say. In fact, he rang several times whilst Zach was with me. All he ended up saying was that we were moving south a bit.

Billy called me to find out where we were; he was at the old house and had come to help. I told him that it was almost all done but that we would be back there soon. I had been ignoring his calls due to the verbal abuse he consistently aimed at me. I had hung up and then refused to answer his calls. He was livid that "the mighty lawyer" had been kept waiting for so long. Had he had the common sense to advise someone of his intent, then perhaps we could have organised things better. He again chose to verbally abuse me; I gave as good as I got but I was in such a mess. I was extremely pleased that he had driven his own car down to the new house and was there for only a very short time before he left. A truly sad indictment when one was so pleased to see the back of their son but I did not deserve the constant abuse he kept handing me and I did not need it.

After much thought and deliberation, I decided that I would speak to the police to get an opinion on what I could/could not do regarding William 's blatant breaking of the law. Jonathon took me to the Logan police station and we spoke to a very congenial police officer. I, again, had to describe my woeful marriage and what William had done to me. When he asked if I had the cameras and I told him that my son, who was a lawyer had agreed with his brother, my stepson, that I should destroy the evidence, the policeman was in a state of total disbelief. 'And he is still practising law?' he asked. Of

William, he repeatedly asked, 'How has he never been diagnosed as narcissistic or psychopathic?'

All I could say was that he was a master liar and had never been caught out and that no one, including my children, had ever believed my concerns about their father. The officer advised me that the recording could not be used to prove his guilt simply because he could lie and say all sort of lies in court as this was blatantly a way of life to him. But he told me, 'You cannot allow him to get away with what he has done to you and the effect it has left on you.' He explained to me, 'By law, surveillance without knowledge and/or consent is classed as "psychological abuse" and I want you to go to the Beenleigh Court to the DVU (Domestic Violence Unit) there and apply to have a DVO taken out against your husband.' The officer apologised that there was nothing more he could do to punish William but he needed to be made to understand that there were consequences to his actions.

I went to Beenleigh Magistrates Court, alone, shaking, darkness all around me. My only other experience of having been in a court had been when Billy was charged, when 17, for trying to remove his $2 coin with a straw from a public phone box when it would not go down so that he could make a call, and when William had been admitted to the Bar as a solicitor. I was drowning in a very deep ocean here. I was directed upstairs to the Domestic Violence Unit and was treated with such kindness and compassion but I was still a nervous wreck. I had explained my situation and the kind lady that was helping me wanted this matter to be submitted that very day, she considered it that urgent. The forms had to be lodged by 16:00 and she was even helping me fill in the forms with the information I gave her. It was such a limited amount of what had occurred in my married life that actually ended up on the forms and I felt that there was no eloquence or continuity due to being rushed but, after she had brought in a second superior team member to check, they both considered that the insignificant amount that was written was more than enough.

We went down to lodge the application and I was given a court time to get a temporary DVO. Again, I went alone as William would not even have received his paperwork as yet. The temporary Domestic Violence Order was granted immediately and without hesitation and a date was set for the next hearing, at which William could attend to defend himself, if he so chose.

I was a nervous wreck, deep in the abyss of my darkness but I knew that William had to understand, somehow, that the way I had been treated by him for more than three decades was both immoral and illegal and if this was the only way to make him sit up and take notice, then I had no other choice but to avail myself of this action.

Your value does not decrease based on someone's inability to see your worth.

-UNKNOWN

CHAPTER 25

THE FINAL INSULT

On Mother's Day in 2014, Billy and Janet came to visit rather late in the day, circa 15:00. They had bought me a beautiful orchid. Janet was very pregnant with their first child, a girl, and she was extremely well and enjoying the pregnancy. I had, despite my financial hardships, managed to layby a selection of baby wear, which I presented to them boxed and wrapped. I would have much liked to have done a second and more but Janet stated that nothing would be going on the baby that was not cotton or wool so I had to be very particular in my selections. They seemed to like and appreciate what I had bought for them, all neutral colours, but one could never actually work out what was going on with Janet as she said so little and there was never any excitement in her voice and her face was almost always expressionless.

They stated that they could not stay long as they were only calling in on their way to Ikea to purchase baby items. I asked Billy to come down to my room and I showed him the paperwork for the second DVO mention. He went rank at me and started to accuse me of all sort of things. He stated:

My trials and tribulations over the last three decades had nothing on what Janet's parents had been through and that he would hear no more of it. He belittled and demeaned my life for the past 32.5 years. I stated that he had no idea what I had gone through, what I had put up with or how often I had screamed silently into my pillow and cried myself to sleep for the sole purpose of preventing my children from growing up in a broken home.

Billy accused me of seeking revenge on Dad as the reason for a DVO against his father. I advised him that it was, in fact, *justice* that I sought for the criminal acts committed against me and other family members.

Billy then went on to state that I was an embarrassment to him for posts that I had put on Facebook and which had been seen by his "friends". In fact, it was only one of his friends, Taps, who was a chef and had worked with Jamie Oliver. I had an email address for Taps to send him a thank you for the wonderful treatment that Isabelle and I had received when dining at *15* in Melbourne. I had also started to develop an online acquaintance with his mother, Emily, a truly lovely lady. Taps and his wife were to give birth to their first child the following month and I anticipated that beautiful event with great glee for all concerned. But after Billy's tirade, I unfriended Taps so as to save him any further wrath from the son I was very fast becoming ashamed of. I did email him some time later to apologise for my own behaviour. His response was so kind. He told me, 'No mother deserves to be treated the way you have been.'

Billy claimed that I would never have come up with the statement, 'I only want what I am legally entitled to', without having been told to say that by my lawyer. I advised Billy that in fact I had gone to my legal team to seek what it was that I was entitled to (first meeting in January 2014) only after the email I had sent to William, Billy, Jasmine, Bianca, Rosemary and Mitchell dated 15 September 2013 had been completely ignored and I had received no reply. I told Billy that as a lawyer, he had never ever advised me on what I should do with regards to family law. The only mention he had made to me, whilst abusing/insulting my intelligence (22 June 2013) had been 'No "I" in marriage' and his 50/50 Rule. I had wondered then about his brand of ethics, especially as a member of the law society. Today, I am certain of the type of ethics he uses.

Billy also claimed that he was a 'professional' and all this stuff 'demeaned' him. He further stated that he did not care to know the intricacies of what had gone wrong with Dad and I, and I should just drop it and move forward.

I was completely gutted by this barrage and gave him a quick cuddle, thank you for my present, then headed back down the hall to say goodbye to Janet. I immediately told Ben what had occurred. He was furious that I had not called him in to deal with Billy but I did not want Billy to have another single reason to stay a nanosecond more than was absolutely needed.

The court date approached quickly and Zach and Ben had both come with me. I was in a dreadful state mostly caused by Billy's abusive tirade earlier that month. The boys were extremely protective of me. Our case was called but there was no sign of William. The judge entered and sat, then stated that he had received a letter to the court from William —he was not well enough to attend court and he neither confirmed nor denied the allegations I had made against him. The judge smiled and granted the DVO without hesitation for a period of two years. After receiving my copy of the "letter to the court", I understood the judge's wry smile. The letter had not been written by William, the manner in which it was written made it completely obvious to me, as it had been to the court, that it had, in fact, been written by a lawyer.

Billy had now at least given up the pretence that he actually wanted me in his life. I had already been left on the side-lines of every single important event and milestone in Billy's life, since Janet had become part of the picture. Billy's siblings continually stated to me that Janet wore the trousers in that relationship and that Billy was just a little "bitch". I had so often told them they were wrong but I was finally beginning to see the truth of their statements, especially with the complete 180 my eldest son had done whilst living in England, the latter part of the time with Janet. I had said to Billy once, 'You left Australia my son but since your return, I have no idea who you are.' He had changed so totally that I could no longer see any remaining evidence of my "Fatman".

With the impending birth of another grandchild, I had thought it fortuitous to send Jasmine and Richard the legal documentation, which fully stated the legal rights of grandparents to see their grandchildren when there were separations, deaths and estrangements in this state and country. My greatest hope would be that they would have the good grace to, at long last, allow me access visits with my beloved grandchildren, Ashley and Emily. Of course, as with every single previous email I had written to my children and/or their father since 19 July 2013, it went unanswered and nothing changed.

Sonia Lee was born to William and Janet on 6 July 2014 just after midnight, as far as I am aware. I did not get a text with a picture until 07:30 the following morning. I knew then just exactly how far down the pecking order I had become. Mind you, it had also been a text to inform of their engagement. Things were just not done the way that I had always experienced in my life. I had been at the hospital from the time that Jasmine had arrived until the birth of both of her children. After Emily was born, it was I who went to get Ashley so that he could come and meet his baby sister. I had also been with Brianna for the birth of both of her children, Steve and Ebony, had cut their cords and given them their first baths. With Jasmine, she had given birth to Ashley in the old Mater Mothers and was then transferred to the new Mater Mothers. The following evening on my way home from work, I had called in to show Richard and Jasmine how to bathe a baby, as requested by them. With Emily, Jasmine had been released sooner so the following day on my way home from work, I had again called in at their home to bathe my beautiful new granddaughter. It was considered that it could become some sort of a tradition for their "Mumma" but Billy and Janet made extremely short work of that. Due to the situation with my other estranged children, I did not feel that I was welcome to go and see my beautiful new granddaughter at her home despite the fact that my heart ached to see her and Billy from the second I had received that original text.

Quite far into the depths of depression, I decided to make one last effort to appeal to my children with an email that stated "very clearly" what my feelings were at that time. Of course, the 9,206-word email was written from the darkness and despair that was engulfing me. We had arranged for William and Janet to bring Sonia Lee to visit us the following Sunday. Although this email had been in the making for a considerable length of time, I felt it was essential, after the verbal abuse that I had endured from Billy on Mother's Day (the last time I had seen him), that he should know exactly how I felt before I allowed myself to fall deeply in love with this beautiful little girl and then have her taken away from me at the whim of the arrogance of Billy and Janet.

Billy's arrogance knew no bounds and I truly believe that he had no idea of how deeply he had been hurting me for many years or I have to accept the fact that I truly was not good enough to be his mother and that he only cared about himself. That made him a narcissist also; what a shame. *The apples do not fall too far from the tree*, as the old Asian proverb states. Billy's reply to my email was swift and harsh. 'Given the content of your email, I am forced to cancel our lunch this Sunday at your house.' He also added, 'I have consistently stated that I would like to move forward with you. This still stands. I will leave it to you to make contact with me.' This was written 17 July 2014 and every attempt that I have ever made to make contact with Billy since that time has fallen on deaf ears. This says to me that he is a liar and never ever intended to have me in his life or that of my granddaughter's, unless it was under his terms. But his total lack of response would suggest that even that was no longer on the table.

I had, in April 2014, had my antidepressant Cymbalta increased to the maximum dose of 120mg/day due to my major depressive disorder for which I had been medicated since 2008. I was now diagnosed with PTSD as well and continued to see my therapist on a very regular basis. I was sinking deeper into the darkness and felt completely alone in my struggle to emerge from the abyss. Neither Isabelle nor Ben were familiar with the extent of the mental illnesses that I was suffering, except for Ben's own depression. I began to seek help online and stumbled across EFT, tapping and through that, meditation. It was an enormous help, I felt I was now taking baby steps in the right direction at least.

In August 2014, I discovered, during a routine round of cardiac checks, that I had a mass in my heart. This just added so much more stress to my life and indeed was just another of the stress-related conditions caused by trauma and abuse at the hands of my family. I was referred from the Logan Heart Centre to PAH to the cardio-thoracic surgeon. I was seen by the consultant, Dr Ura, who ordered more tests. I had a T.O.E. (Trans Oesophageal Endoscopy). Unlike the heart MRI, it showed that, although it was quite large, it was not, as yet, causing any obstructions to major vessels, which had been suggested by all previous tests. It was an atrial/septal lipoma. Dr Ura had been convinced that I would be straight in for open heart surgery following the results of the T.O.E. but I was given a reprieve. He did order an angiogram so that when he did have to operate, he could be aware of any other unsuspected things that may require attention and he could deal with them all in one hit.

The angiogram showed that there was no evidence of arteriosclerosis. I received another reprieve but all the doctors kept saying, 'You have to lower your stress levels.' But when I explain my life history and the way I have been treated by my "family", they fully understand. Of course, it is now common knowledge and has been scientifically proven that 99% of all bodily diseases are caused by stress of and in the body, only 1% is genetic. When one has been traumatised since birth to the point where you are diagnosed with OCD, stress is a constant companion. My mother and sister have everything to answer for in that department. Karma seems to be doing her job where my sister is concerned, at least! In fact, it has been stated to me that through their jealousy of me, my adopted mother and sister and/or someone else very close stole my future for themselves. The exact wording is "I'm certain that someone has stolen **YOUR** life, **YOUR** promised destiny." I was "bewitched" a short time after my birth. Someone close to me had been jealous and had obstructed my path. It could be as simple as someone staring at you with envy, called the "Evil Eye". I believe this to be true.

I ploughed further and further into spirituality and, at least for the time that I was completing tapping and meditation, I felt amazing. I was still having trouble carrying that through a whole day so I did more and more. I even tried yoga but have yet to get into that fully. It transpired that in approximately May of 2015, it was the last time I saw my therapist. Her husband had been diagnosed with cancer and soon thereafter, her mother died. It turned out that she had been unable to deal with the stress of recent events in her life and, in fact, had given up her career altogether and started a B & B on the Sunshine Coast. I cannot speak for any of her other patients, but I was left high and dry without even so much as an explanation, let alone being handed over to another professional for continued care. I found this to be totally unethical and such a disappointment from someone I had thought rather highly of but more than that, I was truly on my own and trying to deal with the darkness. I had been so totally let down by the medical professionals for decades and felt that there was nowhere for me to turn. My GP offered to refer me to another woman who worked in their practice, I declined. I was not prepared to tell the whole tale again just to possibly end up in the same position. I tried to plough on alone. Isabelle did not believe in mental illness and states that one should just be able to 'get over it and move on' and 'it is a case of mind over matter'. Ben, although he has, since leaving the family home, suffered from depression himself, has been my greatest help. He speaks wonderful sense and empowers me but I have always been unable to maintain it when the next crisis hits and the engulfing darkness seems to come thick and fast. When he is down, he accuses me and his father of causing his issues. He truly cannot understand my morals and ethics as he would just have left him. He is a man and has been badly let down by not only his father but his supposed siblings, who have totally abandoned him.

Later that year, in August, my PC was professionally hacked. I had a computer technician come to our house the very next day to see what had occurred. He was unable to retrieve the IP address of the perpetrator but could see that they had hacked in through Team Viewer 7, software that my sons had installed on my PC to enable them to play games against each other. The entry point had been disabled so that it could never be uninstalled. They had also removed many files appertaining to court papers being prepared for family court. It did not take a genius to work out who was behind it all. I reported this cybercrime to ACORN. They have never taken any action in lieu of this crime. I can understand that they have much bigger fish to fry but my PC was only three years old and was my link with the world and my only means to research methodologies that could help me improve my depression, PTSD, OCD and the loss and grief associated with my ostracisation from what I thought at that time to be five of my children and three of my grandchildren. It was also not the first time that things that should not have been known by those five children seemed to come to light. Ben and I were very clear on where we stand regarding the actions of one of that party of five…

November 2015 was family court. William, in his inexpert opinion, had decided that I did not deserve to know where he currently resided. He had also changed his mobile number and his email address. The truth, as I was told by my son, Mitchell, was that if he could not know where I lived, then I did not deserve to know where he lived. William, being disallowed to know where I resided, had been mandated by the Beenleigh Magistrates Court for the term of the imposed DVO. Ironically, two of my sons, Billy and Mitchell, knew exactly where I was, had both been to my home and I have absolutely no doubt that William was fully aware of my address. The real truth was that he was and still is waiting for the police to knock on his door and arrest him. My court papers had to be served on him and it was not actually, according to the Family Law Act in Queensland, allowed to be a post office box address. I again emailed all of my children to advise them of the impending court date and asked that they provide Dad's address so that he may be served with his paperwork. The

ONLY response came from Rosemary, she provided an address for them to be delivered to her work, the Australian Taxation Office, and she would pass them on to him. This was unacceptable as is stated by law, a marriage is between a husband and wife, no third party is to be involved. William would not be receiving his copy of the court papers before the date of the hearing.

In the months leading up to this court date, Ben and Isabelle were advising me that there was something off with the so-called barrister that Jonathon had introduced me to and who was making all kinds of claims and promises with very little in the way of concrete back up. I grew more and more suspicious when I originally tried to get William's address from my estranged children and Jonathon claimed to Andrew that he knew where William was living. Andrew then stated that as I could not be the one to hand them over to William, he would come and collect the paperwork and he and Jonathon would serve it on him. There was something very strange about the way Andrew kept asking me to do favours for him, having me type up letters for him (all of which I have retained), even wanted me to do ironing for him but the biggest problem that made me suspicious was that he kept bad-mouthing Jonathon, his supposed best friend, and constantly asking if I believed all the stories that Jonathon told. I spoke to Jonathon to ask for William's address, he claimed he did not know it. Who was lying here? It was not like Jonathon was not well-known for lying to me. I started to investigate and found that Andrew was a true conman. He would go to a pub on Friday and Saturday nights, handing out business cards, and then when people came to him, he would charge them $200/hour for advice but when the court date arrived, he was nowhere to be seen and these people were left high and dry.

I had received a letter from his supposed boss, Phil, in New South Wales, stating that Andrew was nothing more than a legal clerk who did some work for him. I had a suspicion that the con had been completed with a 2nd person as, when I was there one day with Isabelle, he kept calling someone else for legal jargon and terminologies. Andrew lived in a Department of Queensland Housing property but had a black Mercedes parked in the carport. He also had surveillance cameras all around his property. Very suspicious behaviour for an "honest" man. I sought out the help of a solicitor, who was wonderful. She was worth every penny that was spent.

When Isabelle and I first arrived at the Federal Circuit Court on the day of the hearing, William was sitting alone on the lower level. We had been instructed to go to the court floor and into one of the many available rooms for clients where my solicitor would meet me. William had apparently finally worked out where he needed to be and was sitting in the general waiting area. My solicitor served his papers on him then. He was madly going through them to see what was written. We were called into court and William tried to be his usual "smart arse" self by saying to the judge, 'I have only just received these papers', as if that would make me look bad. Instead, she replied, 'I see that you have made it very difficult for your wife to have these papers served on you by not providing, when requested several times, for an address.'

His tone immediately changed. 'Yes, I have, Your Honour.' The judge then stated that he had 21 days to have his paperwork completed and returned to the court and a copy to me. There was a date set for conciliation for the following February. The purpose of that hearing was to ensure that neither of us any longer had any claim over that which the other held in their possession. No claims would be able to be made by my estranged children for debts incurred by William and the same my way. After we came out of court, William was very busy whinging to my solicitor. He has too sick for this, he did not know how to fill out the forms, etc., etc., etc. My solicitor asked him, 'You have a son who is a solicitor, don't you, William?'

'Yes, but he does not do this sort of law.'

My solicitor advised him, 'I can tell you what the law requires you to do but I cannot give you legal advice, perhaps your son could help with that.' This did not prevent William from calling my solicitor at every opportunity he got until she refused to take his calls.

The paperwork that came back from William was abysmally written, no one had helped him make it look even partially acceptable, it was full of false information that did not add up and I contacted my solicitor to provide the proof of all the inconsistencies and stated that I was no longer interested in seeking the $10,000 that I was more than owed by William and that I would do whatever it took to prevent me from having to see him again in this lifetime.

She prepared the appropriate paperwork and I went and signed all my sections. It was then sent to William but as he had still only provided a PO Box number, time was slipping away and my solicitor had to contact Rosemary to get the ball rolling. By the time William 's paperwork was returned and it was sent to the court, there was not enough time for the Registrar to deal with the matter before the actual date. I was so far into the darkness by now that I was having trouble just getting out of bed. Isabelle and Steve would be coming with me. I had located two envelopes of William 's belongings and they were handed to him when he finally arrived, late, despite having been given the exact same instructions of where to go as I had. William was giving another Academy Award-winning performance that day but you just cannot fake having no cyanosis, no loss of colour or looking clammy or sweaty. Not my fault I am a shit hot nurse even whilst in the abyss!

William completely and totally ignored Steve; I was horrified—the arsehole, how dare he? We were called in to the Registrar and sat. William started carrying on about having to get to the Mater Hospital. The Registrar was no fool. 'Well, if you stop speaking, we can get on.'

He had been put in his place. He made a hasty retreat and it was at that precise moment I knew that it was over. I could no longer remain connected to this excuse of a human being. It was as if I did not even know this figure that stood there. How had I managed to spend so many years living with and having sex with this creature? The acts he had perpetrated against me were unthinkable and yet, my "self-proclaimed intelligent" adult children—unlike the scientifically average adult who only took 2-3 years maximum to see through a narcissist/psychopath—my estranged children have well and truly proved the old adage that *Intelligence and common sense are very rarely good bedfellows,* to the maximum degree possible.

I struggled then as I still do today to understand the rationale behind such adults never having bothered to explain to me, the accused, of what crime exactly I have committed that would be so heinous as to lose their love for me and prevent me from being allowed to see my grandchildren. The fact that William tried desperately to hide himself where I would not find him, which I did, of course, says to me, as I believe it should say to my estranged children, that there is something very wrong with them and their perceptions of anything that I have reputedly done wrong. Clayton also tried to hide himself after we moved to Logan. It was not too long before he and Agnes sold their house in Marsden at a $10,000 loss. It was sold again, for the same price almost a month later. I knew almost immediately that they were living in the units on the corner of Jackson Road and Lang Street back in Sunnybank Hills. His father was no longer there so what was his rationale for that move? Well, Brianna only lives a couple of blocks from there and the Clayton's car, the gold Honda, was often seen going up and down Brianna's Street. What was it that they hoped to accomplish? The new white Honda that Clayton had may also have been seeing driving about.

The fact that everything had been done in secret, behind my back and never ever once discussed with me left only one interpretation. They had, by Dad, Clayton and Tracey, been told the most horrendous lies that they were silly enough to fall for and now, even if there are questions in their mind as to the authenticity of those lies, they cannot drop their egos enough to approach me. Or as someone very close to me said, 'They are afraid to swallow the Red Pill.' In all Western societies, a criminal is assumed innocent until proven guilty in a court of law. There are due processes that must be followed, including in this country. That applies to everyone in the Western world, except me. I still have no concept of what I have been accused of doing. I have never had my day in court, which was and is my right, to defend myself. I was hung, drawn and quartered by simpletons masquerading as the intelligent beings they proclaimed themselves to be. After having been totally ignored by Jasmine and Richard and Emily and Michael at one of Steve's birthday parties in the park, I was sinking into the abyss. Isabelle wrote an email to her siblings explaining just how bad I was and how she feared what I might do to myself. A constant companion on my journey through the torment had/has always been the suicidal thoughts that might at least give me some respite from being treated like shit by my own babies.

The only response was from Rosemary. She claimed she had already dealt with me—a lie. She also claimed that she had a list of all the FB posts and emails I had written. I also had all the correspondence including abusive texts from her and Bianca but I emailed Rosemary nonetheless. I am a mother who gave 150% of myself to my children and I will never give up on them, ever.

I told her, 'We BOTH have said and done many extremely nasty things in the heat of the moment. I know I regret this and I thought as my daughter, you may too.' I further stated:

I have never blamed YOU or ANY of my children for my marriage breakdown because that would not be the truth

The person to blame is not you or I

You are the victim of a broken family

I am a victim of crime

I asked your father on 16 October 2013 to call a family meeting so that all this crap could be sorted—he refused

Rosemary's response: 'I really don't have the energy or time to continue this email trail. If you think there would be value in us meeting to discuss, I'd agree to do so; however, I think it would be best conducted with a mediator—someone outside the family.'

Bianca had, in one of her nasty texts, written, 'The whole situation is a joke and you have only yourself to blame.'

For what exactly is my question, has always been my question. What is it that I am being accused of doing? How can I ever move forward, with or without my children, without knowing what I am being accused of? I want my day in court; I want the opportunity to prove who is really responsible for this charade I now call an existence. The fact that siblings have been cut out of the "inner sanctum" and are not privy to the reasons reeks of the many secret societies in this world but they, at least, have codes of conduct that they must adhere to. They seem, at least to themselves and their followers, to have morals, ethics and integrity. Something I find there is a total absence of in my estranged children. As I am the one that raised them, I know I taught them these values so I am left to believe that the contrary ways of the dark side of the father seemed to make more sense than the true and honest way to conduct oneself that I tried desperately to instil in them. They, therefore, must have been lying to me their whole lives and that is a very difficult realisation to make. Such a sad indictment indeed...

*When someone in your life is a narcissist or sociopath,
it takes people around you a long time to realise the
true culprit in the relationship. Deception is at the core
of a toxic person's game.*

-SHANNON THOMAS

CHAPTER 26

THE GAME PLAYERS CONTINUE TO WIN

Both my physical and mental health deteriorated drastically in the period since 2014 and only continued to decline more at every turn. I had next to no interest in life and everything I achieved was only managed by pushing myself beyond my capabilities at any juncture. Isabelle always tried to make all occasions a big deal as if to make up for the total ignorance and stupidity that she saw as her estranged siblings. To me, there was no point in any celebration of any event without all of my beloved children with me. I had to feign interest, excitement and even happiness because Isabelle would have gone to so much trouble and effort that it would have been totally and completely unthinkable of me not to show my gratitude and appreciation for her efforts. All I wanted to do, and very often did, was cry.

For Mother's Day, May 2015, Isabelle had taken me to get acrylic nails done, and also to have my eyebrows and moustache done. I actually looked forward to having my nails done for the first time in many, many years. We went on the Saturday before Mother's Day. By the time I got home, I was feeling a little itchy around my hands.

By tea time, it was increasing. Overnight, I started to develop itchy areas on my face and at varying points on my body. Ben took me to Mt Tamborine to *The Codfather* for lunch with Steve, I could not stop itching. Mitchell had rung me whilst we were there. It was such a lovely surprise to hear from him, as it always was. Later that day, I was itching all over my body. Isabelle rang someone but I was not feeling up to going to a hospital so we applied calamine lotion. By Monday morning, I knew I was in trouble as I was having difficulty breathing. An urgent medical appointment was made and I was diagnosed with anaphylaxis. I was put on a large reducing dose of Cortisone and a second appointment was made for later that day, should I require it. If I was to suddenly worsen, of course, it would be straight to the hospital. We managed to buy a calamine lotion that had Lignocaine in it so, at least for a short while, I would get a reprieve and be able to rest. It took 6-8 weeks for the rash to even look like leaving. I had been due a haircut and the itching of my head was driving me insane. I went to get a haircut to my regular hairdresser of many years. After hearing what had occurred and seeing the remaining evidence for herself, she advised me never to dye my hair again and considered it a near miracle that I had not already lost all of my hair. I was devastated as I had never planned on growing old gracefully but then, I could no longer run the risk of going bald either. I chose the lesser of two evils.

After this event, my physical health seemed to be declining rather rapidly but without a real cause that one could put their finger on. I had eczema on my wrist when I had the nails done and had connected the two events as to something getting into my system through the very tender cracked skin on my wrist. It was so bad that I had to stop wearing all of my bracelets. It became equally as acidic to my skin as my wedding ring had been to me for years. Every time I put the ring on, it would become immediately inflamed and I would itch as if trying to put a fire out. I had put my ring on for Billy's wedding just before we had left the unit and before he was even married, I had been in agonising pain but had to last until the reception was over. I have never worn it again, from that day to this, but it is still plain to see where it used to sit as if I have been branded by it. My doctor told me that I am grossly allergic to white gold and silver. The only bracelet I can now wear is yellow gold; one Isabelle had given to me many years ago. All the others, in fact, all of my jewellery is now gone, given away.

On 18 September 2015, having completed vacuuming and washing the tiles, I was taking the bucket and mop down the hallway to the laundry. I had the bucket in one hand and was using my other hand to unlock the deadlock when my feet started to slide. I had not realised that there was still a slight amount of dampness on the floor. I could not correct myself in time and did the complete split sideways and hit the deck. I had to try and get my left leg back into a more natural position as the pain was excruciating. Miraculously, I had not dislocated my left patella but I could not get up off the floor and had to extremely painfully and slowly move as best I could to get to the PC room to ring Ben and Isabelle. Ben had not left that long and he came straight back home and helped me get onto the couch. He confirmed that I could walk, in a manner of speaking, to ensure there were no broken bones. As soon as Isabelle arrived home, she took me to the Logan Hospital. I had tried to lay down but was in too much pain so off we went. The staff there had been wonderful. I had done in my hamstring on my left leg. There was a lot of soft tissue damage as well. Due to my inability to take any painkillers other than paracetamol, I was left to deal with the excruciating pain until it righted itself. It has now been over two years and it is still not right. I suffer sudden excruciating cramps in that hamstring muscle and have suffered severe nerve pain since that day as well.

In 2012, after the scare with the neurosurgeon, Rosemary and I had gone to Garden City Shopping Centre to claim back some of the money they had outlaid for my private specialists from Medicare. I was so grateful to them, William, Bianca and Rosemary for not allowing me to be under further stress, not knowing what might be brewing in my head. We were at a café outside of Big W enjoying morning tea. I spoke to Rosemary about the concept of writing a book about my life for my children so that they would have a written history, so to speak. Rosemary had thought this was a wonderful idea at that time. I also tried to broach the subject of Dad by saying, 'Rosemary, there is a very strong possibility that Dad and I will not be together for very much longer and I would like to talk to you about that.'

'Oh no,' she said. 'I do not wish to talk about anything like that.'

I was let down again. And the more I was let down, the more the concept of my autobiography developed. I had written and rewritten the opening chapter in my head thousands of times and in 2015-6, I even started putting pen to paper, so to speak. Well, actually, putting fingers to keys in Microsoft Office actually.

In October 2015, I had completed a month-long mindfulness summit organised and conducted by an Australian, Mellie O'Brien. She had speakers from all over the world, one each day, and my mind was awakened and hungry for more. Throughout this summit, I was taking notes, names and any information that I felt could further my healing journey. I will, forever, be grateful to Mellie for opening my eyes to a whole new world. I immediately widened my modalities through this summit as one person would lead to another and another. I realised that I had regained the spirituality that I had developed in my teens, despite the Catholics doing everything they could to get their hypocritical claws into me. I had stopped believing their rubbish in 1968. That truly was the best month I have had in many; many years and I found a new exuberance for life.

Today, 10 December 2017, as I write this, I am in a very dark place. It has been 37 years since I made the biggest mistake of my life—marrying William. There are all sorts of things taking place here today and I am feeling about as low as I have ever felt and have already shed many tears today, not a single one of them for William. I am also acutely aware that he will be sitting in his 4th floor apartment, thinking just how wonderful he is to have fooled my children with his lies and left me with only the memories of the children I would still give up my life for in a nanosecond. Mitchell has given me the strength I need to carry on today, I can always rely on him to be there when I most need him. It is a true comfort to me. But that was a digression and I have tried, for the main, to keep things chronological and must return to that now. I am, however, reminded here of a post on Pinterest I saw and it just so aptly describes my ex-husband:

Beware the person who STABS you
and tells the world they're
the one who's BLEEDING.

-JILL BLAKEWAY

This was just so William, like the boy who cried wolf.

I undertook the writing of my autobiography in earnest in late 2015-6 whilst at the same time trying to undertake an online diploma course in mindfulness. I was also still tapping and meditating every day as well but it was a game of fits and starts as I slipped into and out of the darkness that constantly engulfed me. I also was dealing with the emotions involved in reliving my extremely traumatic childhood and beyond. I would, after writing something that had triggered a particularly bad memory, just curl up in a ball and cry. It would be weeks, sometimes months before I came back to both writing and completing my course.

I was getting nowhere fast on either front due to my mental illness; a new issue raised its head halfway through 2016. On 1 June, Isabelle had a day off work and had received some good news so we decided to go for a celebratory lunch at *Sizzler*. As a diabetic, I only had the salad bar as fruit and vegetables are my most favourite foods. We really had a most enjoyable time and a lovely afternoon afterwards. Later that night, I began to feel unwell and developed diarrhoea. Through the night, it became worse and I started to feel very unwell. Isabelle had gone off to work well before I got up and when I arose and tried to eat something, I realised just how nauseated I was. It was not long before I was heaving like I had never ever done before in my life. The interesting, although rather ghoulish, fact was that I was vomiting totally undigested foods from the salad bar, most notably the sundried tomatoes that had for 20 hours sat in my stomach, now were much larger than when they had gone in. I advised Isabelle that I was in a bad way and heading back to bed.

The vomiting settled through the afternoon and I tried dry toast at dinner time in order to take medications. Overnight, I became worse again and the gastroparesis that had long been suspected was a thought that came back into mind in the hours I spent sitting on the toilet whilst holding a bucket. Another thought was pyloric stenosis (a narrowing of the pylorus, the first part of the small intestine) and as I was projectile-vomiting, it truly seemed a possibility as well. The water diarrhoea went on almost constantly for 49 hours. I was completely dehydrated and so weak that I could barely walk.

Isabelle had made contact with my GP, in her capacity as my senior power of attorney, to establish which medications I needed to keep trying to take as I was becoming extremely lightheaded and almost collapsed many times. It was considered that I had experienced food poisoning from something that I had eaten at *Sizzler* but as I was taking hydrolyte and anti-diarrhoea medications, it was hoped that I would recover quickly. I did not, I lost the entire month of June 2016, only having left the house twice for visits to the doctor; I had lost 7kg in five days. Returning to feeling like my old self took even longer as I really did not know any more where my conditions ended and I began.

After this episode, I made the decision that I would fully concentrate on completing my mindfulness course and then plough into writing the rest of my book. I completed and submitted the assessment for my course work and was so excited when I received a distinction. The very first person I thought about was Bianca. I was reminded of the same level of excitement that I was experiencing now when she had passed her blood collections course. I had been so happy for her and could not stop crying that day as all I truly wanted to do was hug her, feel her beautiful soft skin on mine, smell her gorgeous hair and feel the love that always made me feel safe when Bianca hugged me. It had a basic truth to it and I knew that I could always trust her to love me as much as I loved her; well, times had changed. As happy as I was, it again became a trigger for yet another PTSD episode.

I was determined to move forward, millimetre by millimetre. I had been due to have surgery on 22 December 2016 for carpel tunnel syndrome and focal ulnar neuropathy of my elbow. Late on the Saturday evening prior to this date, I started projectile vomiting again and the diarrhoea followed. I had eaten only a home-cooked meal. This episode was not quite as severe as the one in June but was enough to prevent me from having surgery for the 2nd time. The first had been due to probable imminent open-heart surgery but luckily, I have managed to keep avoiding the knife as my lipoma has not, as yet, decided to grow at all, thankfully.

I was becoming concerned about what was causing these episodes as was Isabelle so we sat down and worked out a FODMAP/ low GI diet that I followed religiously. It had little to no impact on the oesophageal reflux or the IBS and I was constantly nauseated. On 6 April, I made soup for lunch. It was tomato-based with one carrot, one sweet potato, one slice of pumpkin, one can of corn, one can of tomatoes and one can of water. I had not even finished consuming this soup when I started feeling the now familiar feelings that preceded an episode of vomiting and diarrhoea. I went to bed and when Isabelle got home from work, I asked her for a bucket. I started projectile-vomiting at 18:30, the diarrhoea had already begun. Once the water diarrhoea started, I was in for a very rough ride. It would last for 60 hours and no amount of rehydrating fluids or anti-diarrhoea medication was going to stop it before it was done with me. My doctor truly wanted me in hospital receiving IV therapy but I was not going to soil myself en route to the hospital, which is exactly what would have occurred had I tried to leave the bedroom when I could barely make it into the en suite without having an accident.

I did, eventually, start to return to a somewhat normal state. What was normal for me and my body any more, I was not certain. But I was certain that something was amiss and each episode had involved tomatoes and other fruit and vegetables. Isabelle reminded me that tomatoes were a nightshade vegetable. We had already considered this but then followed on with FODMAP. Upon further investigation, it seemed fair to at least try to eliminate nightshades from my diet and assess the response from my body.

It has been an exceedingly long and difficult journey but I have never, since the soup, eaten another tomato—my absolute favourite food. Whether fresh, whole, sliced or cooked, nothing beats the taste of a tomato. Unfortunately, I will never again enjoy that simple pleasure. As time and experimentation has progressed, it would appear that I have had an intolerance for nightshades (any plant of the genus Solanum—family Solanaceae and all foods that contain Solanine not classed as nightshades) for many decades. It is stated that if you are a person who struggles with food sensitivities, allergies, autoimmune disease, inflammatory bowel disease or leaky gut syndrome, there is a greater chance that you will have nightshades contributing to your health issues.

It is not for me to give all the scientific information here other than to say that my sensitivity is not only to nightshades but to all plants that contain Solanine. I have been allergic to morphine, codeine and all its derivatives for decades—morphine is a nightshade. I first experienced this allergy in 1981. I smoked for many decades— tobacco is a nightshade—I now know why it had such an effect on my bowels. Yeast contains Solanine, it is incomprehensible how many foods use yeast, yeast extract or yeast flakes to enhance their food. I can no longer even use oyster sauce on my Chinese vegetables. My first-hand experience with anaphylaxis turns out to have been caused by the nail polish, which was a shellac polish; this comes from the Lac Beetle that feeds on wolfberry plants, which are a nightshade fruit, along with blueberries, another of my favourite foods. After having seen a wonderful dietitian at PAH, I have discovered that I am also allergic to salicylates, amines and glutamates. So, my diet is extremely limited. I am 80% plant-based, minus all nightshades and

Solanine-containing foods, low GI, GF and yeast-free. I do not eat eggs or dairy; I do not eat any soy-based products or corn (they are all GMO). There is precious little left. I eat a lot of salad, vegetables and fruit minus potato, capsicum and all other peppers, onion, garlic, aubergine, okra, goji berries, cherries and many of the spices I used on a daily basis. I love my smoothies and do eat chicken and fish. My body can no longer process beef but rarely, I have a piece and always pay the price with the severe abdominal pain and resulting diarrhoea. It is becoming rarer and rarer, believe me. I also take a lot of supplements.

I had an endoscopy and colonoscopy in February 2017, which discovered that I suffered from a duodenal ulcer, and I had four bowel polyps removed, all were suspicious but two were pre-cancerous. No matter how difficult my life has become from a dietary perspective, I have the nightshades to thank for narrowly avoiding a diagnosis of bowel cancer. I now have to have a colonoscopy every year instead of the usual three years but if it keeps illness at bay, it is a small price to pay.

In January of 2017, I had to request a referral from my doctor to see a psychiatrist. He knew exactly what state I was in but had never again, since 2015, offered me any mental health alternative treatment. I found this to be extremely lacking on his part. I saw my psychiatrist, a lovely man, and he read all of my information, asked me many questions and stated that I suffered from PTSD and major depressive disorder caused by the 'sexual and emotional abuse' I had received from my husband. I had also taken him a poem that I had written when I had been 10 or 11 and living in Chinchilla. I had entered it into the show and received a second prize for it. My psychiatrist stated that I had been an extremely intelligent child and that I am a very intelligent adult. This was a shock to me as I had never seen myself in that way, mostly because of the treatment I had received at the hands of my mother and my husband but I was so very grateful to him for helping me to see ME the person at last. I was placed on a low dose of Valium as well as my Cymbalta and requested to get a referral to a psychologist. The irony was that the psychologist I see is in the building directly behind where my ex-husband lives. The two carparks back onto each other and every time I go to see my wonderful psychologist, I could check out who was parked in the carpark under his building. The irony was not lost on my psychologist and as she also worked weekends, I got to see a fair bit.

When I first started with the psychologist, she stated that I was so damaged from my treatment by "family" that it could take two years just to scratch the surface of the issues I had. She has copies of all correspondence between myself and my estranged children and finds it almost impossible to understand their actions towards me without any form of explanation to me as to why I have been cut off. This, she now knows, is the one thing that I will never recover from. I am a mother who loves all of her children unconditionally and cannot ever get over their loss from my life or that of my grandchildren. I spent all of 2017 progressing through therapy with her whilst still seeing my psychiatrist and both were amazed at how quickly I made a turnaround. PTSD never leaves you and all I can do is remove all the triggers from my surroundings that will take me back into the abyss. I have culled all of my belongings from furniture, clothes, jewellery, perfumes, trinkets, gifts, photos, etc. Anything that triggers a memory goes. I have very little now and I do not need things any more. I am now an awakened, aware, mindful, conscious, spiritual empath who, moving forward, has only one true wish—to save as many children as I can from homelessness, cold, hunger, fear, loneliness and, most importantly, sexual and physical abuse. I want to save their mothers from a life of low self-esteem, being forced to believe they have no worth and could never cope without their narcissistic partner out in the big world, believing they had to settle for the bottom of the barrel because they were not worthy of better, as I did. The children need to be taught in primary schools just how important they truly are in this universe and know they are valuable members of the human race.

I had my fair share of stress in 2017, including a breast cancer scare in August and before I had received the results of all the testing, on Father's Day, Ben had a high-speed crash off his motorbike and, thank God, came out of it with grazing and severe soft tissue damage to his left knee only. Ben had never been hurt before and found it difficult to come to terms with the pain, the crutches and the inability to fully care for himself. What did help was his finding of spirituality through the realisation that he could very well have died that Sunday if a car had been coming in the opposite direction, if the 4WD trailing a horse float behind him could not have stopped in time, if his friend with whom he was out riding had not been able to slow down before running straight over the top of him or if he had not had the common sense to purchase very expensive protective gear for riding, but mostly if he had not known how to place his body whilst sliding across the tarmac, the outcome may very well have been a totally different story. The motorbike was written off, Ben was not. He had been taken via ambulance with full spinal precautions to the hospital where he was told that he would require six weeks recovery time before returning to work. Ben was bored as the 3rd week came to a close. He had to see his doctor weekly and at the end of that 3rd week, Ben begged to be allowed to return to work. The doctor agreed. Ben went to work the following Monday on light duties— was there such a thing in a steel fabrication factory? He was lucky enough that the workplace physiotherapist had been there that day and he administered acupuncture to Ben's knee. This continued for the first few weeks. Ben's physical ability was very quickly returning but his depression was much more obvious. There had been a few arguments within the house around issues that Ben previously had no knowledge of and he was determined to leave. I have always felt that it would be so much better for my baby boy to be away from me and my mental conditions, for his well-being. The last thing I wanted was for him to leave but his welfare was uppermost in my mind even though his father and siblings had left him high and dry.

He came home one Wednesday afternoon stating that he could not return to that workplace ever again. He felt that if he did, he would end up in jail. After much to-do, I advised he call the surgery and see the doctor and get two days stress leave to think. I also advised he go to Mt Barney, one of his favoured spots, to put distance between him and all the issues he felt were dragging him down. After four days, he was due to start night duty on Sunday evening but still felt he could not return. He called them to inform that he would see the doctor again the following morning. He was referred to a psychologist from whom he gained benefit and insight into what he needed to do. Mostly, I believe, from that which he already knew to be true of and within himself. He also went and saw the bosses at his work and they were extremely understanding with Ben, putting him on paid leave. He checked in with them each week. He managed to get himself a different job and has been there ever since. He is deciding now on his life path and I feel he is still a long way from being truly happy but he is so much better than he was. It warms my heart to know that after all he has been through and how badly he has been let down by those who professed to care, that he, above them all, will be the cream that rises to the top and will make himself proud of his life and achievements.

Brianna has also been diagnosed with PTSD and major depressive disorder and sees a psychiatrist and psychologist. She also has been on antidepressants for years and has had Valium and a 2nd antidepressant added to her regime. She is making major progress towards happiness despite continuing relationship failures. She has been unable to work for over two years. There were a lot of times when her problems were becoming triggers for my PTSD but we have worked through much stuff from the past and are the closest we have ever been and it is truly a beautiful relationship that I have with my baby girl again. I am the only one who can answer all her questions honestly, and that is exactly what she needs as her memories very slowly return to her from wherever the trauma had been stored for so long. I now have enough information from her to be absolutely certain of what had happened to my baby girl but it is staying very firmly where it is stored, in its little box, until the appropriate time for its release.

It is really difficult for her to know the truth that her beloved grandmother, Uncle Jonathon and Aunty Emma, all of whom she had adored once, knew from 1984 that William had been accused of sexually abusing his daughter, Tracey, but ALL chose to keep that information to themselves. They thought so little of Brianna, truthfully, and her safety and well-being that they never told me what they believed to be true. What sort of a family keeps that information from their own daughter and sister, especially when Brianna was his stepdaughter? Was their hatred of me so deep that they were willing to sacrifice not only Brianna but Isabelle, Jasmine, Bianca and Rosemary to a probable paedophile? If he could abuse his own daughter, what could he do to a stepdaughter, and more of his own daughters? It was just after Jasmine had been born in January 1985 that Mum told me that she would no longer be visiting whilst William was at home and refused to say why. Did she honestly believe that if she was not there, Brianna would not be harmed? On one occasion only, Brianna recalls Mum telling her that she was never to allow anyone to touch her private parts. How dare she speak to my child without my permission and my knowledge? I knew we should have left that house as originally planned when Brianna had been two weeks old and maintained a healthy distance for both our sakes. I hold Mum, Jonathon and Emma totally responsible for the alleged sexual abuse of my baby girl and for all the hardships that she now endures as life deals her shit because of what has been done to her. She asked Emma once if she knew about William and the allegations made against him. Emma's response was that she had "suspected"; the woman and her lies have never ceased to amaze me. She has three daughters of her own and Jonathon has two. If the tables had been turned and I had not given them the information I received, what would that have made me? How would they react especially if it later turned out to be true and they could have saved their child from decades of trauma and abuse and a lifetime of mental illness?

I will lay everything out very clearly so that there are no misinterpretations or mistakes here. Once I was under the care of a therapist, I discussed my guilt over what had obviously happened to my baby girl at the hands of her stepfather without my knowledge. I wanted to talk to her about it but the therapist stated, in no uncertain terms, that no one was to bring the subject up with her as it could very easily cause her to "implode mentally". My brother, Jonathon, had this explained to him very clearly and fully. Why? Because he has always thought he knows better than everyone, especially me. Unbeknownst to me, he decided that he not only knew better than I did but also the therapist whose advice I had very meticulously passed on. He went to visit Brianna and brought up the fact that William had probably sexually abused her and proceeded to give her his advice on how she needed to handle the situation and what she needed to do moving forward.

Brianna IMPLODED, as it had been stated that she would. It was the most disastrous time in her life. It was due to this wonderful advice from her supposed uncle who claimed to love her that Brianna was placed on antidepressants, had to give up her beloved job and, for the first time ever, her children feared for her life and their future well-being as a family. Well, thank you Jonathon, your ego has really shown who you really are. Nothing and nobody matter other than you and your ability to ensure that you show everyone that you are right! You could not have been more WRONG. You have cost Brianna so much. Precious time with her children that can never be regained whilst she is in the midst of the abyss. You have cost her years' worth of wages that, as you are unable to manage money, you will never repay her. You took her, the happiest, most fun-loving person, and turned her into an unrecognisable moody, sad, depressed little girl who did not know which way to turn or how to regain her true self. I do hope you are very proud of what you have managed to do to my daughter, Jonathon. I could not live with myself if I had ever done anything like this to any of my nieces, it would have become an untenable situation for me. You were not finished there though, Jonathon. You had to add more fuel to that fire. The following year, you went to Brianna and gave her the address of the man that you believed to be her abuser. You decided that she did not need the phone number and told her that if she chose to give the address to me—after you had told me that you had no knowledge of where William lived—she was to lie to me about where she got it from. Just make something up, you said to her.

Karma is a beautiful thing and if you are really lucky, God will let you watch it happening… Sometimes you can get a glimpse of Karma in action vicariously through social media.

It doesn't end there though; it has already reached the next generation. My beautiful granddaughter, Ebony, was being very badly treated by her boyfriend and then he dumped her. Ebony was so smitten and then devastated that after this, she started cutting herself. That rocked me to my core, how many generations have to be affected by this narcissistic psychopath before he is made to account for his actions? Ebony had been very small when she had told me, 'Dadda touched my bum.' I had flown at him, again unable to prove a thing, but I had made it perfectly clear that I would not hesitate to call the police if I ever heard anything of that nature ever again. Oh, how he must have been laughing at my stupidity and all I was doing was trying to be a protective grandmother. He was too clever for me; he would not be caught again whilst I carried on believing I had thwarted something awful from happening. There had been so much more that I had not realised was happening right under my nose when I was at home. I believe that time is a man-made construct and no such thing exists but the flowing and evolving of my period in human form has revealed so much more than I am mentally capable of comprehending could possibly have occurred in MY family home whilst the patriarch of the family was in charge. If I had been shocked and disbelieving before, I was in for a real roller coaster ride of new information…

Eyes are useless when the mind is blind.

-UNKNOWN

CHAPTER 27

SECRETS AND LIES

Ben turned 21 in November 2016. I had wanted to take him to dinner, have a BBQ, whatever he thought was most befitting the youngest of 12 children turning 21. He was not interested in celebrating this day in any way. Every other member of his family had celebrations of their 18th and 21st, which the entire family had attended. His own father had refused to attend his 18th for which he would never be forgiven and neither had Clayton. This would not be an occasion that he could remember with fondness but that did not stop me asking repeatedly for months and weeks leading up to the day. He did not want any gifts either as there was nothing to celebrate without the whole family. I was happy for him to have his mates over, do a BBQ, get pissed and collapse and slumber on the floor. His birthday was a Sunday and he had to start work at 10 pm that evening so I wanted to have a celebration on Saturday night.

Zach and Charlie were going to come over on Sunday to see Ben. They had been to New Zealand the month before and were bringing all their photos over to show us. The day arrived and nothing was planned, it felt so wrong to me but it was Ben's birthday and his decision so I had to go with the flow. Isabelle had bought a mud cake from Coles. I had bought him a crystal decanter and two glasses along with a bottle of alcohol, which he seemed to love. Zach and Charlie arrived and had bought a New York pizza on the way. I suggested we get more pizza and Isabelle went down to collect it but Ben said no to that too. His mates, Allen and Shane, had arrived and they were sitting out back having a drink and talking. We took the cake out with candles and sang Happy Birthday but Ben was not happy. I offered him pizza and he took some.

It turned out that he had not liked the fact that Zach and Charlie had brought all their holiday photos on that day, his birthday, and occupied me with explaining them all. He felt we should have all sat around sharing anecdotes about Ben as had been done on all previous 21st birthday occasions for his siblings. I shared his pain; it was the saddest and most disheartening thing to see your family disintegrate without explanation and to know that you meant nothing to those for whom you would give your life so readily. But the hardest thing for me was to watch the pain on my baby boy's face knowing that, through no fault of his own, he had been thrown into the rejection pile by most of his family.

That day was also the very first time that I learned some more home truths, of which I had absolutely no prior knowledge. Zach said that he felt compelled to tell me about the game the children had played when they had been younger, called "The Three Little Bears". He explained that it was a game he knew for a fact had involved Mitchell, Ben, Jasmine and possibly Steve. It involved genitalia and he had overheard Jasmine say to Mitchell on one occasion, 'No Mitchell, I do not want to play that game anymore.' I was absolutely mortified as I listened to what had occurred in MY home whilst William had been in charge. My mind was going crazy. William was a voyeur; he had used surveillance cameras on me as well as Brianna and Bianca for certain but had he been watching some sick incestuous game being played out by his children? Zach had felt sure that Dad did not know about it. I think otherwise. Where would they even get the idea for such a game? Bianca's favourite song at one point during her childhood had been a particular rendition of the Three Little Bears—*once upon a time in a nursery rhyme there were three bears...* Had she and Rosemary also been involved? I could not comprehend the volume of what I was being told. Trying to put all the different pieces of information together that I had received since Isabelle returned from UK early in 2013 created a dreadful picture in my mind, one that I found hard to accept BUT William had constantly been sending me out to do things or forcing me to go lie down. It became apparent that William would drug me to ensure I slept in the afternoons when, after having eaten lunch and feeling fully ready to complete an afternoon's work around the house and garden, I would drink my Pepsi and suddenly feel so tired that I could not stay awake. Brianna had found a crushed-up pill in her Pepsi when she came back from the toilet one day. She suddenly knew why both she and I would suddenly need to lie down and sleep whilst being surveilled, unbeknownst to us at that time. She did not let me know at the time as she lived in fear of what William would do to her once he realised that I had found out another of his truths. As previously stated, a narcissist controls by threat of further trauma, either to the person or to a family member that they dearly love. Well, William had already broken both of her arms and smashed her head and face into steel bunks. I believe her now when she tells me that she lived in fear of what he would do to her if she came to me with what he was doing to her. I freely admit that I would immediately have confronted him, which, of course, would have caused more trauma to be rained down on my baby girl.

Trying to remain silent with what I was being told and trying to carry on with what was already a horrible 21st birthday for my youngest child was, to say the very least, extremely difficult. I said to Zach that we needed a far more in-depth conversation about this subject at a later time, which has not occurred as yet. I kept this info to myself until everyone had gone home and Ben had gone to lay down. I told Isabelle but she seemed, rather curiously, not to think it to be that bad. I was livid that my children had been allowed to behave in this manner and/or believed it to be acceptable. They were more than likely encouraged by their father or another family member. It does throw into question exactly who had been the instigator of this game and if that was what William held over their head by way of a threat. It has often been asked, 'What is it that Dad has on Clayton and William that they would act the way they have?' I think that question could be posed for all of the older children. William certainly seemed to be quite certain that I would never be able to prove things against him in 2013 when he came to me once he knew for sure that I was leaving him. The biggest question to be asked here is, why would Clayton and Billy, who both vehemently accepted that their father sexually assaulted/abused Tracey, put their own daughters' safety in jeopardy by having this man they believed to be a paedophile anywhere near their own daughters? Many, many times William would be watching Rhianna after having forced me to go for a rest.

I was in a state of shock and disbelief. Is it even possible that William and I were on such completely opposing frequencies that he could get away with living an entirely alien life to the one that I was living? Had he dragged our beautiful children into his seedy existence as well without my knowledge? Is Clayton actually a part of this whole dreadful ordeal and willing to sacrifice his own daughter? Has Billy some inner knowledge or is he too part of this scenario? He was so desperate for me to forget my life with his father and move forward, stating that this was the only way he would have me in his life. It was becoming clearer and clearer to me that my ostracisation by my children was much deeper than previously realised but I still fervently believed that William, Clayton and Tracey were deeply entrenched in the reasons they had chosen to stop loving their mother.

I was in a never-ending abyss as we moved closer to Christmas that year. It held no meaning for me at all. As Christmas approached, I had an email from Mitchell wanting to try and come for a visit. I took this as an opportunity, as I was so sick at that time and in the depths of a PTSD episode, to state my truth as clearly as possible. I was in a place, mentally, where I needed to know where I stood with Mitchell as many of our previous visits had been marred by minutiae or Ben playing the dutiful and protective son. I could no longer play games. I needed to put my mental health first followed by my physical health and in order to do that, I had to start being truly honest with myself and with everyone else in my life. I could not take any more rejection in my life and I wrote a heartfelt email back to Mitchell. I asked if he would like to visit over the Christmas/Boxing Day period of time off but I did not hear back until the 28th.

Mitchell had felt that I had rejected him and had not checked his emails. Nothing could be further from the truth. I had so hoped that he would respond favourably and that we could reconcile properly and return to the relationship that we had once had. It was the outcome I prayed for and longed for but was living in fear would not eventuate. I find it impossible to fully explain the depth of my feelings of love that I hold for each and every one of my children. There do not seem to be adequate words to appropriately express just how I truly feel. I always feel that I have not been understood whenever I have tried to express that love in the past. But thankfully, Mitchell had understood what I meant and we arranged to meet. At the eleventh hour, Ben informed me that he would not allow Mitchell in our home. I was shocked and devastated by this revelation for several reasons. It was not HIS house, it was the house that Isabelle, he and I shared. I felt he had no right to disallow his mother to have visitors, especially when it was another son that would be visiting. Further, Mitchell had always visited in the past, why was this one any different? Did Isabelle not also then get to have a say as Mitchell was her brother as well?

I let it go and organised with Mitchell to meet out. After many last-minute changes, again due to my health issues, we met at the Coffee Club at Meadowbrook for what felt like a reunion of mega proportions on my part and I believe that Mitchell felt the same. Gone, on my part, was all pretence or minutiae. This was me, the mother, meeting up with her beloved son. I could have held Mitchell in my embrace for the rest of my life that day, and every time I have seen him since. We talked for hours and it was the most beautiful experience of my life. To regain my son was truly beautiful and I will treasure that time forever. I did not want to leave. I had never, ever had the experience of one-on-one time with any of my children for such in-depth conversation before. To be able to sit in a bubble of mutual love and respect was an exhilarating and profound experience. It was the most fulfilling experience I have had, just to speak to another human being from the heart and with such love going both ways. It was the turning point in my life. I knew, from that day forward, exactly how I wanted my life to be. I still had much to achieve with my health, both physical and mental, but I was no longer the victim of abuse and crime, I was the survivor and I would heal, fully, no matter how long that took.

Our next meeting was even longer, more intense and loving and I enjoyed it even more. I was now on the right path to healing and I was truly happy. I turned 60 late that January and I did not wish to celebrate the day without my children and grandchildren but Isabelle had other ideas as always. Isabelle and Steve took me to *Sizzler* for a celebratory lunch and I had a wonderful time with them both. We looked around the shops and did a few groceries at the end. Whilst I was in Woolworths, my mobile rang. It was a mobile number and under normal circumstances, I would not have answered it but, in recent months, many of my appointments had been advised and confirmed via mobile numbers so I felt duty bound to ensure it was not important. Even with my hearing aid in situ, the noise from the supermarket and the people around me made it almost impossible for me to hear who was on the other end of the line. I handed Isabelle my cards to pay for my shopping and left the supermarket in search of a slightly quieter spot.

It was my brother, Jonathon, whom I had not spoken to for a long time. He had called, on my 60th birthday, to inform me that my daughter, Bianca, had sexually assaulted his daughter, Shelley, effecting penetration with a foreign object, when they were quite young and we had been living in Sunnybank Hills. He also claimed that William had sexually assaulted Bianca. I was still barely hearing all of this so I made him repeat what I said back to him. I was left to wonder why he had chosen THIS day to make this call. Why was he calling me at all? Why had he not called Bianca? Or William? Or the police? Why was he making the call? Shouldn't any action taken be completed by Shelley as she was now an adult? What did any of this actually have to do with me? If he was looking for sympathy, he had called the wrong number. If he was expecting me to feel guilty, again, he was calling the wrong number. If, it was in fact true, what did he think that I would do about it when I had been ostracised by not only Bianca but also Billy, Jasmine and Rosemary? What did he expect me to do with this information?

Mitchell called me for my birthday later that evening. I spoke to him about the call as Jonathon often called Mitchell as well. Yes, Jonathon had also called him that afternoon with the same sorry tale. I spoke at length with Mitchell about what was expected by making this revelation to us. The very least that I felt Bianca deserved was a heads up regarding this piece of information. If it was true, she should be aware that they may take action. If it was untrue, then any actions taken would be for Bianca to consider.

I also chose this occasion to mention to Mitchell what Zach had told me regarding their childhood game at the end of the previous year. I explained it all as I had been told by Zach. Mitchell remained silent for a long while. I explained that I had eventually told Ben about the conversation and whilst he had no memory of what had actually occurred, he most certainly knew that something had indeed happened. He did not wish to discuss it and became agitated by the very mention of it, a clear indication that most certainly there had been something that I should be concerned about. My hope for it being some huge mistake was fading.

Mitchell confirmed the story as well. He, unlike Zach, did not believe that Dad had known or that the girls were involved. He was, however, totally and completely relieved that it was now known by me at last. He had carried an enormous amount of guilt in the ensuing years believing, although he had no physical memory of it, that he was to blame for the whole thing. I reassured him of two things. I was now certain that this game had come from much higher up on the sibling chain and that I could do nothing about what had been perpetrated against my children when they were younger, especially without my knowledge. It certainly was an extremely dangerous game to play given the previous involvement in our lives by children's services, whoever was the original instigator. Perhaps that was exactly where William had gotten his thrills from, the more dangerous and closer to the edge, the better. If anything, I felt an incredibly huge weight and burden added to my shoulders for, again, not having seen this or heard even a whiff of what was happening in my own home. I now fully understand why I was allowed to have so many children. I was always and forever busy doing for the family whilst William did as little as possible. He never did anything right anyway so I was happier just to have to do it all and know that it was done right the first time. But then he had always made sure he mucked it up as I would never allow him to do those things again. This may be due to the fact that science has now proved that having a traumatic childhood produces OCD in the traumatised and, although I had always called myself a perfectionist, OCD was very much closer to the truth. This also explains why Brianna has OCD to almost the same extent that I do. I was, sickeningly, giving him more victims. It makes me feel physically sick to think about it now, as it did then. It is incomprehensible just how blind and naïve I have been over the past almost 40 years.

I considered the whole sick and sorry situation overnight; there was no way that I would be able to sleep. Bianca was my daughter and I love her dearly, whether she liked that fact or not. She had a right to know that there had been an allegation made against her good name. I would prefer to tell someone this type of news face to face but that would not occur so my only other option was to send a text. I chose to text Billy, Jasmine and Rosemary as well so that if she needed comforting or legal advice, neither of which I was allowed to give, she would have people there for her even though it was my right as her mother to be there for her.

The text read:

'I have been informed of an allegation against you, Bianca, which I feel you have the right to know about. It is alleged that you sexually assaulted a female relative causing penetration with a foreign object. This is incest, and it is further alleged that you were sexually assaulted by your father. He was observed watching surveillance footage from a camera he had set up on you, as he did to Brianna and myself for many years. I have never and will never abandon my children as you have all done to me. My concern now is for the true welfare of my grandchildren. I will need to think about how best to ensure their protection from what is a continuing sick situation. Clayton tried to sexually assault me when he was a teenager. Tracey will tell you what suits her. I was pregnant with Jasmine when she claimed her father sexually assaulted her in an effort to prevent me from having any more children to her father. I had been warned! After the birth of my first three children. I am sorry that you have been caught up in this sad, sick saga. All because their father never allowed them to properly grieve after the death of their mother. I feel as much sadness and pity for them today as I did in April 1980. Vengeance is a very lazy form of grief and I am sorry I dragged myself and my children into this situation. Please understand that Dad used drugs to achieve his goals. On me, Brianna and goodness knows who else. I love you, Bianca, unconditionally and eternally, as I do all of my children and will always be here for you when you finally work it all out. xxx'

I had truly hoped this would elicit a response from Bianca so that we could start a dialogue and I could be there for her, whatever the truth of the matter turned out to be. As always, I was to be treated as a mushroom, left in the dark and fed a load of bullshit!

The only contact, as always, was from the mouth of the group, Rosemary. It read:

'Contact me again and I am going to the police. I am not playing. Stay the fuck away from me.'

Wow, that would be all of my Christmases come at once. I would so love the police to become involved and have her finally tell me why it is a crime to contact my own daughter. I could then drag William down to where he belonged, especially with all the new information that I was receiving. I laughed so hard that I almost wet myself. I slept extremely well that night. She had not really given that response a lot of actual thought… The following time Mitchell and I met up, he advised me that Jasmine had changed her phone number. That I also saw as a knee-jerk reaction and it smelt equally as heavily of guilt to me.

After this tumultuous start to the year of 2017, things continued along rather smoothly. I was enjoying my renewed relationship with Mitchell whilst making every effort to get my physical and mental health onto a more even keel moving towards healing. As my consultations with the psychiatrist and psychologist progressed, I thought of my estranged children less and less, even though they were often the subject of our discussions. I realised that I did not need them in my life even though I dearly wanted them to be there. All respect and trust had evaporated many years before and although I would welcome them back with open arms, I could never trust or respect them again. The biggest reason for me feeling this way was the fact that, not even once, did any of them ever speak to me, as a person, face to face, and ask why I felt I had to take the actions that I did, or tell me why they had chosen the course of action that they had. I have been oblivious to the reasons I have lost my children and grandchildren since 2012 when I first saw a change but could not comprehend what was happening or why because I was so deeply entrenched by then in the abyss of PTSD and depression. By the vicious texts that I received from Rosemary and Bianca, it seemed that they made an assumption that I knew exactly what I am reputed to have done wrong, which was totally inaccurate. Actually, it was the fact that I have no knowledge of my perceived wrongdoings that has kept my mental illness affecting me so badly and for so long. What annoys the heck out of me on a more intellectual level is that none of my estranged children can actually have read my emails or texts, or they are not endowed with the common sense that I had thought they were. Of course, the only other way to understand their reactions to said communications is to know that they were so totally living in the EGO, so totally unconscious and unawakened that it was not in their capabilities to understand what they were doing and how deeply they were hurting the one person who would willingly die for them in a heartbeat. This takes me back to a very learned doctor who had studied in Britain and had, after learning everything William had done and also knew of the actions of my children, vehemently believed that William had brainwashed them all against me. I argued that they were self-professed intellectuals who surely would not be able to be manipulated in this manner but he went on to cite many facts and studies and patients that he had seen in England and was totally convinced that this was the fate that had befallen my children. Many other professionals, some of whom had also trained and/or worked in England, confirmed that they believed this to be the case. English is by far the hardest language to learn but, as it is their native tongue, it should be easy for them to understand and yet they never actually either read or understood anything I wrote to them.

2016-7 was also the period of time during which Isabelle was looking to build her first home. It was a long and time-consuming process of looking at parcels of land, checking out display homes, poring over house plans and inclusions, deciding on the best financial institution and working out how all the elements would come together logistically to suit Isabelle, Ben and myself. I was easy, I could live anywhere. It is Isabelle and Ben who work in Brisbane, for now.

Isabelle chose the land and the builder and then undertook to get the finance arranged for which she was given tentative approval quite quickly. The holdup was the building company, who decided that Isabelle would be their test case in offering house/land packages for the first time. Thankfully, Isabelle had her deposit down on the land as the process was going to prove rather long and drawn out with all the toing and froing between the financial institution, the building company, Isabelle's solicitor and the company's solicitor.

The building of the house commenced on Ekka Show Holiday, 16 August 2017. If not for the communication between Isabelle and the new soon-to-be next-door neighbour, she would have been none the wiser. From the following weekend, Isabelle began the long trek back and forth to check the progress of the building and take photos of every stage of the same. She did, for quite some time, take Steve with her as he has a keen eye and had studied architecture as a subject at school so his informative knowledge was invaluable to Isabelle. Isabelle and I and Isabelle and Steve had gone through the process of selecting all the tiles, carpets, colours, etc. that would be used. Isabelle was getting the increased package, which upped the quality of parts of the building and she had also added many extras to the tiles, electricals, etc. to suit her requirements. The piles of paperwork were growing exponentially but Isabelle was so on top of it all with her spreadsheets and whiteboards full of information. I did all that I was capable of to assist by buying new furniture—dining table and chairs, entertainment unit, buffet, coffee table and lamp table. I also bought the roller blinds for the bedrooms, dining and kitchen and bought the curtain material and made up the curtains for the back door and laundry door. Ben had hired a trailer to take a huge amount of rubbish to the dump; we had St Vincent De Paul come and collect some furniture, some we gave away. It was going to be a very new and clean start for us all; we were ridding ourselves of the dreadful past we would no longer entertain. I had been packing and culling for many months.

2017 was also the year I finally became a person in my own right again, but for the first time in my life, without having to answer to anybody. I had bought myself new furniture for my 60th birthday and was paying some of that off until July. This left me with an inability to save for the divorce I desperately needed for me. I had mentioned it in passing to Mitchell and he immediately transferred the money to my bank account so that I could have what I needed to start healing. He had offered earlier in the year but the last thing I had wanted him to be accused of was enabling me to divorce his father. I accepted his gift in the spirit in which it was given, with love to his damaged mother. I made my application and sent William's paperwork off to him, for him to sign and return. He did not. The court date was set for 11 July 2017.

The date was fast approaching and, as always had been the case with William, he was making this final action between us as difficult as he could for me. Isabelle had reprinted the required paperwork and she and Zach headed to Dad's to get his signature. When they arrived, and tried to alert Dad to their arrival, the voice that answered was, of course, Rosemary's. She wanted them to leave immediately and did not allow them to see Dad. Isabelle was insistent. Rosemary and her new boyfriend came down. Again, there was a lot of toing and froing between Isabelle and Rosemary. Isabelle made it clear that she was not leaving without that which she had come to get. Dad finally came down but was anything but pleasant to two of his children that he had not seen for years. He signed the paperwork at last and Zach tried to engage him in a conversation, but Dad was uninterested. Zach wanted a hug from his father; William treated him as if he had leprosy. Zach wanted to give Dad his mobile number as he and Charlie had purchased a brand-new apartment less than 10 minutes down the road but William refused to take it. Zach said he could pop in for another visit now that they also had a brand-new car but again, he was rejected by his own father. William babbled on about there being another form to be signed, which he could have mentioned by advising Isabelle at an earlier juncture or by returning what he could sign to me and stating that there was another form to be signed. He does not suffer from PTSD or depression, just self-inflicted medical conditions but, true to form, he was going to make this as difficult as possible to the bitter end.

And yes, for the very first time in his entire life, he was actually right. There was another form that I had not been advised of. It was one week until the court date. Isabelle went and collected Steve after work and they set off to get Dad's signature on the extra form. They pressed the buzzer 8 times over a 30-minute period but William refused to acknowledge them. Isabelle dropped Steve at home, with the paperwork, and called me, she then headed home. I called Mitchell asking if it was normal practice for dad to not answer the ringing doorbell unless he had prior knowledge of who has coming to visit. That answered a lot of questions for me. William so lived in fear of the police being the ones on the buzzer as time went on and more of his truths came out to be discovered by everyone. Mitchell went and collected Steve and the paperwork and went to Dad's. They were not allowed into his unit, they had to stay downstairs. The paperwork was signed, lodged and the divorce would finally become a reality. As with my entire married life, everything was made so much more difficult than it needed to be by William.

The divorce was granted and I was truly amazed at just how wonderful I felt to be free of abuse and control at last. I was so grateful to Mitchell for having helped enable the divorce to occur at all. Steve and I went out for a celebratory lunch at a buffet restaurant. I could now put the past squarely where it belonged and get on with living the rest and best of my life. For the first time since my birth, I truly felt free, no longer having to "do this for my sake" nor did I have, any longer, to walk on eggshells waiting for the next bomb to drop or worry about explaining my every movement or stress about what my husband would do to me next. Truly free and at peace is an amazing feeling, one that until now, I had never experienced before.

After the divorce, Ben made the decision that he would like to go and visit his father and make his peace. I advised him that he would need to call Mitchell to announce his arrival due to William 's bizarre ritual of not answering to anyone without prior advice. He did and Ben ended up with his father's mobile number. He was not allowed to go up to his unit either. He had to remain downstairs in a "Visitors Room" to speak to his own father. He had ridden his bike over instead of taking his 4WD. William seemed to be, at least superficially, pleased to see Ben. The only thing I asked of Ben upon his return home was, 'Are you okay? Did it go well?' I had no interest in my ex-husband other than how he treated my beloved children. Ben told me that he had told his father that he wanted to be informed when he died as he would attend his funeral.

I learned just before Christmas of 2017 that William had supposedly dropped his phone and broken it and had to get a new phone but he also claimed that he had to get a new mobile number! He also refused to give that new phone number to Mitchell. All mobile companies allow you to keep your existing number, if you choose to. The only reason that one needs to get a new phone number is by choice or if you are trying to hide from something, some criminal act perhaps.

If he thought for one nanosecond that I had his mobile number, then he was wrong. I have absolutely no interest in him in any way and most certainly do not need a mobile number. If he thinks that the way he has acted towards his three youngest sons is acceptable on any plane of existence, then he is irrefutably wrong in so many ways. I am disgusted to have chosen this man to father my children, I have to accept the responsibility for their sperm donor and I do. I am grateful for having been allowed the honour of having each and every one of my children in my life and I am more than enough for the ones he has not brainwashed/programmed against me. He knows full well that his two youngest sons have already written affidavits stating what they witnessed their father doing when they were younger and they will confirm this in any court. That is the real reason William is scared of them. William, Billy, Jasmine, Bianca and Rosemary are scared of Mitchell and have not allowed him into the inner sanctum because he has maintained a relationship with both of his parents, as was my request before I had even left their father. Why should he be condemned for a completely natural and loving act?

It must be a very lonely life hiding away from the world in your fourth-floor unit, not game to answer any ring at your door for fear of who it might be. That is not a life; that is a very sad existence. Mice, not men, hide away where they cannot be found. Well, mice and criminals.

My comfort comes from knowing that Karma is doing its job.

In the Karma Café, there are no menus. You get what you deserve…

May I become at all times, both now and forever
A protector for those without protection
A guide for those who have lost their way
A ship for those with oceans to cross
A bridge for those with rivers to cross
A sanctuary for those in danger
A lamp for those without a light
A place of refuge for those who lack shelter
And a servant to all in need.

-14TH DALAI LAMA

CHAPTER 28

THE PATH TO ENLIGHTENMENT

The house build was not without its hiccups, it was a cause of much frustration for Isabelle at times. But truthfully, as we would be breaking the contract on our house rental, the longer the new build took, the better. Finally, it was stated that the build completion date would be 15 November 2017 and settlement date would be 6 December 2017. Then Isabelle could book movers, bond cleaners and fence builders for the one side that had a neighbour and required negotiation between the two parties. The other sides and the return were already completed. Isabelle had advised Ben and I that we would be moving on 16 December as she had to attend work on 15 December for a particular governmental meeting that required her expertise and she could not avoid after which she would be taking some of her long service leave to get everything sorted with the new house. It was all hands-on deck then to ensure we were fully prepared for the off.

On Friday, 8 December 2017, after the settlement date had come and gone without settlement having occurred, Isabelle, through no fault of her own, had to be the one to drive to the Gold Coast to the builder's solicitors with the final paperwork from solicitors and financial institutions to ensure settlement would occur that afternoon at 14:15. Having completed all that she needed to do there, as she was leaving, Isabelle fell down a stair she had not seen. She called me stating she had good news and bad news. Firstly, all the paperwork was finalised and settlement would go ahead. Secondly, she had fallen and had broken her arm again in the same place as almost six years earlier. An ambulance had been called and she would be unable to drive the car back to Brisbane.

I immediately called Ben at work and he came straight home and we drove to the Gold Coast, reaching Isabelle before the ambulance did. Apparently, there was an enormous amount of need for the ambulance service that day on the coast. I was unimpressed nonetheless that Isabelle had been left in agonising pain for so long. Ben drove straight back and I brought Isabelle to the Logan Hospital. She asked that I go home, two minutes away, to be with our dogs as it was a miserable rainy day and I had just run out leaving them outside in the wet weather. Isabelle would let me know what was going on. All the way back from the coast, I kept saying that she could not have broken the bone in the same place as previously due to the fact that once a bone is broken, the healing process then ensures that the bone is much stronger than it was originally and it is extremely rare for it to be broken again.

However, the Logan Hospital did state that the radial head was fractured again and even though Isabelle also had enormous pain in her wrist, they stated that they could not see a fracture in the wrist. Isabelle was sent home in a sling and had been referred to the Ipswich Hospital as we were moving closer to there. It dumbfounded me, all that I knew as a nurse said that something was not right. Isabelle has private health insurance but with all of the last-minute costs of moving, she chose not to utilise it. As an adult, that is her right and I again focussed on assisting my daughter with everything from showering, bathing, cooking, doing her hair, making certain she was comfortable for the night and also still packing and cleaning ready for the move.

Ben and I had to drive out to collect the keys and all the paperwork for the new house the following day. We had also taken the first load of packing to the new house. The following day, Ben and Mitchell took several loads out to the house. The following week went by so quickly but no matter how exhausted I was, I refused to let my meditation go. I meditated for 1½-2 hours every evening before going to bed. On Friday, 15 December, Brianna, Daniel, Ebony and I headed out to the house to unpack everything that had already been taken out there before the movers arrived the following day with everything that remained, particularly the large items. The fence that had been built between the new house and the neighbour was so far up off the ground that our dogs would not even have to lower their ears to be under it, so Steve and I had bought all the wood we thought we would require to adjust it and Daniel set to work actually doing it with Brianna's assistance whilst Ebony and I emptied box after box, container after container and bag after bag. Thank goodness for ducted air conditioning as I would surely have collapsed otherwise. It was a wonderful day, although totally exhausting for all involved but I had not spent so much time with my daughter and granddaughter in so long. Brianna was finding it very difficult, to say the least, to accept that I was moving so far away from her. She did not believe that she could cope and had opted not to be at the new house or the rental on the day of the move as it would have been too much for her to handle. Through the process of Brianna's psychology appointments and her renewed ability to ask me any question and feel comfortable, we had developed the closest relationship we have had since she became an adult. It is one that I cherish with all my heart as much as Brianna does. She is remembering many things now and asks me to explain them all to her.

As I dropped them off that afternoon, I too shed tears for when I would see my baby girl again but this was a move that I had to make for me. I had also had my doubts about moving so far away from my estranged children but, with help, came to realise that it was they who had totally and completely abandoned me, never having given me any reasons for their actions. It was time for me to put the past where it belonged, well behind me. By the time I arrived home, I was exhausted but ready for the following day and the big move.

I was up at 06:00, Zach was already at the rental and after having breakfast and packing the final few items I still had to use that morning and having our vehicle fully packed, Zach and I took off from Loganlea for the very last time. I did not even give it a backward glance as I headed for the motorway. We arrived and unpacked our load. I set about putting everything where it belonged whilst waiting for Ben to arrive with the next load. I did the same with that load. Next to arrive was Mitchell. He had been delegated to drive back to Logan in our car after the movers had left. The movers arrived and were extremely pleasant. Mitchell and Ben had nipped out earlier to buy some beer in order to be able to give them each a six-pack; they were very appreciative of this. Isabelle was in agony and had reached breaking point so we sent Mitchell back to collect her and the boys. She had, again, been on the phone for hours with Telstra. Again, they were letting us down. The NBN would not be up and running until 28 December 2017. I would revert, for the interim, to just doing mindfulness and loving kindness/metta meditation.

It was, for a while, a flurry of people, furniture and white goods. Once the movers left, we were able to get everything set up. Once

Isabelle was here with the dogs, we were all in a rush to get beds sorted for the evening. Exhaustion was very quickly setting in on us all. It had been a truly wonderful day for me personally with my three sons back having fun together, just as it had always been. I was the happiest I had ever felt in my entire life. Mitchell drove Zach back to Logan to collect his car and they both headed to Sunnybank to get an iced tea, then Zach asked Mitchell to call in and see his new apartment, which he did for a short time. It brings a tear to my eye to finally have Zach and Mitchell back on speaking terms. I know that Mitchell is also over the moon.

The Ipswich Hospital had wanted Isabelle in their OPD first thing Monday morning but Isabelle had the bond cleaners coming and decided that she was capable of driving back to Brisbane. I totally disagreed but she insisted. She took the dogs who had a playdate with Bubbles, Brianna's dog, whilst Steve did all the driving for her around Brisbane and Logan. The following day, she was off to the Ipswich Hospital and took a cab. There were to be X-rays, CT scans, consultants' visits and surgery. Yes, the radial head was, in fact, broken in the same place as almost six years earlier. It had not been correctly treated by QEII Hospital at the time and would now need to be re-broken, re-aligned and have screws inserted. There was also a wrist fracture and the surgeon was to check the CT of the wrist on the day of surgery. This was on 3 January 2018. Ben had dropped Isabelle at the hospital on his way in to work. I had communicated with Isabelle before she went into surgery. She had five screws inserted into her elbow and the wrist was fractured and there was a piece of bone pressing on a nerve. This may also require further surgical intervention in the future. She could not drive, could not move her elbow or arm in any way. Things were extremely difficult for Isabelle and still are. She has been back to the hospital for a check-up and for OT (Occupational Therapy). They are pleased with her progress thus far but put a 12-week recovery in place from the date of surgery. Isabelle had originally been due back at work on 30 January 2018. She will, from Monday, 29 January 2018, be working from home and taking things one week at a time. As it is my belief that there are no coincidences in life, that everything occurs for a reason—to teach us a lesson—it is for Isabelle to work out the lesson she is to learn from this experience.

I have spent 60 years looking for my Shangri-La. Life always seemed to throw lemons at me when all I wanted and strived for was a bed of blooming flowers. I wanted to be able to give love and receive love, that didn't seem like a big ask to me. I feared for such a long time that I would never find that peaceful place that I sought without returning to my true home, that place in all of us that we know exists but we are unable to find. When I had first left William, I so longed to go to that home that I had even set the date on which I intended to return there. I truly did not believe that I could survive without my estranged children, particularly Bianca. I was incapable of understanding how the person I felt so close to and loved so dearly could have turned against me in the manner that transpired. Suicide had, at that time, been the only response I could come up with to the way they were treating me and the way their actions made me feel. It had cut me sharper than a chef's knife when, at Ben's 18th birthday party, Bianca had walked straight past me without even acknowledging my existence. After that night, I would have welcomed instantaneous death. I could barely breathe for the grief and loss I was experiencing. All my mind kept saying was why? I had been asking that same question of life since 1968, I was yet to receive a response.

Slowly, and with the help of my therapist, those thoughts were put to the back of my mind. I had always been a fighter—a stubborn mule—and I was not yet prepared to give up on those who did love me despite my inability to see a way forward without all of my beloved children. Isabelle felt as if she and the children I still had should be enough for me and she had not been the first person to raise this question. It is impossible to put feelings into words adequately enough to make people understand the depth of my love for ALL of my children, without whom I am no longer whole. A mother falls in love with each of her children and I know that I did from the moment they were all born and I find this difficult to explain, especially to those who have not had children or those who do not have that same depth of feelings that I have always experienced. I have, since the birth of my eldest child, been prepared to give up my life for any of my children and that has never changed for me. This is the reason, I have been told, that I am having such a hard time dealing with the loss of those children, made much worse because I have no reason that can, in time, help me accept that loss and learn to move on. To be prepared to take a bullet for someone, then just to have them disappear from your life and take your grandchildren with them, is the most horrific and heinous act that can be bestowed upon a mother and grandmother, this one in particular.

Finding tapping, meditation and mindfulness was the only way that I have been saved from living my remaining days in the darkness of the abyss or returning home, perhaps prematurely, to escape the all-encompassing pain that has devoured me since I lost my babies and grandbabies. Despite all the trials and tribulations that have occurred since leaving William, all of them caused by stress, I kept coming back stronger to my spiritual practices that, inch by inch, made me feel stronger and more able to cope. I would fall backwards constantly but I refused to give up and kept trying to get a better foothold in consciousness. Through the power of the Internet, I have had access to so many of the world's best spiritual teachers and have even been honoured, through Isabelle and Ben, to have been able to attend an evening with Eckhart Tolle, ranked as #1 of the most spiritual people of our time. It inspired me to keep going with my practice. Every time I listen to Eckhart, Tara Brach, Wayne Dyer, Jon Kabat-Zinn, Deepak Chopra and so many more, I hear something new that inspires me to continue towards fulfilment and to have the belief that I can cope with a life without all of my children.

Of course, I would be completely within my rights to have a case brought against William, Billy, Jasmine, Bianca and Rosemary for the violations of my human rights, particularly with regards to their discrimination of me because of my disabilities; i.e., hearing loss and mental illnesses—PTSD and major depressive disorder. Where Billy is concerned, I am certain the law society's ethics department would be very keen to hear of his infractions regarding advising a person to destroy evidence; though he had believed his father was a paedophile and that he was in full possession of the fact that his father had broken the law regarding surveillance of his wife and children without their knowledge or consent, Billy had failed, even when begged for help by me, and sent his mother off to "talk to his father" and never did another single thing to ensure the well-being of either his mother or siblings. I am ashamed of the way he has acted in this regard towards me but to put the well-being of his siblings, nieces and possibly his own daughter in jeopardy is completely beyond any reasoning to me. Again, I have to ask the question, what does William have on Billy that is causing him to break the rules of his chosen profession so blatantly?

I have, for many months now, been meditating for at least 1½-2 hours per evening. This does not include my mindful meditation through each day or the many hours I spend listening to summits and special events that further enhance both my spiritual and physical well-being. On the day we moved to the new house, I felt completely at peace and blissfully happy. It is said by some that sometimes when your suffering has been so intense, the universe will pick you up and put you into a blissful sanctuary. I believe that this is exactly what has happened to me. I finally feel completely safe, a feeling I have never experienced before. My gratitude to the universe and to Isabelle for allowing me to find this peace is eternal.

I believe that before we come into each incarnation, we choose every detail of the lives that we will live. It seems incredulous that anyone would choose to have lived the life I have for 61 years but we are here to observe and, by observing, create, and I have begun to see the purpose of my journey even if it has been a particularly difficult one. We can change our reality whenever we choose and I have chosen to change everything about my life. All of the clutter is gone from my life and I now take full responsibility for everything that I have lived, the people that I have known along the way and the experiences that I have had—both good and bad. There were points along my journey that I can now see offered me choices but I was too traumatised to make what ultimately would have been the best choice. Regret is a useless emotion and I choose to learn from my life and keep moving forward towards my true life's purpose. I accept that I was only ever the custodian of my children; that they, like I, have free will choices but that will never prevent me from loving them unconditionally.

I am truly grateful to all of my children but I must especially thank Billy, Jasmine, Bianca and Rosemary for causing me such pain and suffering, as without that, I would not have been able to find my true spiritual path. I wish you all a wonderful life filled with health, wealth, happiness, joy, bliss and love in abundance.

I have found my Shangri-La and I wish the same to every single living being.

May you be happy,

May you be well,

May you be comfortable and at peace.

Namaste.

www.ingramcontent.com/pod-product-compliance
Lightning Source LLC
Chambersburg PA
CBHW020915140626
46545CB00015B/43